**Illinois Central College
Learning Resources Center**

GYPSY & ME

GYPSY & ME

At Home and on the Road with
Gypsy Rose Lee

by

ERIK LEE PREMINGER

Little, Brown and Company
Boston — Toronto

FIRST EDITION

Library of Congress Cataloging in Publication Data
Preminger, Erik Lee.
  Gypsy & me.
  Includes index.
  1.Lee, Gypsy Rose, 1914-1970   2. Preminger, Erik Lee.   3. En-
tertainers — United States — Biography.   4. Mothers and sons —
Biography.   I. Title.   II. Title: Gypsy and me.
PN2287.L29P7   1984   792.7′028′0924 [B]   84-12584
ISBN 0-316-71776-2

VB

Designed by Patricia Girvin Dunbar

Published simultaneously in Canada
by Little, Brown & Company (Canada) Limited

PRINTED IN THE UNITED STATES OF AMERICA

For Brigid and Christopher,
my wife and my son,
so that they might come to know her

PART ONE

CHAPTER ONE

WE TURNED onto Collins Avenue seven blocks from the club, but even at that distance Mother's name was the biggest and brightest thing in sight. It had been sewn in four-foot-tall, sequined letters on a huge, floodlit banner that hung from a flagpole on the club's roof down to the top of its front door. The sequins caught the light as the ocean breeze ruffled the banner so GYPSY ROSE LEE sparkled over the street against the night sky.

It was nine o'clock on the night before New Year's Eve, 1956. The following evening, Mother was opening for a week at the Cavern, and we were on our way there to drop off the costumes and scenery that were presently piled high in the luggage trailer we towed behind the Rolls. It had been a grueling thirty-six-hour drive from New York to Fort Lauderdale. Mother was exhausted, but opening days were long and hectic, so she always made a point of stopping at the club when we arrived in a new town. In addition to unloading the trailer, it gave her a chance to size up the room and stage for problems as well as to establish her relationship with the club's manager.

Mother had earned her living with her strip-tease/comedy act for her entire adult life. Because she felt a child belonged with its mother, I had trouped with her since I was six months old. I had just turned twelve, but the first glimpse of her billing at a new club still gave me goose bumps, and that night I found it especially thrilling.

It had been nine months since our last tour, nine months of living a more-or-less conventional life in our Manhattan townhouse while Mother wrote her autobiography, and I had missed being on the road. Until this layoff, we had always spent at least six months of every year on tour, often more. We had crisscrossed the United States countless times — once with a carnival — spent two years in Europe, and even

3

played Australia. The New York house was where we stopped to do our laundry; home was the front seat of the Rolls or backstage in the dressing room. I had been excited since we left the city, but the banner was the clincher.

"Oh, Mother, look!" I cried.

"Modulate your voice, dear. I see it." She hated loud noises, and my voice was still a bit shrill, particularly when I was excited.

"Don't you just love it?" I continued more softly.

"Hardly."

Her tone was serious, but I looked at her to see if she was joking. Next to a big salary, big billing had always been of paramount importance to her. She looked grim, too; and when she parked the car in front of the club, she began staring out the window at it. That added to my confusion. Usually she bounded out of the car and went inside to take care of business. I followed her stare, but could see nothing worth looking at. The club was a large, two-story brick building in the commercial section of town with a windowless ground floor, the facade of dirty brick broken only by the entrance, which was flanked by two empty display cases for billboards. The second floor was ringed with windows, all but one of which were dark, and the one with a light behind it was too dirty to see through. A typical provincial night-club, no different from thousands of others we had played over the years.

It was best not to disturb Mother when she was thinking, but after a while I could contain my curiosity no longer. "What's wrong?" I asked.

She sat a moment longer, then shook her head and started to get out of the car. "Oh, Erik. It's all so depressing."

Her dog, Fu Manchu, whined to go with her, but she patted him on the head and said, "Not now, darling." Then, as an afterthought, she looked at me and said, "Erik, be a darling and take Fu for a walk while I go inside. The poor dear must be ready to burst."

My curiosity disappeared in a burst of resentment. I hated Mother's dog, and I hated the way she used "darling" interchangeably for the two of us. We had always trouped at least one pet; Mother claimed it was for my benefit, but in fact she loved animals while I merely tolerated them. This was only a one-week date, so we had agreed to leave everyone at home, but at the last moment she had changed her mind about Fu, claiming "I just know he won't eat if I leave him alone." The argument was logical because he was a new addition to the family and hopelessly devoted to her, but in truth she brought him along because she adored him. Why she did was beyond me. She had a soft spot for the unusual and offbeat, but Fu Manchu was, without doubt, as repulsive an animal as ever set foot on earth. A Chinese Crested Hairless, he was bald except for tufts of hair on his head, tail, and paws. His mottled gray, pink, and black skin was rough to the touch but quite sensitive and prone to acne. My flesh crawled whenever I had to touch him, and he must have sensed my revulsion because he certainly reciprocated it. Fastening his leash to his collar was a test of my reflexes: without warning he would make a lightning-fast snap at me, and when he connected, his razor-sharp teeth always drew blood.

That night, however, he was either in a rare good mood or desperate to relieve himself because aside from a low growl, he gave me no trouble whatsoever. And once outside, I even had to admit to myself that I didn't mind walking him. It was a lovely evening, and it felt good to stretch my legs. Best of all, it gave me an excuse to get far enough from the car to risk sneaking a cigarette. Mother had caught me once. She hadn't punished me or even yelled, but she had made her disapproval quite clear, and her disapproval could really sting. I didn't want to get caught again, so I was very careful.

I was half a block from the car and had just finished my cigarette when I saw Mother march out of the club followed by a man in a pale blue dinner jacket. He was struggling to catch up with her so I knew he was the manager.

Most nightclub managers were unintelligent, harried, professional "nice guys" who were hired to make sure the joint showed a profit, take care of the dirty work, and keep everyone happy. Mother knew this, and she made a point of letting them know, right from the start, that to keep her happy they would have to fullfill, promptly and without question, her every demand. She wasn't being arbitrary; she simply felt that the customers were paying to see her and that she knew, better than anyone else, what she needed in order to give them their money's worth. And besides, she was the star.

The manager was out of breath when he caught up with her at the car. "Believe me, Miss Lee, it'll be all right," he said, panting. "We'll take care of everything tomorrow."

"I have a show to do tomorrow, Mr. Taylor," she instructed him, accenting his name as a teacher would that of a naughty student. "Not to mention a band to rehearse, scenery to set up, and two new girls to break in. I can't do all that and worry about the goddamn bandstand at the same time. It's out of the question."

5

I had watched her play this scene, with slight variations, on our arrival at every club we had ever played, and it never ceased to amaze me that she could carry it off looking as she did. When Mother drove, she dressed for comfort. That night she was wearing the same clothes she had worn during the entire trip: a faded denim skirt, a man's plaid flannel shirt, sandals (without the heavy wool argyle socks which she had removed when it began to get warm, halfway through Florida), and a scarf tied around her hair. This outfit had been clean and pressed when we left New York, but now it was wrinkled, smudged with cigarette ashes, and spotted with the tea which she drank by the thermosful as she drove. It was also a little ripe. But if Mother was the least bit self-conscious about her appearance, no one could have guessed. It was all in the way she carried herself. She was 5'9", but unlike most tall women, she never slouched. Never. Her back was always ramrod straight and her head high. Even dressed as a charwoman, she had the bearing of a queen.

Royalty, of course, need their vassals, and Taylor seemed to understand his role. "You don't have to worry," he assured her. "I'll take care of it. I promise. And please call me Jack."

"Another thing," she waved her arm in the general direction of the empty display cases flanking the front door. "Where are my photographs? How the hell can you expect any customers if no one knows I'm here?"

"The flag —" he began meekly.

She interrupted him. "That vulgar eyesore?!"

A look of intense hurt crossed his face. "It's drawn a lot of customers," he said proudly. "We're sold out tomorrow night."

"Of course you're sold out. It's New Year's Eve." He started to say something, but she cut him off. "Oh, never mind. I'm too tired to argue." I hurried back to the car. Her "too tired to argue" line was a sure sign that she was winding down.

"Of course you are, Miss Lee. Now don't you worry about a thing. It'll all work out."

"Oh, no," I thought, slowing to a walk, "we'll be here all night." Mother hated being patronized; usually she reacted with a long, sarcastic tirade.

But she let it slide. And moments later when he told her that we couldn't unpack the costumes because he had left the dressing room keys at home, she calmly agreed to leave the suitcases and scenery locked in the liquor storeroom until morning. I had rarely seen her so complaisant.

She was oddly quiet on the drive to the motel, as well, and I was reminded of her strange reaction to the club when we arrived, so I finally asked her if something was wrong.

"No, darling, I'm just tired."

"Are you upset about the flag?"

"I just told you, Erik, that I don't wish to discuss it."

I knew better than to persist, but I also knew by then that she had something on her mind.

Taylor had reserved rooms for us at the Sun & Surf Motel. Mother didn't care where she lived when she was working as long as it was close to the club, cheap, and had a kitchen. The kitchen was the least important because we could make do with our hot plate and electric frying pan. Club managers could never imagine a star of Mother's magnitude living in the type of motel she felt she could afford, however, and they invariably booked us into motels that cost too much. One look at the Sun & Surf, and I knew that Taylor had made the usual mistake. It was new and clean, so it had to be costly. I had already found an alternative in the Automobile Club guide when Mother came out of the office and announced that we'd spend the night and find a cheaper place the next day.

Relieved as I was that we wouldn't have to drive around half the night, Mother's extravagance was so totally out of character that it confirmed my suspicions about something being wrong. I went to bed hoping she'd be back to normal by morning.

She was. At six she was wide awake and making her first cup of tea. I tried to pretend sleep, but she knew.

"Darling, it's time to get up," she said softly.

"Not yet. Please. Five minutes more," I pleaded, pulling the covers over my head. Mother always got up early, and I hated it. I dozed off.

"Come on, now, Erik. I gave you ten minutes, five more than you asked for, so hurry and get up. Enough is enough." This was her no-nonsense voice, sharp and abrupt. It was such a normal morning, I completely forgot my concern of the night before.

Mother was furious when we couldn't get into the Cavern at seven-thirty. True, the previous evening she had notified Taylor that she would arrive at eight, but she was anxious to unpack and get settled in her dressing room, and when she was anxious logic was irrelevant.

"That son-of-a-bitch," she complained after five minutes of pounding on the front and stage doors. "If he hadn't told me the friggin' janitor lived here, I would have relaxed at the motel and had another cup of tea." It wasn't true, of course. Mother never relaxed, least of all on opening days. She had been dressed, packed, and ready to go by seven this morning. Then, after ten minutes of nervously pacing around the room, she had remembered Taylor's comment about Roy, the janitor. Five minutes later we had checked out and were on our way.

"Well," I commented, "he's dumb enough; maybe he's deaf, too." The night before, Roy had helped us unload the car; and we had both noticed that he was severely retarded. Mother had evaluated him as "a slow nine in a thirty-year-old body. But sweet. Nine's a good age for boys."

Nevertheless, she rebuked me sharply for my comment. "That's enough, Erik. Don't make fun of those less fortunate than yourself. It's in very poor taste." Then she took the sting out of her reprimand by adding, "Speaking of the less fortunate, let's find a phone and call Taylor at home."

We were pulling out of the parking lot when Roy finally opened the door. He was obviously going to be slow at everything. Mother cursed Taylor softly as she parked the car by the stage door. "Christ! What a sanctimonious idiot. Hiring that poor man for a job that's clearly beyond him."

"At least he gave him a job," I said. I was always trying to soften Mother's judgments.

"He has no business soothing his conscience at the expense of others. Wait until you need Roy to help you today. You'll see."

I hadn't thought of that. It was my job to set up the scenery, arrange the lights, and so on. Unless there was a stagehand, rarely found in regional clubs, Roy would be my assistant.

Mother's opinion of Taylor was further diminished when she discovered that he had the only keys for the liquor storeroom where we'd left the costumes. "What in God's name did he think I was going to do here at the crack of dawn? Sit and stare at the goddamn walls?!" She noticed Roy cringe at her outburst and lowered her voice. "Roy, would you please call Mr. Taylor and tell him that I must see him right away. Tell him it's urgent." Roy was afraid to disturb Taylor before eleven o'clock, so Mother had to make the call herself. Even getting Roy to part with the phone number was an uphill battle.

While Mother phoned, I looked around. I didn't get far; the main room stopped me cold. Regional clubs were usually unattractive — at best, plain and dark; at worst, gaudy — but the Cavern was a new low. Designed to resemble the interior of a cave, its walls were craggy and uneven and large plaster stalactites hung from the ceiling; the tables were imitation rocks, and the chairs were covered with phony zebra skin. The bar, walls, floor, and ceiling were painted a uniform textured gray, and over the years soot had filled the grooves, giving the room a seedy, run-down air. It was also huge, and the decor accentuated its size, making it very cold and forbidding.

Although grotesque, the room's appearance was at worst unaesthetic. The bandstand, however, presented a very serious problem. It was set on a raised platform behind the stage, and since her burlesque days Mother had insisted that no one be in back of her when she performed. Her strip was designed to be viewed by an audience, from the front; from behind, parts of her were visible that she didn't want seen by the audience, stagehands, or musicians. Mother was actually a very modest woman.

So the band would have to be moved, but the only place available was the floor, which would mean eliminating some of the tables that were crowded next to the stage. In spite of Taylor's promise the night before, I doubted he would do it. He had also said that the club was sold out, and nightclub managers never removed paying tables. Never! The day had started badly, and I sensed it was going to get a lot worse.

It did, too, but not because of Taylor. He did all he could for Mother, but the more he tried, the more impossible and demanding she became. It started the moment he arrived. We were waiting in the dressing room when he rushed in, spewing apologies.

"Oh, Miss Lee, I'm so sorry. I don't know what —"

"I do. You forgot, and it's inexcusable."

"Roy's bringing your things right now —"

She wouldn't let him finish a sentence. "I've never been treated like this in all my experience." She waved her arm around the dressing room.

"Don't you like your dressing room?" he asked. Even I didn't understand. Compared to most, it was lovely, with two large windows and excellent lighting.

Where's my sofa?" she demanded. I still didn't understand. Aside from Vegas, Reno, and a couple of large hotels, dressing rooms never had sofas.

"I'll try and get you one."

"I must have someplace to rest . . . if you expect me to go on." The threat was obvious, and it surprised me. Mother never threatened, only demanded.

Roy arrived with the first load of suitcases, and she turned her back on Taylor. "Now leave me alone. I have to unpack." Her curt dismissal was also strange, but soon we were busy setting up the dressing room, and I forgot it.

We had barely finished unpacking the costumes when Taylor asked her to come downstairs and see his solution to the problem of the stage. It was ingenious — he and Roy had simply dismantled it and moved the band onto the floor in its place, leaving the band's original platform as the new stage. Mother couldn't have asked for more: no one was behind her, the new stage was wider and deeper than the old one, and in effect the band was now set in an orchestra pit, which was ideal for many of the gags in the act.

But rather than compliment him — and it was her custom to praise any job well done — she ignored the stage and instead began yelling at him because the stairs leading to the dressing room were filthy and would soil the hems of her costumes. She worked herself into a rage, and he listened in hurt silence. The expression on his face reminded me of a faithful dog who had unknowingly displeased its master. I felt sorry for him; he had done a good job and Mother's anger seemed totally unreasonable.

She interrupted her tirade when the four showgirls arrived from Miami. Mother's act hadn't changed since the thirties: she opened with her strip, changed costumes, and then did a comedy routine that was, basically, a reverse strip. After introducing four scantily clad girls, she draped them with panels of brightly colored silk while doing a comedy monologue. The girls had no lines; all they had to do was walk across the stage and look sexy. Still, I was glad two of them had worked with us before. Walking across a stage isn't as easy as it sounds, and they would be able to rehearse the new girls, which would take some of the strain off Mother.

I had hoped the girls' arrival would end Mother's attack on Taylor, but it didn't. After greeting them, she started in on him again, this time about the "deplorable" condition of the upstairs toilet. The girls smirked as she reviled and belittled him. I couldn't watch any more of it, so I went upstairs to the dressing room.

I was very upset. Mother was acting like a stranger. She was often difficult, especially when she was working, but she wasn't cruel and her tantrums always had some justification. I had never seen her wantonly humiliate anyone as she had Jack Taylor. It wasn't her nature. But suddenly it was, and I was confused and disturbed by the change. I considered discussing it with her, tactfully of course, but as soon as she came upstairs, she sent me off to begin assembling the shadow box.

In their heyday, nightclubs had a number of different acts on every bill, and Mother used to change her costume while they performed. As the cabaret business declined, new booking policies made it Mother's responsibility to provide an entire show. Rather than pay someone to perform while she changed, she incorporated the change into her act by doing it on stage in a shadow box.

The shadow box was a frame of aluminum two-inch L-beams six feet wide, four feet deep, and eight feet high. A white translucent scrim, painted around the edges to resemble an old vaudeville drop, was stretched tightly across the front, and Mother's shadow was cast on it by a spotlight behind her. For privacy, the sides were draped with pink satin. A matching curtain covered the scrim except during the change. The whole structure disassembled so we could travel with it, and my biggest job on opening days was putting it together.

It was a relief to go to work. Constructing the shadow box was like doing a giant jigsaw puzzle, and it totally occupied my mind. Roy turned out to be an excellent assistant, more than making up for his limitations by his willingness to work and to follow directions. Still, it was a big job, and we were barely halfway through it when the band arrived and we had to stop. Mother didn't permit any activity onstage or in the club while she was rehearsing; it disturbed her concentration.

When she came downstairs, Mother had Fu in her arms and a look on her face that I knew only too well. "Darling . . ." she began.

"I know. You want me to take Fu for a walk."

"Oh, Erik, how sweet. Actually I was going to ask you to buy me some grapes for tonight, but there's no reason he can't go along. That way, both of you can get some fresh air." He growled as I took him from her, so I quickly put him down. "Fu! Be nice," she told him sternly; then, handing me a dollar, she said, "Don't be too long. And try to get seedless."

Mother was quite superstitious. As a child, she had read the tea leaves of one of the boys in their old vaudeville act and foreseen his violent death; three days later he had come to a messy end in a car accident. After that, she stopped reading tea leaves and insisted on observing a number of bad- and good-luck rituals: no hats on the bed, no whistling in the dressing room, and eating twelve grapes on the twelve strokes of midnight every New Year's Eve were among them.

I knew that Mother took her grape ritual very seriously. Given her mood I certainly didn't want to return to the club empty-handed, so

I became quite nervous when, after searching and asking about for over half an hour, I was unable to find even a grocery store, let alone the grapes. It was a hot day, and Fu was exhausted from all the walking. Finally, he simply refused to go any farther. I was in no mood to put up with him, so I tugged at his leash. It was a mistake. He dug in his heels, and his collar slipped right over his head.

He didn't run away, but when I approached to replace the collar, he bared his teeth and moved just beyond my reach. I called to him, but he didn't respond. We stood on the street, eyeing each other suspiciously. I was desperate. If he got hurt or lost, Mother would be beside herself. When he moved to a streetlamp and lifted his leg, I saw my chance and lunged, but he was too fast. I got his spray, but I missed him, and the chase was on. For what seemed an eternity, he led me around Fort Lauderdale — across busy streets, down to the beach, and under the boardwalk. He never stopped for lights, of course, so I was constantly dashing into the street, arms waving, to keep the cars from crushing his ugly little body. Through it all, I knew he was tormenting me. He conserved his energy by staying no more than five or six feet out of reach and by resting whenever I did. Eventually I managed to drive him into an alley and corner him. He snapped at me, drawing blood when I grabbed him, but I didn't let go. I put the collar around his neck, tightened it until it was almost strangling him, kicked him, and dragged him back to the club.

"Where have you been, Erik?" Mother's voice rang through the club. "I've been so worried about you. Why must you do things like this when you know I'm trying to work?"

It was not the greeting I had expected, but I answered her calmly. "Fu slipped out of his collar, and I had to chase all over town after him. Look what he did to my hand." I held my hand out, but by then most of the blood had dried, and there wasn't much to see.

She didn't look anyway. Instead, she picked up Fu and began petting him. "Poor darling," she cooed. Then she turned on me. "Why weren't you more careful? You know how easily he slips out of that collar. He might have been killed." Her accusation seemed too unfair to answer, but my expression must have told her I was hurt because she added, "Remind me to buy a harness for him."

I knew that was her way of apologizing, but it wasn't good enough. I mumbled, "Okay," and turned to go upstairs in an obvious sulk. I should have known better; Mother hated petulance.

"Wait a minute, Erik," she stopped me. "Where are the grapes?"

I had forgotten them completely. Lamely, I offered, "I couldn't find any."

"Goddamnit all, Erik! What's the matter with you today?"

"But there aren't any grocery stores in the neighborhood."

"That's ridiculous."

"The boy's right, Miss Lee." Taylor came to my defense. "The closest is over a mile away." I knew I had been right about him; he was a nice guy. "Tell me what you need, I'll go get it for you."

She told him, he left, and I went up to the dressing room, angrier than ever after being yelled at in front of the whole club. The first thing I noticed when I entered was the addition of a green sofa. "Taylor's really trying to make peace," I thought. "I wonder if Mother yelled at him because it's green." She considered green an unlucky color backstage.

I had nothing to do, so after leaning out the window to sneak a few drags on a cigarette, I lay down to take a nap. The sounds of the rehearsal filtered upstairs.

"No, no, no . . ." Mother was saying impatiently. "You there. Mister Drummer . . ."

"Sid."

"Very well, Sid. You've missed your cue three times in a row now. Please pay attention. And I want the cow bell on the pin drops just a little softer. . . ."

"God," I thought, "they're still working on the first number. Mother must be pissed." I was delighted. I enjoyed her having problems when I was angry with her — and dozed off reveling in my secondhand revenge.

"Erik! . . . Erik, do you hear me?"

Mother's call from downstairs woke me. I stuck my head out the door and yelled back. "What do you want?" I was still angry.

"Come down and finish the shadow box. It's getting late."

"Rehearsal over?"

"Good God, no! And at the rate it's going, we'll never finish."

"I'll be right down." It was late, there was work to do and a show to put on. My anger vanished. I splashed some cold water on my face and went downstairs.

It was chaos: waiters were setting tables, the bartender was clanking glasses, the showgirls were working together, and Mother was still rehearsing the band. I grabbed Roy and soon we were adding to the noise and confusion. Everyone in the room was charged by the pressure of getting ready in time; it was exciting, and I loved it.

Roy and I were almost finished with the shadow box when I noticed Taylor and a very well dressed, gray-haired man in his fifties enter the club. Taylor introduced him to Mother, and the three of them talked for a while. They spoke softly, but I could tell from Mother's expression that she was complaining, and from Taylor's that he was defending himself. The gray-haired man's face remained impassive, and after a few minutes he shook her hand, bowed his head politely, and left. Taylor walked him out, and Mother resumed working with the band.

"Who's that?" I asked Roy.

"Mister Silverstein."

"Who is he?"

Roy got very close and whispered, "The boss."

Mother gave up with the band around six. She was not pleased, but she knew they could make it through, and she wanted to rest before the show. As she headed upstairs, she called to Taylor, and when he came over, she said in a voice loud enough for the whole room to hear, "I think you should know, Mister Taylor, that in all my experience I have never worked with a less professional group of people. And you are, without a doubt, the least professional of them all." With that, she turned and started to leave the room.

"Oh, Miss Lee," he called to her as he ran back to the bar, picked up a paper bag, and then ran up and handed it to her. "Your grapes." Without a word, she took them and went upstairs.

By seven-thirty, I was ready to go: the shadow box was finished, the props and costumes were arranged inside it, and the correct gels were in the spots. I took a quick look around to double-check and went upstairs feeling quite pleased with myself.

When I got to the dressing room, Mother was just starting her preparations to go on. I sat down and kept her company. We didn't talk. Peace and quiet were part of the routine, a pre-performance routine that hadn't changed in my entire life. Mother began by applying body makeup from her neck to her feet. After it dried, she used spirit gum to glue on her G-string and the black lace bows that covered her breasts. Then she did her hair, and finally her face.

I have often been asked about my reaction to seeing Mother naked, but it was such a normal part of life that I never gave it a second thought. She was very modest with everyone but me, and even with me she never paraded around without clothes; that just wasn't her style.

But we lived together in the cramped confines of hotel and dressing rooms where modesty between us would have been so difficult and so awkward, it would have been unnatural.

Taylor knocked and gingerly announced, "Half hour, Miss Lee." That was my cue to go downstairs. It was another of my jobs to help Mother with her change in the shadow box; however, she wanted the audience to assume her dresser was a maid. The spotlight was set so only my arms cast a shadow on the scrim, but in clubs like the Cavern where the only access to the stage was through the audience, I would have to wear a busboy's jacket and sneak into the box half an hour before the show and remain in it for another half hour afterward in order to maintain the illusion.

Mother fastened the front of her blouse with straight pins. As I was leaving, I noticed that she was having trouble with them because her hands were trembling.

"Mother, what's the matter?"

She dropped the pins on the makeup table and sat before answering. Her voice was tired. "I've had it, Erik."

"What?"

"The act. I'm forty-two years old. Too old to be taking my clothes off in front of strangers." She said it simply, it was a fact, and I didn't know what to say. She took a deep breath and willed herself to be calm. I had seen her do it before, but it always impressed me. She was never without control. When she stood and began pinning her blouse again, her hands were steady. "You better go down now."

I didn't want to leave, but I could think of no reason to stay, so I kissed her on the cheek and left. I walked downstairs, put on the busboy jacket, and threaded my way through the club. It was jammed full of gaily dressed women and men in plaid dinner jackets, all drunk, but I hardly noticed them. I was too busy trying to assimilate what Mother had just said. I sensed it would affect the core of our lives and was frightened, but I couldn't think about it or analyze it. Dumbly, I took my place in the shadow box and waited.

The next thing I remember, I heard the opening drumroll, and when Taylor made his introduction, my heart soared. This I knew and understood, it comforted me, and I clung to it. "Ladies and gentlemen, good evening. Tonight, the Cavern takes great pleasure in presenting the Queen of Burlesque, the One and Only, Miss Gypsy Rose Lee!"

Before we began using the shadow box, I used to stand in the wings or at the back of the audience for every show, and I knew each move in the act by heart. That night, as the audience applauded and Mother's music began, I was out front, watching with my mind's eye.

Holding herself proudly erect as always, she walked gracefully and slowly across the stage, looking at the audience and showing off her costume. Her dress was demure, almost Victorian, in the way it covered her from head to toe. A full floor-length black velvet skirt, belted at the waist and worn over a four-layer lace petticoat, contrasted sharply with her pure white, loose-fitting organdy blouse with its black lace fichu. She wore her hair pulled straight back into a chignon but softened its severity with Gibson Girl–style bangs which peeked out from under a large black velvet hat decorated with two large satin roses.

After crossing the stage twice, she paused at the microphone until the applause died. Then she began her routine, speaking her lines in time to the music, almost like poetry:

> Have you the faintest idea about
> the private thoughts of a strip teaser?
> Well the things that go on in a strip-teaser's mind,
> would give you no end of surprise.
> And if you're psychologically inclined,
> there's more to see than meets the eye.

She walked across the stage, removed her hat, and handed it to the band leader. How ironic the routine seemed that evening. I wondered what she was really thinking. Whatever it was, it didn't affect her performance. She sounded as she always had.

Mother's act emphasized tease over strip: she remained covered for almost the entire act. After the hat, she raised her dress and petticoat, unfastened her stockings from her garter belt, and rolled them down.

> For example,
> When I raise my skirts with slyness and dexterity,
> I'm mentally computing just how much I'll give
>   to charity.

> And though my thighs I have revealed,
> And just a bit of me remains concealed,
> I'm thinking of the life of Duse.
> Or the third chapter of the *Rise and Fall of the*
>   *Roman Empire*.

The music's tempo became faster, and she removed the petticoat from under her dress.

But there's the music,
And although it's my cue;
I can't help thinking,
Of all the things I really have to do.

Cable regrets to Elsa Maxwell,
Forget-me-nots to Edith Sitwell.
Call Mainbocher about my fitting,
Match the wool for mother's knitting.
Ask Maximillian my furrier to bring,
A muted mink lining for next winter's g-string.

Oh, yes. At noon, I'm laying a cornerstone.

On "cornerstone" she dropped the petticoat over the head of the drummer. It was one of her biggest laughs, and the primary reason she liked having the band in an orchestra pit. No one ever asked the drummer his opinion.

The music slowed again, and she walked back and forth across the stage, removing the pins from her blouse, one by one, throwing them into the orchestra pit. With each pin, the drummer was supposed to lightly tap the cow bell. Sid was still a little loud, and I thought that Mother must be cursing him to herself.

When I lower my gown a fraction,
And expose a patch of shoulder,
I'm not thinking of your reaction,
I'm not even feeling colder.

I'm thinking of a landscape by Van Gogh,
Or *The Apples* by Cézanne.
Or the charm I found in reading,
Lady Windermere's Fan.

When all the pins were removed, she slowly opened one side of her blouse, revealing the huge black lace bow that covered her breast. Then she did the same with the other side. The second bow, as always, was crooked.

"Oh dear!" she said, straightening it. The audience howled.

Mother's strip lasted twenty minutes. She also removed her black velvet sash and her garter belt, but she kept on her blouse, which hung loosely covering the bows, and her skirt.

At the end she unhooked the skirt, held it in front of her, and said, "And then . . . I take the last thing off."

Suddenly one of the girls from the act who had sneaked into the audience screamed, "NO!"

Mother laughed, and the audience laughed with her. After it subsided, she grabbed the curtain of the shadow box with her free hand, still wearing her open blouse and holding her skirt, and continued:

> And stand here shyly, with nothing on
> at all — well, practically nothing —
> clutching an old satin drop and looking
> demurely at every man. Do you believe,
> for one moment, that I'm thinking of
> sex? . . . Well, I certainly am.

Mother pulled the skirt away from her body and simultaneously pulled the curtain in front of her. For an instant, the audience glimpsed her black-lace G-string. Over her applause, she stuck her head out from behind the curtain and said, "Oh, boys, I can't take that off. I'd catch cold."

That was my cue to turn on the spotlight. I waited until she was in position before opening the curtain, but when she entered I noticed there were tears in her eyes and forgot all about it.

"Mother, what's wrong? Are you all right?"

She nodded and wiped her eyes, but her voice was a hoarse whisper. "I've never been embarrassed before." She shivered. "It was awful." Then, for the second time that night I saw her will herself to be calm, and as she continued her voice returned to normal. "But it's over now. Tonight's the last time. Never again." She got into position. "Open the curtain. Let's get this show on the road."

The change went perfectly. I concentrated all my attention on my job; it was an easy way to avoid unpleasant thoughts.

Mother's second-act costume was spectacular — a black monkey fur coat over a tight, gold-beaded fringe dress — and the audience went wild when she walked on the stage. I had closed the curtain, turned off the spot, collected the old costume and props, and was looking for something to do before she delivered her opening line:

> Many years ago,
> A burlesque show,
> Was a riot on Broadway.
>
> Many years ago,
> I joined that show,
> And look at me today.

I heard no more of the act that night. Mother's nostalgic line reminded me that twelve years earlier I, too, had joined a burlesque show. It had provided much of the continuity in my life, and now I was going to be leaving it behind. I hated partings. As a small child, I had made a new friend in every town and then been miserable at the end of the date when I'd have to say good-bye, so I stopped making friends. But this was a farewell I couldn't avoid. After tonight there would be no more clubs, no more music, no more act. The tears came, and I cried — quietly, of course, so it wouldn't be heard out front.

The show was over at 11:45, but rather than wait the full half-hour, I sneaked out while Taylor was counting off the last minute before midnight. "Happy New Year!" I shouted when I entered the dressing room. Mother nodded, smiling. She couldn't answer because her mouth was full of grapes. She already had her makeup off, her driving clothes on, and one suitcase packed.

"We're leaving tonight as soon as we can get loaded," she said as soon as she swallowed the grapes. She pointed to the closed suitcase. "Bring that one down to the car, but don't let anyone see you. I haven't told them yet."

The intrigue was exciting. "Are you going to, or are we going to sneak out?"

"Don't be silly, Erik. Of course I'm going to tell them."

"What if they don't let you go?"

"They will. They had me for tonight, and that's all they really wanted. The rest of the week will be dead. Besides, after the way I treated him, Taylor will be glad to be rid of me."

Then I understood. She'd known all day what she was going to do. Probably even the night before, which was why we had stayed at the expensive motel.

There was a knock on the door. Taylor called in, "Are you decent, Miss Lee?"

"One moment," she answered. Then, whispering, she told me, "Let him in, then take that down to the car."

I opened the door, and Taylor rushed in, gushing with enthusiasm. "A great show! Great! The best New Year's business since I've been here, and they loved it. Loved it!" I left, closed the door, and listened from outside.

"It was lousy," Mother stopped him. "Your band missed damn near every cue, the electrician on the follow spot must have been drunk, and your goddamn waiters kept serving while I was on."

"It'll be better tomorrow."

"No it won't. I'm not going to be here tomorrow. I've never put up with this type of treatment before, and I'm not going to start now. That's all there is to it."

"Now, now, Miss Lee. You're not serious."

"Of course I'm serious."

"But you can't leave. We have a contract."

"Sue me."

"Miss Lee, please. You wouldn't want me to call Mr. Silverstein, would you?" Taylor said it almost apologetically, but the sinister undertone was obvious.

"Are you trying to threaten me?" she demanded in her deepest, most severe voice. "How dare you!"

"Not at all, Miss Lee. Believe me . . ." He was stammering, trying hard to regain the advantage he thought he had lost but in fact never had.

"I insist you call him. Immediately. This is obviously beyond your authority."

I decided to take the suitcase down to the car before Taylor came out and found me listening. The interview was over.

It was two-thirty before the last customers left and I could begin striking the shadow box. In the meantime, everything else had been packed and loaded into the car. Mother hadn't left her dressing room, and there had been no sign of Mr. Silverstein.

He finally arrived shortly after three. Two young men with greasy hair, wearing cheap fluorescent suits, walked a deferential three steps behind him. Roy and I were on the stage, finishing with the shadow box; Taylor was behind the bar, counting the night's receipts; and the four girls were sitting at one of the empty tables playing cards. Otherwise, the huge room was deserted.

As if on cue — she had probably been watching for him from her window — Mother entered the room. Silverstein waved his flunkies away and watched as she stopped at the stage, told me to hurry, and walked down the long aisle to the bar where she joined him and Taylor. If his stare made her nervous, she didn't show it. She walked purposefully, head high, at a steady, deliberate pace.

I would have hurried even if Mother hadn't asked. The weirdly decorated, almost empty room was sinister in the glare of the bright house lights. Silverstein's flunkies, one of whom made a show of removing his jacket to reveal the gun he wore under his arm, had joined the four girls, and their laughter seemed jarring as it echoed through the room. And there was Mother, talking with the two men responsible for all of it, so far away from me at the darkened bar. I wanted to get out of there as quickly as possible.

Minutes later, Roy and I had finished with the shadow box and loaded it into the car. There was nothing left for me to do; so I went back inside the club. Silverstein and Taylor were off by themselves, talking, and Mother was alone. I told her the car was loaded, and she nodded.

"What about the girls?" I asked softly. They were having a wonderful time, passing a bottle around the table and taking turns sitting on the flunkies' laps. I felt they were traitors, siding with the enemy.

"Stupid," Mother answered. "They'll learn."

Just then, Silverstein approached. I took a step closer to her. "Very well, Miss Lee. I've decided to let you leave, but I'm warning you, don't try to work in Florida again."

She ignored his threat. "There's still the matter of my salary." She took a slip of paper from her purse. "According to my calculations, you owe me one thousand four hundred and twenty-eight dollars." She nodded toward the bar where Taylor was standing with the night's receipts. "I'd like it in cash."

Silverstein was visibly surprised by Mother's demand, and it took him a moment to decide on his answer. "I can't very well force you to work, but if you think I'm going to pay you, you're out of your mind."

"That's the most dishonest thing I've ever heard," Mother said indignantly.

"*I'm* not breaking our contract."

"Oh, don't be ridiculous. You're tickled pink that I want out. The rest of the week will be dead whether I'm here or not. I did the only important show, and you owe me for it."

"And you owe me six more nights, so that makes us square." He smiled, quite pleased with himself.

"Very well, If you insist, I'll finish the week." He stopped smiling, and Mother continued. "And while I'm here, I'll have AGVA send a steward up from Miami to inspect the working conditions — I'm vice-president of the guild, you know. I might just contact the state liquor authority, as well."

He glowered at her, furious. I doubt anyone had ever threatened him, let alone a woman. But Mother stood her ground, and after a moment he turned on his heel and marched out of the club, yelling to Taylor as he left, "Give the bitch her money." His flunkies hurried out after him.

It didn't take long for Mother to collect her salary and pay the girls. When we had been in the car for a few minutes and were settled, I turned to her and asked, "Weren't you scared?"

She smiled. "A little."

"Then why did you do it? Ask for the money, I mean."

"I worked for it, didn't I?"

CHAPTER TWO

MOTHER arrived home in a panic. She had been quiet for the entire drive, so I suppose it had been building ever since our departure, but the first I knew of it was in Virginia, on the second morning out. It was nine-thirty and bitter cold. We had stopped for gas, and after filling the tank, she went into an outdoor phone booth, called someone, and yelled for at least ten minutes. I knew she was yelling by the huge vapor clouds coming from her mouth. I could also hear her, even through the closed car windows and the glass walls of the phone booth. She was still furious when she got back into the car. "Goddamnit all! Five bucks shot to hell and nothing to show for it."

As she started the car, she noticed a large truck approaching on the highway. She hated driving behind trucks, so she threw the car in gear and pulled on the road directly in front of it. The truck's squealing brakes and blasting horn seemed right on top of us, but she ignored it and continued her train of thought. "That son-of-a-bitch! Three months I've been waiting for him to start the friggin' floor, but now when I want to cancel it, he tells me it's too late. I knew I shouldn't have given him that deposit."

Nothing she could have said would have surprised me more. We lived in a townhouse on East 63rd Street in Manhattan that was the pride of Mother's life. It had been built in 1919 by Barbara Rutherfurd, a granddaughter of Cornelius Vanderbilt, the railroad and shipping tycoon, and was known at the time as "the Rutherfurd Palace." Palace was an apt description. It was really two houses, one behind the other with a patio in between, and contained twenty-eight rooms. We didn't occupy all twenty-eight. Because we had no live-in staff, Mother had long ago converted the original basement kitchen and upstairs servants quarters in the front house into three apartments. We managed very nicely in the original six-room "master suite," which consisted of an entrance foyer and dining room on the ground floor of the front house and four large rooms, one to a floor, in the rear house: a drawing room, my room, Mother's room, and a library. There were also assorted baths, closets, an elevator, stairs, a tiny kitchen that Mother had installed in a closet off the library to replace the one she had turned into an apartment, and a marble-floored hallway that ran alongside the patio connecting the front house to the rear.

For as long as I could remember, Mother had wanted to extend the marble floor from the hallway into the drawing room, and when she had finished the first draft of her book, she had ordered it as a reward to herself. I couldn't imagine her canceling it. "But I thought you wanted the floor," I said.

"Of course I want it; affording it is something else."

"How come?"

"Good God, Erik! Isn't it obvious? Without the act, I haven't the faintest idea of how we're going to survive, let alone pay five thousand dollars for a goddamned floor."

Mother was forever pleading poverty. I had once seen over two hundred thousand dollars' worth of annuity policies on her desk, so I didn't believe her, but I let the matter slide. Money was one topic I had learned to avoid whenever possible. Like many survivors of the Depression, she was neurotically obsessed with a fear of going broke; at the same time, however, she loved beautiful and expensive things. As a result of this inner conflict, her behavior and attitude toward money was often irrational. Once, for example, while earning $10,000 a week at the Riviera Hotel in Las Vegas, the manager had to ask her to stop cooking in the room because the other guests were complaining about the smell in the hallway. But rather than pay the "outrageous" prices for room service, which she insisted she couldn't afford, she moved us to a cheap motel on the other side of town, spent forty minutes commuting every day, and had to pay for gas and parking as well. Two weeks later, back in New York, she bought herself a sable jacket for $7,500.

In retrospect, however, there was a rationale to these decisions. She would spend money on something of lasting value or use — our house, the Rolls, her sable jacket, my school — but she cringed at throwing it away on ephemeral luxuries like room service. Had I understood this, I might have realized that her trying to cancel the floor was very much out of character and that her concern for our future was not just another phobic reaction.

This time, she had good cause to be afraid. When she gave up the act, she also gave up the only security she had ever known. For twenty-six years, stripping had fed her, clothed her, housed her, and above all, sustained the fame that nurtured her soul. Everything else she had done since 1930 — Broadway, films, mystery novels, even a radio show — had been marginally successful at best, and that had derived primarily from the novelty value of a stripper working in her clothes instead of out of them. By putting the act behind her, she left herself a middle-aged woman, alone in the world, with no career, limited savings, and an enormous overhead. It was not an enviable position.

Fortunately, she was far too premeditating to embark on something so drastic without a plan for the future, and in this regard her comment about our survival was exaggerated. She had decided to use her autobiography, *Gypsy*, to launch her in a new career as a writer and had already started her next book: *The Gypsy Rose Lee Cookbook*. Of course, for the plan to work *Gypsy* would have to be a success. Its prospects appeared excellent. It was a well-written, often hilarious account of her childhood in vaudeville and her rise to stardom in burlesque. Harper and Brothers, her publishers, were convinced it would be a major best-seller and were rushing it into production.

Mother had learned the hard way, however, that a huge gulf exists between a publisher's expectations and cash in the bank. Back in the early forties, after the success of her first mystery novel, *The G-String Murders*, both she and her publisher felt the second, *Mother Finds a Body*, would be a smash. After all, the writing was better, and she had already established an audience. They were wrong. It was a total disaster, financially and critically.

She was determined to avoid a repetition of that failure and began working eighteen hours a day on *Gypsy*'s release as soon as we returned from Fort Lauderdale, even though the actual publication date was still months away. She handled the normal author responsibilities of correcting galleys, selecting photographs, and preparing excerpts for magazines, but she spent most of her time orchestrating every facet of the publicity campaign. Publicity is free advertising, and while Mother was good at getting anything for free, publicity was her forte. It always had been.

When she first arrived in New York as an unknown stripper back in 1932, it was her knack for getting free press that put her on the map. In those days, Walter Winchell was the most important columnist in town; he could make or break an established star, let alone a new-comer. One night, she noticed him in the audience and sent him a note after the show. In it she apologized for her poor performance, blamed it on being flustered at seeing him in the theater, and asked him to please return the following night and give her a second chance. He did, but what he saw was not her usual act. Instead, she did a routine she had written that afternoon, based on his column of that morning. Winchell was charmed, and from then on he mentioned her in his column at least once a week, always favorably.

Mother used a similar tactic on a nationwide scale for *Gypsy*. Advance copies of books were always sent to the country's literary critics, but she sent autographed copies, along with personal notes, to all the entertainment columnists as well. They were very flattered and responded with a flood of column items praising her and the book.

Mother's interest in publicity also had an emotional aspect. She, like many vaudeville performers, measured her success in large part by the weight of her scrapbooks. Every mention, every review — good and bad — was tangible proof of her fame, and she had kept them all. They filled seventeen volumes of scrapbooks, the first beginning with the newspaper story of a Healthy Baby contest she won when she was a year old, and the last ending with the clippings from our Australian tour in 1955. Subsequent material was stored in a number of boxes waiting for her to begin volume eighteen. Mother loved being famous. It was as vital to her well-being as air or water; and now with the act behind her, she was especially interested in establishing a reputation as an author.

It was for this reason, more than to sell copies of *Gypsy*, that she was particularly excited when her publishers arranged for her to appear on Edward R. Murrow's *Person to Person*. It was not a run-of-the-mill talk show where anyone with a book to plug could appear. *Person to Person* was one of the highest-rated shows on television, and one of the most prestigious. Murrow was the dean of American newsmen, and the people he chose to interview were established celebrities who had already made it to the top of their profession — people like Duke Ellington, Norman Rockwell, Eddie Cantor, Marilyn Monroe, and John F. Kennedy. Simply being invited was an honor.

It was the show's format, however, that most appealed to her. Murrow from his studio interviewed his guests in their homes through a live television hook-up. It was the first show ever to permit the audience a glimpse of how the famous "really lived"; and it presented Mother with an ideal opportunity to correct any misconceptions the general public might have about her being just another stripper. She was, in fact, a woman of taste, intelligence, and style — an intellectual in the best sense of the word — and the house, which was filled with books, antiques, and fine paintings that she had painstakingly collected over the years, reflected all these facets of her character.

There was, however, a problem: the marble floor. With the contractor's assurance that it would be finished on the fifteenth of January, she had agreed to do the show on the seventh of February. Since the floor was now going to be seen coast-to-coast, she had even reconciled herself to its cost. But it was not finished on the fifteenth, nor on the twenty-fifth, and only by threatening a lawsuit was she able to get them to finish it by the fifth — thirty hours before Murrow and his crew were coming to see the house and lay out the show.

When I arrived home from school that day, the workmen were just removing their equipment, and I stopped at the drawing room to see the finished job. Mother was already there, walking around, testing the tiles with the toe of her slipper. I stood in the doorway quietly. Cool blue winter daylight filtered into the almost empty room through the french doors leading to the patio. The black grand piano stood in one corner, and the eight-foot-tall Victorian nude by Bouguereau hung on one wall. Both objects had been too large to remove, and now they were covered with a thick film of marble dust, as were the walls and floors. The room looked as if it belonged in a long-neglected French château with Mother as the concierge in her ratty blue housedress, worn slippers, and threadbare bed-jacket.

I couldn't imagine being ready in time. It would take days just to clean up the marble dust, but we also had to move all the furniture in from the hall, replace the curtains, wash the windows, and rehang over eighty paintings. Had I been Mother, I would have pleaded sick and canceled the show, but nothing motivated her like a challenge, and when she finally noticed me in the doorway, she said, "Well, don't just stand there. Let's go to work." It was a call to action, and when Mother called, doubts vanished and adrenaline flowed.

"Where do you want to start?"

"Find Mrs. Mitchell and help her clean up this friggin' dust. I'm going to call Boyd and invite him for dinner. He can help with the furniture."

"It's after three. She's probably cleaning the china cabinet."

"Go check anyway. Maybe we'll get lucky."

I crawled over the furniture piled in the hall and went into the dining room where I found Mrs. Mitchell, our cleaning lady, sprawled on the floor, head and shoulders inside the lower shelf of the china cabinet, sound asleep. She was at least seventy, arthritic, blind in one eye, and an alcoholic. Every day around three she passed out in exactly the same place, then at five she'd get up and go home. Mother felt too sorry for her to let her go; besides, Mrs. Mitchell brought her own booze, and even in those days it was hard to get a cleaning lady for seven dollars a day.

Mother was tying a rag around the brush-end of a broom when I returned. "Passed out?" I nodded. "One of these days I'll have to do something about her."

"Did you reach Boyd?"

She shook her head. "No answer." She began wiping the wall with the broom; but instead of sticking to the rag, half the dust fell on her head and the rest billowed into the air and finally settled right back on the wall. "Goddamnit all!"

"How about the vacuum cleaner?" I suggested.

"Oh, darling, that's a wonderful idea." I tried it, and although it was still quite messy, it was an improvement. "What a smart son I have," she said, heading for the elevator. "While you do that, I'll go upstairs and try Boyd again." After she'd been gone about an hour, I realized that she had bamboozled me into doing the whole job, and I decided to watch for my chance to even the score.

It came later that night, after dinner. The dusting was finished, and she had been unable to reach Boyd, so she asked me to help her move the furniture. "Oh, Mother, I'm sorry, but I can't," I said, trying to look as apologetic as possible. "I have an English test tomorrow, and I have to study for it." It was a lie of course. I rarely studied for tests even when I did have them.

"A test? Ummmm." She lifted her right eyebrow to let me know that she was wise to my game. "All right. You can stay home for the rest of the week and take a make-up on Monday. I'll need you to help out here anyway."

I hated school and thought I had gained a major victory, but as the evening progressed I realized the victory had been hers. She was an incredibly hard worker, and she pushed everyone to keep up with her. We stayed up until two, working without a break. When we finally went to bed, the curtains were hung, the windows had been washed, and all but the three heaviest pieces of furniture had been moved back into place. The next morning, she was up at six. By six-thirty, we were back rehanging the paintings and tending to other odds and ends. I was exhausted, but her energy never flagged. Then, on the second wall of paintings, disaster struck.

I was cleaning the crystal candelabra, so I didn't see it happen, but

I heard Mother's sharp gasp and, immediately after it, a loud crack as the hammer hit the marble floor. I looked up. She was standing, holding the Chagall in one hand, looking at her feet. "Oh, Erik! Look what I've done to my new floor." I stood up, but before I could get there, she walked to the elevator. "It's too much," she continued, her voice a mixture of anger, disappointment, and fatigue. "I can't do it all alone. I just can't." Then she got into the elevator and went upstairs.

She looked so tired and defeated as she left that I wished I could put my arms around her and tell her that everything would be all right, but Mother wasn't the type for that kind of comforting. She was a realist and had no patience for glossing over the truth. Instead I inspected the damage. The hammer lay where it had fallen, and two large cracks radiated from it through four tiles. I asked myself what I could do, but I knew the answer was nothing, so I stood there, dumbly looking at the floor, feeling depressed and useless.

"Yoo-hoo, where is everyone?" Boyd's lilting voice echoed in the hallway, and I immediately felt better. Like a court jester, Boyd always put Mother in a good mood.

Most stars surround themselves with servants, agents, business managers, secretaries, assistants, and other paid sycophants to ease the burdens of everyday life and massage their egos. Maintaining this staff costs anywhere from 10 to 50 percent of their gross income. Mother, too, had her entourage, but it was much less expensive. She had no exclusive agent. She paid the standard 10-percent commission to anyone who got her a job, but club owners often called her directly, then she negotiated her own contract and saved the commission.

In addition to Mrs. Mitchell, the household staff consisted of Esther, Erica, and Boyd. Esther was Mother's personal maid. She took care of Mother's clothes and costumes, and she also doubled as our cook. She had only ten recipes and all her sauces separated, but even Mother didn't expect perfection for $32.50 a week. Erica, Mother's secretary, came in only on Wednesday. She paid the bills, handled the correspondence, made the unpleasant phone calls, did the taxes, and so on. She put in a long day for $10, and eventually Mother gave her a raise to $12.50. Boyd did everything else, and he was paid nothing. In fact, he paid her $60 a month for the dubious privilege of renting the basement "apartment" in the front house: two dank, unfinished, subterranean rooms that flooded whenever the sewer backed up, which it often did. His duties included shoveling snow off the sidewalk, tending the balky furnace, laughing at Mother's jokes, and helping with any heavy jobs around the house. But it was not as inequitable as it sounds. When they first met, in 1945, Boyd was a small-town, eighteen-year-old boy from Oklahoma with no education who had come to the big city looking for excitement and acceptance of his homosexuality. Mother gave him those plus a role in her glamorous life, an education in the social graces, and, most important, a feeling of being needed. These were far more valuable to him than money, and he reciprocated with a love, devotion, and loyalty that would last as long as he lived.

He came into the room carrying an armful of rhododendron leaves for the vases. Mother felt cut flowers were too expensive. "The leaves work just as well," she often explained. "As long as there's something around that's alive."

"Where's Mother?" he asked.

"In her room. Upset." I showed him the cracked tiles and explained what had happened.

"Oh, that's nothing. They can be replaced. Go upstairs and tell her I'm here. I'll make myself a drink and get to work on these paintings. This is no time for hysterics." Then, as I was waiting for the elevator, he asked, "Get laid yet?"

My relationship with Boyd was, of course, completely different from Mother's. As the only man present in the household throughout my entire childhood, he had become something of an older brother. If he felt it necessary, he wouldn't hesitate to correct me, as, for example, he had when he noticed I was adopting some of Mother's mannerisms and told me they were too effeminate for a boy. For the most part, however, he was simply my best friend. I spent hours in his apartment, discussing Mother, school, and, lately, sex. I had just discovered it and was anxious to experiment, but I was also very shy, and in spite of his continued urgings, I had yet to ask a girl for a date.

"I wish," I answered.

"You can't get in their pants until you take them out." It was our standard exchange these days, provided Mother wasn't around.

When I got upstairs, she was lying on her bed, convulsed with laughter. She managed to control herself enough to tell me why. "I called to complain about the floor — after all, they must have done something wrong if it cracks so easily — and you know what the son-of-a-bitch said! 'Madam. Ladies with marble floors do not go around carrying hammers.' " Repeating the line broke her up all over again. Between laughs, she continued, "So I said, 'Well, buster, this one does, and she's not paying you another red cent until it is fixed.' Of all the nerve."

"Boyd's here. He's started on the paintings."

Her mood changed completely, and she jumped off the bed. "Oh, my God! Why didn't you tell me? He'll do it all wrong." There were certain jobs that she never trusted anyone to do without her supervision; hanging the paintings was one of them. As she got into the elevator, she asked me to make her a pot of tea.

They were having a wonderful time when I arrived downstairs with the tea. She was telling him the story of her conversation with the marble contractor and at the same time directing him as he held a painting against the wall. "Up a little, darling . . . and you know what he had the nerve to say? . . . now over to the right . . . 'Madam, ladies who go around carrying hammers shouldn't have marble floors.' . . . Perfect . . ." Mother loved directing people almost as much as she loved perfecting her stories.

So the crisis passed, and thanks to Boyd the room was ready when Murrow and his staff arrived at seven. From then on, *Gypsy* seemed blessed by the gods. The next day, Mother learned that the advance reviews in the two most important book-industry publications, *Publishers Weekly* and *Kirkus Reviews*, were raves, and that night, *Person to Person* was everything she had hoped it would be.

The show opened with Mother, in a pink Charles James ballgown, and me, in a dark suit and tie, seated at the piano as I played "On the Ice at Sweetbrier," a composition for first-year piano students. I had been studying for three years, but I never practiced, so it was the only thing I knew. Mother often asked my teacher why, as long as I was going to keep rehearsing the same piece, it couldn't at least be Chopin; but that night she managed to look every bit the proud, doting parent. From there, we moved over to the sofa where she showed off my stamp collection. It was really hers, but stamp collecting, like piano, was her idea of an acceptable pastime for a well-brought-up young man. It was an elegant and proper family portrait. It was also pretentious, but she carried it off so well that no one noticed.

A camera had been crammed into the elevator, which was only five by three, and after Ed said goodnight to me, she squeezed in with it and they rode up to the library on the fourth floor. The room was paneled in walnut and lined with books and the mounted heads of the muskies she had caught on a fishing trip in Wisconsin. It was warm and relaxed, a perfect contrast to the stark elegance of the drawing room, and an ideal place to talk about *Gypsy*. But Murrow wouldn't let her dwell on the book. Instead they spent most of the remainder of the show discussing fishing. This had been his idea, and during the rehearsal Mother had resisted it, but much to his credit, he kept at her until she gave in. It gave her an accessible, real quality that, according to most of her friends, made the show. The show was made for Mother, however, when she told CBS that the four marble tiles had cracked under the weight of the camera, and the network paid to replace them.

By publication day, the book had taken off. Andre Deutsch bought British publication rights, it was serialized in newspapers around the country, and offers began pouring in for the motion picture and dramatic rights. Still, she didn't let up. Together with Stuart Harris from Harper's publicity department, she embarked on a three-month, cross-country public appearance tour that included press interviews, book and author luncheons, autograph parties in bookstores, writers conferences, local television and radio shows, lectures, the works. Stuart kept trying to slip in a rest day here and there, but she wouldn't let him. "I'll rest when we're on the best-seller list. Now I'll work."

Nothing was too petty or insignificant if it would sell books. The weekend before she was scheduled for an autograph party at our tiny neighborhood bookstore, she mobilized the entire household to put announcements in the mailboxes of every house within a twelve-block radius. And when my school had its PTA benefit, she arrived with twenty-five copies of the book and auctioned them off. The PTA got the profit, but she deducted the publisher's cost — which included her royalty.

With all of this, Mother still made time for me. It was during this period that she decided I should start learning about women. Her lessons had nothing to do with sex — no doubt she assumed I would handle that on my own. Rather, she wanted me to learn how women should be treated. I had been going on and on about Janet, the belle of my class, so one day she suggested I invite her to the house for dinner.

"Oh, Mother!" was my only reaction. We used to eat off a tray in her bedroom, and it seemed unnecessary to amplify my objection. Besides, I didn't want to admit that I was too shy to ask her over. But Mother understood and made the offer irresistible: an intimate, candlelit dinner for two with a split of champagne served by our cook in the library.

It took me three days to screw up the courage to ask, and when I did it was a blurted "How would you like to come over to the house for dinner on Saturday?" but Janet immediately accepted.

On Saturday, her father dropped her off at seven. Things started off exactly as they did with all my male twelve-year-old friends. On the way upstairs, we talked about school and stopped off at Mother's room to say hello. But when we arrived at the library, everything changed. Janet saw the table, the candles, and the champagne in its silver bucket, and she was immediately transformed into a young woman.

Somehow, I rose to the occasion, and we spent the evening being grown-up. At ten, her father arrived to take her home, and the moment we heard the doorbell, we reverted to being twelve-year-olds. We never dated again, but I learned something that night that has always served me well: women love romance, and there is nothing as romantic as champagne by candlelight.

Mother's next venture in preparing me for my social responsibilities wasn't nearly as successful. Prompted by a commercial she had seen on television, she enrolled me at the Arthur Murray Dance Studio. Ten private lessons for $85. It wasn't *the* Arthur Murray Dance Studio; he had sold it years earlier, and it was now a franchise operation. At any rate, once a week I put on my good suit and rode my bicycle downtown to the "school," which was really nothing more than a refurbished rehearsal hall. There, a perfectly charming older woman — she must have been twenty-two — taught me the basic steps of the tango, fox-trot, samba, mambo, cha-cha, swing, and a few other hope-lessly old-fashioned dances that no one else my age had even heard of, let alone danced.

I didn't bother to tell Mother that the whole thing was a waste of time and money, nor did I pass on my teacher's invitation for her to attend my "graduation." Mother had never attended my real school's commencement exercises; I hardly imagined that she would troop all the way downtown to mark my completing ten dancing lessons. The manager of the branch phoned her, however, and made it into such a big deal that she agreed to attend. I was, to put it mildly, surprised.

It turned out to be a come-on, pure and simple. After my instructor put me through my paces for ten minutes, the manager of the branch — who was also seeing me do my stuff for the first time — pronounced himself "extremely impressed" at the progress I had made in only ten lessons and assured Mother that I had "the potential to become an accomplished ballroom dancer." All it would take was another hundred or so lessons, at ten dollars each, although considering my age he suggested that a lifetime membership at $2500 would be a much wiser investment in the long run.

Mother didn't let the s.o.b. have it for enticing her downtown on false pretenses. She let him finish his spiel, then politely accused him of underestimating the excellent job his instructor had done with me.

"From what I've just seen," she said, "my son already is an accomplished ballroom dancer. I'll bet there's not another twelve-year-old boy in all of New York that can do a tango like that. And all thanks to this charming young lady.

"No," she added, standing, "further lessons will be quite unnecessary. Now we really must be going." Two polite handshakes, a haughty "Come along, Erik," and we were out the door. By the time we hit the street, we were both laughing. I may not have learned much about dancing, but Mother got a story that she used for years afterwards.

On May 20, Stuart called from Harper's to tell Mother that the book was going to be on that Sunday's *New York Times* best-seller list. For the first time that year, she rested: she went to her favorite antique store and bought a $300 lamp that she had coveted for months.

CHAPTER THREE

W E-E-E-'RE OFF!" Mother and I shouted in unison as the winged lady on the front of the Rolls emerged from the Lincoln Tunnel. It was a family tradition. Few things infuriated Mother more than retracing her steps; she liked to move forward in everything, especially driving. It was, therefore, an unwritten law that we never returned to the house once we passed through the tunnel. Anything we had left behind could be mailed to us or, more likely, done without. New Jersey meant we were on our way, and the shout affirmed it. It also helped release the tension that built up during the frantic routine of getting out of town: eighteen hours of packing that lasted until eleven or later the night before our departure, waking up at four the next morning, Mother frying chicken for our picnic lunch while I ran around the house collecting the animals, loading the car, gulping a quick breakfast, and dashing cross town by five A.M. in order to miss the rush-hour traffic. After that, New Jersey always brought a sigh of relief.

"Take the New Jersey Turnpike south. We stay on it till exit six." One of my jobs when we toured was to read the maps and give Mother directions. She called me her "co-pilot" and I took my responsibilities very seriously. That morning, I was particularly careful; she was in no mood to take a wrong turn. It was January 17, 1958, and we were going to Palm Beach, Florida, where she was giving the first performance of her new one-woman show, A Curious Evening with Gypsy Rose Lee. Once again, she was launching a new career; and as with her book, Gypsy, the year before, she was convinced that her future depended upon its success.

Actually, Curious Evening was less a new career than a new approach to the old one. Mother had been a comedienne all her life;

35

but unlike a stand-up comic who reels off jokes, Mother's brand of comedy required a gimmick on which she could hang her humor. The strip-tease had been such a gimmick. It was, in fact, the only one she knew, which was why she turned to writing and gave up appearing on stage when she retired. But writing wasn't her métier. She was good at it, and she enjoyed it, but it didn't provide the gratification that she received from appearing in front of a live audience.

Then in April, while publicizing the book, Arlene Francis had invited Mother to appear on NBC's *The Home Show*. Arlene had been to the dinner parties Mother gave during the early fifties where, after the bribe of an excellent dinner, the guests had been subjected to an hour or more of home movies. Unlike most of the other guests, Arlene remembered them fondly and suggested that Mother bring five minutes of clips to run on the show. Mother loved the idea. She had done so many talk shows for the book that she was desperate for new material, and her film collection seemed like the perfect solution. She had been making home movies since the thirties and had over fifty thousand feet of 16mm film, roughly twenty-four hours' worth. Getting five usable minutes from it was, however, quite difficult. Much of the earlier material had been edited for the dinner parties into long reels dealing with various subjects — "Hollywood 1937," "The Carnival," "Erik," and so on; but since 1950, she had done nothing with the film she shot but put it in boxes marked "film for editing." There were six of these boxes as well as over fifty cans of outtakes and "precious bits" left over from the edited reels. Worse, it was stored in various places around the house, and most of the labels had fallen off over the years. Her projector, too, left much to be desired. A circa 1939 Bell and Howell, it had been lent to the army during World War II and was used in the Pacific to show films to the GIs. It still bore a little tag that read, "Fumigated and passed for return to U.S."

Nonetheless, by working eighteen hours a day and concentrating on the older footage, she managed to assemble five minutes showing her working with Fanny Brice in the *Ziegfeld Follies*, practicing one of her early strips on the roof of the Republic Theatre as the chorus rehearsed in the background, and doing laundry on the carnival with the bearded lady from the freak show. It was a fair five minutes, but her narration was a perfect blend of wit and nostalgia. She received a lot of fan mail from the show, all asking to see more, and it inspired Mother's new gimmick. She decided to assemble a ninety-minute documentary on her life, write a witty narration, and play it on the lecture circuit and in small theaters around the country.

It was a massive undertaking. Not only did she have to wade through and organize every foot of film she had ever shot, she had to spend hours searching for and making films of stills from her scrapbooks to cover her early life, put together a tape-recorded music track for background, and write the narration. But Mother thrived on hard work, and in June, right after she finished promoting the book, she converted the dining room into her base of operations, covered the windows with blackout curtains so she could project film during the day, collected all the film from around the house, and went to work. Now, six months later, she was going to find out if it was all worthwhile. Would it play?

That was only one of Mother's concerns that morning as we set out for Palm Beach. As soon as I was sure that we were headed in the right direction, I turned around to check on the others. They were riding in the back seat: four two-day-old Siamese kittens, Lichee their mother, and Gaudi their father. The cats were supposed to stay home this trip, but two of the kittens were runts and had to be fed warm formula with an eyedropper every four hours. Mother wouldn't trust anyone else to take care of them, not that she could have found someone anyway, so along they came.

Lichee and her kittens seemed quite content in their carrier, but Gaudi, the oldest member of our animal family, was used to having free run of the car. He had been complaining since we left the house, and his screeching "meows" were unbearable. Unfortunately, he and Fu Manchu, who was comfortably curled up on the front seat next to Mother, didn't get along, and I had visions of a bloody dog and cat fight as we rolled down the highway at fifty miles an hour.

"What should we do about Gaudi?" I asked. I knew what her answer would be, but I wanted her responsible for whatever happened.

"For godsakes, let him out so he'll shut up! He's driving me crazy."

I opened the box. Gaudi jumped on the back of the front seat, saw Fu, and hissed. "Gaudi, that's enough!" Mother said, pushing him back to the rear seat. He didn't try to return to the front, but before he settled down, he used the sand box. It was his revenge. The acrid smell filled the car, and for the rest of the trip he made sure the odor stayed with us no matter how often we changed the sand. Fortunately, we were used to animal smells, and after a few minutes no longer noticed it.

"Fix me a cup of tea, would you please, Erik?" Mother was addicted to caffeine and cigarettes. When she had to give up coffee because of her ulcer, she simply switched to tea and drank more so her caffeine intake remained the same. So did her ulcer, for that matter.

Another of my jobs on the road was to pour her tea from the thermos we carried and then to "season" it with cream and sugar. It couldn't be pre-mixed because she claimed that ruined the taste. It was quite an operation, but I rarely spilled a drop — as long as we didn't hit rough pavement.

"Now reach me a cigarette, would you please," she asked as I handed her the tea. She was always polite with me and demanded the same in return. She felt it was good training, and I liked it because it made me feel like an equal. Manners and respect notwithstanding, I was dreading this moment. Since Fort Lauderdale my occasional smoke had developed into a pack-a-day habit and sitting in the car for hours on end while she chain-smoked was going to be torture. I considered asking for frequent toilet stops, but she hated pulling off the road and had trained me early to hold my water. A sudden attack of weak bladder would be obvious and unappreciated. I knew I'd just have to suffer, but I wasn't looking forward to it.

I took the cigarette from the pack and held it out to her, but instead of taking it, she glanced at me and asked, "Would you please light it, darling? I can't manage while I'm holding my tea." She had managed for years, but she understood and wanted me to be happy without retreating from her position. I could have kissed her. From then on, I lit her cigarettes whenever she was driving. It was an ideal solution . . . almost. I didn't really like her menthol cigarettes.

Mother loved touring by car. She didn't have to worry about her appearance (in those days, the press still met stars at train stations and airports), it freed her from rigid schedules and animal restrictions, and it saved the expense of redcaps, overweight charges, and tickets for me. It also meant she could deduct the depreciation and maintenance on the Rolls from her income tax. There were drawbacks, too — bad weather, traffic, breakdowns, detours, and speed traps to name just a few — and it was a rare trip that we didn't encounter at least one. When we did, Mother would become short-tempered, tense, and intolerant of the slightest mistake or irritation. Sharing the front seat became hell. So when I noticed a few snowflakes fall as we sat in a diner outside Washington, I said a silent prayer for a brief flurry.

Mother also noticed them and was immediately on edge. The moment the waitress brought our lunch, Mother gave her the thermos to fill with tea and the kittens' formula to warm. As soon as she returned with them, we left, leaving half the meal on our plates.

Outside, it was already snowing hard and the temperature had dropped at least fifteen degrees. While Mother fed the kittens with the eyedropper, I went back inside and had the waitress fill their hot-water bottle. The heater in the Rolls wasn't very good, and Mother didn't want them to catch cold.

Before long, the snowstorm grew into a blizzard. The wind shook the car, and the road became a slippery white sheet defined only by the guardposts at the edge of the shoulders. Most drivers pulled over; we couldn't. The kittens' birth had delayed our departure by twenty-four hours, and we hadn't a moment to spare if we were going to arrive in time for the show. I watched Mother leaning forward in her seat, straining to look through the windshield, her knuckles white from gripping the wheel as she fought the wind for control of the car, and wondered what had happened. Seven months earlier, when *Gypsy* was on the best-seller lists, life had seemed so promising. Ever since, she had suffered one bad break after another.

It had begun with what seemed at the time to be a stroke of good fortune: Early in July, Harry Joe Brown called from Hollywood to offer her a part in a film he was producing for Columbia Pictures. *Curious Evening* was progressing slowly and its expenses were mounting quickly, so Mother didn't wait to see the script or even ask its title. All she wanted to know was "How much? . . . What's my billing?" and "When do you want me?"

He didn't need her for three weeks, but we flew to Los Angeles immediately. Mother had heard of an excellent but inexpensive plastic surgeon there, and with the film and *Curious Evening* ahead of her, it seemed like the ideal time for "a few tucks here and there so I won't look like a road map in my close-ups."

We were living in a secluded house at the beach while she recuperated, and I was making myself some lunch when the script arrived from Columbia. Mother wasn't eating — she wanted to be thin for the camera as well as wrinkle free — and the moment the messenger left, she began reading her part. She finished reading before I finished eating, and I could tell by the way she closed the cover that she wasn't at all pleased.

"Not very good?" I asked.

She shook her head. "Even the title's ridiculous. *Screaming Mimi!* Good God!" She tossed the script on the coffee table and stared at it morosely. It was a serious moment, but I found it difficult not to laugh. The hundreds of tiny black stitches around her eyes, across her forehead at the hairline, and under her chin, coupled with her gloomy expression and the bikini she was wearing, made her look like a musical-comedy version of Frankenstein's bride. Finally, she stood up and shrugged. "At least it will pay for the operation." She put a towel over her head to keep the sun from swelling the incisions and went out to work on her tan. Normally, she didn't take disappointments that lightly, but she was used to them in Hollywood. It had happened twice before.

The first time was in 1937. From Minsky's, she had made the unprecedented leap to Broadway as a co-star with Fanny Brice in the *Ziegfeld Follies* when Darryl Zanuck, head of 20th Century–Fox, offered her a contract. She didn't hesitate. Like every other young woman of her generation, it was her dream to become a movie star, and she had every reason to think stardom was right around the corner. Zanuck hadn't asked for a screen test, he was paying her more than she had ever earned in her life, and he had even paid the producers of the *Follies* $20,000 to release her from her run-of-the-show contract.

But neither she nor Zanuck had considered Will H. Hays, the head of Hollywood's powerful self-censorship board. He was outraged when he heard that Zanuck had signed a "strip woman" and vowed to the press that no film in which she appeared would ever be shown in a theater. "I have been charged to protect the morals of America's youth, and it is exactly what I intend to do."

In an effort to salvage his investment, Zanuck appealed Hays's decision, and they compromised: Mother was allowed to appear in films, but not as Gypsy Rose Lee. She had to use her maiden name, Rose Louise Hovick. Without her stage name, she had no marquee value, and Zanuck lost all interest in her. The star treatment came to an abrupt end. He switched her to the B-picture unit, let her make five very forgettable films, and dropped her when her contract came up for renewal at the end of one year.

Her second disappointment had come in 1944. Bill Goetz, head of the newly formed International Pictures, hired her for his first major production, *Belle of the Yukon*. She returned to Hollywood in triumph. Behind her was a string of record-shattering appearances for Michael Todd at the New York World's Fair and in *Star and Garter*; ahead was the co-starring role with Randolph Scott in an expensive, costume epic. Best of all, the name that would follow Scott's on the screen and in all the ads was Gypsy Rose Lee. Hollywood welcomed her with open arms. The press ran story after story, each more favorable than the last. She was invited to every party, and before the film was even in the can, Goetz began negotiating a long-term contract with her lawyer. Now she thought she had made it.

Like all contracts, this one took a long time to finalize, but she wasn't worried. Both she and the film got excellent trade reviews, and when it opened to the public the critics agreed. Then suddenly, everything went wrong. The picture died at the box office, Goetz stopped returning her lawyer's calls, reporters no longer waited outside her door, and the party invitations dried up. She left town unnoticed; her departure didn't even rate a mention in the trade papers.

With those memories, Philip Carey and Anita Ekberg for co-stars, and a small role in a lousy script, Mother wasn't expecting anything to come from *Screaming Mimi*. So it came as a pleasant surprise when, in the middle of shooting, she was offered another film. *Wind Across the Everglades* had all the ingredients for a good commercial film with blockbuster potential. The story, which told of the efforts of a federal wildlife agent, played by Christopher Plummer, to eliminate the poaching of exotic birds in the Florida swamps at the turn of the century, had lots of action and a little social relevance. The script, written by Budd Schulberg, who had won an Academy Award for writing *On the Waterfront*, was excellent. Nicholas Ray, the director, had recently completed *Rebel Without a Cause* and was at the height of his career. And the budget was ample to permit full cinematic utilization of the savagely beautiful locales. Mother played the madam of the local brothel, and although her role wasn't large — "mostly visual" as she said — it required her presence for three weeks, which at $2500 a week was the kind of money she never refused.

She did, however, hesitate. There was a lot of work left to be done on *Curious Evening*, she had already agreed to show it in Palm Beach on January 19, and she knew it couldn't be postponed. Finally she decided that she could make up the lost time by working extra-hard during the layoff between the two pictures. As it turned out, she didn't have time even to look at it. When she wasn't getting costumes fitted for *Everglades*, she was in meetings with her lawyers deciding what to do with the dramatic rights to *Gypsy*. There were four offers pending: M-G-M and Warner Brothers were each offering around $200,000 to make it into a film, while David Merrick and the team of Lerner and Loewe wanted to use it as the basis of a Broadway musical. She finally sold it to David Merrick for $4000 against a percentage of the box-office gross.

I was stunned when she told me. "You turned down two hundred thousand dollars?"

"It's a risk," she explained, "but if the show is successful I'll get royalties from it for the rest of my life as well as at least that much when it's sold for a film."

"But why David Merrick instead of Lerner and Loewe?" They had written *My Fair Lady*, and I was always impressed by success.

"I like David. He's young and aggressive." Her face took on a wistful expression. "Reminds me a lot of Mike [Todd], and God knows I was always lucky with him. Professionally speaking, that is."

She hadn't mentioned what would happen if the show flopped, nor that the odds on Broadway were against her. I couldn't believe that she was taking such a risk; it was so unlike her. I was afraid she had made a terrible mistake.

Without question she had made one when she agreed to *Wind Across the Everglades*, as she discovered on the first day. Right after the first take of the first shot — not even the first "print" — the director celebrated the start of filming by treating the entire cast and crew to champagne. Mother disapproved of drinking on the job, and when lunchtime arrived without another frame of film being shot, she decided to complain to the producer. Unfortunately, he was in the bar celebrating with the director. Furious, she returned to our room in the hotel, took off her costume, and lay on the bed. "I'll be goddamned if I'm going to wait around in the hot sun while that son-of-a-bitch slops up booze. When they want me, they'll just have to send for me and wait until I get there." They didn't. The celebration lasted until after dinner, and no one even noticed her protest. That was the only party, but the director had a serious drinking problem, and if the morning wasn't lost to one of his hangovers, the afternoon suffered because he drank his lunch.

That was only one of the film's difficulties. Because it was made on location in Everglades, Florida — right in the middle of the largest swamp in the United States — before location shooting was common or perfected, it was beset by every problem imaginable: costumes were lost en route from New York (Mother ended up making many of her own), the cameraman was bitten by a poisonous snake and had to be hospitalized for a week, tropical thunderstorms interrupted shooting almost every afternoon, the heat and humidity were staggering, and the equipment constantly malfunctioned because mold and mildew gummed up the works. It was, in short, a disaster; one compounded for Mother as each delay postponed her return to New York and to work on *Curious Evening*.

It was November before we got home. She had only two months in which to bring order from the chaos of film that filled the dining room. She drove herself mercilessly. Every waking hour was spent working on the project, she slept less than four hours a day, usually in cat naps, and I was pressed into service after school and on weekends. By the day before we were scheduled to leave, she had something to show, but it was a far from finished product. The film was rough and full of splices which often broke going through the projector, the taped music score was uneven and punctuated by "bloops" and "wows," and the narration was a bare outline. And she was exhausted. Then the kittens arrived, which postponed our departure and added both to the pressure on Mother and to her exhaustion. To be hit now by the worst blizzard of the season seemed like a cruel blow. Perhaps even the last straw.

Fortunately, Mother was used to foul weather driving and knew how to make time in the worst conditions. "Find a speed you can maintain, then stick to it," was her motto. Nothing ever stopped her. She'd keep going even if it meant sliding down the highway at fifteen miles an hour. We were doing precisely that when a policeman stopped us at a roadblock. He was standing in the middle of the highway. Because the Rolls had a right-hand drive, I lowered my window, and he leaned in front of me to talk to Mother.

"Snow's real bad up ahead, ma'am," he said, quickly pulling his head out of the car. The animal smell must have been too much for him. "Can't let you pass without chains."

Mother hated using chains; she was afraid they'd break and scratch the paint. "I have snow tires," she argued, lying.

"They won't do you any good today."

"Well, is there someplace up ahead where I can have my chains put on?" Not that she would.

"Lady, I just told you, you can't pass here without 'em." He looked at the car skeptically. "Al's garage is just back a few miles; he might be able to help you out."

"I can't turn back. I'm Gypsy Rose Lee, and I have a show to do in Palm Beach tomorrow night. If you don't let me pass, I'll miss it." As always, she announced her name regally so the cop wouldn't have to recognize it to know its importance.

"You won't make it if you have an accident, either. And then you'll blame me for letting you through."

"That's the most ridiculous thing I've —"

"No point in arguing," he interrupted. "I ain't going to do it."

Mother turned the car around and started back down the highway. "That son-of-a-bitch! Ten to one, he and Al are in cahoots." Mother hated not getting her way, especially after using her name. She'd never admit the policeman could be right; he had to have an ulterior motive.

Al did nothing to prove Mother's suspicions. Just the opposite. He took one look at the car, shook his head, and said, "Can't help you, lady. Never seen a car like this before."

"That's all right. I have the chains. You put them on just like any other car."

"Maybe, but I ain't fooling with it. There's a place in Washington that handles these foreign jobs. Try there." He turned and started back inside.

"Wait!" Mother yelled after him. She was leaning in front of me, and the shout rang in my ears. Al came back. "I can't go to Washington; it's fifty miles in the wrong direction. At least let me pull inside, out of the storm. I'll put the chains on myself." Al stood in the snow, thinking; Mother pressed on. "I'm Gypsy Rose Lee, and I'm opening in Palm Beach tomorrow night. If I don't get chains on the car, I'll never make it."

"I don't know." Al shook his head again. "If something happened to you in my shop . . ."

"Nothing will happen; believe me. Please. It's very important." I noticed an edge of desperation in her voice but couldn't decide if it was real or simply for effect. Then she said, "I'll pay you," and I knew it was for real. Mother only offered money as a last resort.

Al must have sensed it too. "Oh, you don't need to do that. Come on." He opened the garage doors, and we pulled inside.

Mother disdained the ordinary, and her Rolls typified the inconvenience she'd suffer to avoid it. One of the first designed to be owner-driven, its body was built entirely by hand in 1949 and retained the height, elegant shape, running boards, and separate headlamps of the classics. However, there was no interior partition, and instead of basic black, it was painted maroon over gray. Mother bought it used on our first trip to Europe in 1951, added her initials in gold leaf to the front doors, an antique crystal bud vase to the dash, and told everyone it had been built especially for her.

It was beautiful, luxurious, and unique; it was also totally impractical for cross-country touring in the United States during the fifties. Most highways, for example, were still only two lanes, and the right-hand drive made it impossible for Mother to check approaching traffic when she wanted to pass. I'd look for her, and she'd trust my judgment; we had a number of close calls. Passing, however, was a minor irritant compared with the problems we encountered in getting the car serviced. Outside of the major cities, few Americans had ever seen a

Rolls at the time; mechanics capable of working on them were non-existent. Most, like Al, were even unwilling to try.

But Mother would manipulate anyone without the slightest compunction. "I'm a woman alone in the world with a child, and I'll do whatever I must to survive." The Rolls broke down a lot, so she had become something of an expert with recalcitrant mechanics; and as we pulled into the garage, I was looking forward to watching her finagle Al into installing the chains. It would be a welcome break from the tense monotony of driving through the storm.

Even before turning off the engine, however, she told me to take Fu Manchu for a walk. I was afraid I'd miss the show and considered arguing; but I knew that I'd lose and decided instead to hurry. Of course, the spiteful animal wouldn't cooperate; he just stood in the snow and shivered. I gave him until I finished a quick smoke, and then I went back inside.

I hadn't missed a thing. Mother was taking the chains from the spare tire compartment, and Al was nowhere in sight. I took the leash off Fu, and he ran to her.

She petted him and cooed, "Does my little darling feel better now?" Returning to the chains, she asked me, "Did he do everything?"

"No, just peed; but he was getting cold," I lied. To ease my guilt, I added, "I'll take him out again before we leave."

"Ouch!" Mother yelled. "Goddamnit! Broke another fingernail." Her timing was a godsend. Fu was just proving me a liar by lifting his leg in the corner, but she never noticed. "Would you do this for me, darling; I don't want to break another one." I was so relieved, I would have gladly done anything.

Under her supervision, I laid out the chains behind the rear wheels. Mother's plan was to back the car over them, then wrap them around the tires. It was logical but unorthodox, and I doubted it would work. I didn't know it wasn't supposed to.

When I was almost finished, Mother took the carrier with the kittens from the car over to Al's office door, knocked, and called in to him. "Pardon me, Al?"

He opened the door. "Yeah?"

"My son's kittens have to be fed," she said, pointing to the box. "The mother cat's dry, and we've been keeping them alive by nursing them with an eyedropper. Would you mind if he did it in your office? It's so drafty out here, they might catch cold." Then she lowered her voice. "If anything happened to them, he'd be heartbroken."

I cringed at "heartbroken." Although I understood that Mother was only using me as a foil, she did it all the time, and I hated the way it made me look weak and helpless.

If Al thought I was a sissy, he didn't show it. "Sure. Come on in, son."

Then Mother added insult to injury. "Be careful, Erik. Don't give them too much at one time." She explained to Al, "He's not used to doing it alone. I usually help." God, I felt like such a jerk.

That's when Al noticed the chains. "You'll never get them on that way."

"No?"

"Got to jack the car up."

"But my jack's buried under all the costumes in the trunk. Unloading everything would take hours." The jack was in the spare tire compartment and easily accessible.

"Use mine," Al offered, right on cue. He pointed to a large, garage jack.

"Oh, thank you, but it looks much too complicated. I wouldn't know where to begin." Mother was just as willing to play the fool as she was to cast me in the part. Whatever worked.

Al looked at the car, the jack, the chains, the kittens, and finally at Mother. "Why don't you go inside and help the boy take care of those kittens. I'll have your chains on in a jiffy."

"Oh, *thank* you. You're a lifesaver. Erik, get the formula out of the car." As she picked up the carrier and walked into the office, she turned back to Al with a final thought: "Be careful not to scratch the paint."

We were back on the road by six. Mother had called the Automobile Club from Al's and learned that the storm extended halfway through North Carolina and was expected to continue until late the next day. She hated driving at night, let alone in the snow; but at the rate it was falling, she felt the roads could be closed by morning. We couldn't afford to get snowbound, so there was no choice but to drive through the night.

Crises were an inevitable part of our life, and we were used to them, but that night's drive was as torturous, nerve-racking, and exhausting as any we'd ever made: the glare of the headlights reflecting off the falling snow; the incessant, hypnotic beating of the chains and windshield wipers; the precarious road conditions; four kittens that had to be fed every four hours, and a dog that had to be walked in the bitter cold. We even lost one of the runts from the litter. Mother was sad but realistic. We buried it in a trash can at a gas station. For the rest of the trip, however, she paid particular attention to the surviving runt. "One death is about all I can take tonight," she said.

Through it all, she maintained a steady thirty miles per hour (which she finally admitted would not have been possible without the chains), stopping only to refill the thermos, buy gas, or feed the kittens. I kept her company so she wouldn't fall asleep, rubbed her neck to ease the tension, poured her tea, and lit her cigarettes. By seven-thirty, the storm was behind us.

We stopped for breakfast in Fayetteville, North Carolina, and Mother remarked, "We were supposed to spend last night here. If we keep on going now, we'll be right on schedule."

I wanted to go to sleep, but it would have been useless to argue. Whatever she did, Mother always pushed herself to her limit and then still farther. It was amazing.

At four, after thirty-three hours on the road, she decided to stop for the night. She would have gone on until sundown, but she'd just been caught at a speed trap in a one-light town by a redneck sheriff. It cost her forty-five dollars, and losing money always drained her energy.

After replenishing our supplies at the local grocery, we checked into a third-rate motel (the forty-five dollars had to be made up somewhere) outside Statesboro, Georgia. Mother cooked dinner in the room in our electric frying pan, made our lunch for the next day, fed the animals, and was sound asleep by seven. We were back on the road at five-thirty the next morning and arrived in Palm Beach at four that afternoon. Close, but we'd made it.

We drove directly to the art gallery/boutique of William Alexander Kirkland. Bill ran the lecture series that was sponsoring Mother's appearance. He was also the second of her three ex-husbands and my father. Mother had called him from our last fuel stop, and he was waiting on the sidewalk when we pulled up.

It was a moment I had dreaded for months, ever since I had told him about *Curious Evening* during one of our divorced-father-and-son Sundays together, and he had asked if I thought Mother would like to try it out in Palm Beach as part of his lecture series.

I was appalled at the idea. Bill had always struck me as something of a failure. His boutique sold a hodgepodge of gift items ranging from the corny to the tasteless, the art gallery was nothing more than a hallway leading to the shop in which he hung overpriced paintings by unknown artists, and his lecture series had barely limped through its first season. I felt it was all terribly beneath Mother's stature.

But I couldn't say that to Bill. He was the second father figure in my life. The first had been Mother's third husband, Julio de Diego, a Spanish painter. I had known from the start that Julio wasn't actually my father, but it hadn't mattered. He was everything I could possibly want: warm, affectionate, flamboyant, and loving. I adored him, used the name Erik Lee de Diego in first grade, and was a devastated six-year-old when he and Mother separated.

That's when I learned about Bill being my "real" father. I took his name and began seeing him. It was a totally different relationship from the one I'd had with Julio. Bill was a reserved, almost courtly, New England WASP. I doubt we ever used the word "love" between us. We saw each other only on weekends and I always felt the relationship was tenuous. But he was the only father I had and I wasn't about to risk losing him by telling him what I thought of his suggestion. Instead, I took the only safe option: I told him I'd pass his invitation on to Mother.

I briefly considered not telling her and then reporting to him that she wasn't interested. They never met when he came to collect me for our visits — in fact, I had never seen them together — but they did talk on the phone and I was afraid the subject might arise. So I waited until she was in a bad mood and then mentioned it very casually. It didn't work. She loved the idea.

Now, seeing him on the sidewalk, I realized again that she was going to see the crummy shop with its gold-colored telephones, its vinyl place mats inscribed "Doggie Diner," and all the other crap. I was positive she would regret having gotten involved and blame me. Or, that she would make fun of it and offend Bill. As it turned out, my fears were unnecessary and unfounded.

Mother stopped the car at the curb, opened the window, and called, "Well. We made it."

Bill came over, gave her a kiss on the cheek, and said, "Hi, princess. How are you?"

"Oh, God, Bill. Don't ask. Just look at me. Princess, indeed."

"I like your new hair style." Leave it to Bill, I thought, to notice. When Mother had first had it cut a month earlier, I hadn't noticed until she called my attention to it.

"It'll look a lot better after a few minutes with the curling iron. But you look wonderful. I love those madras jackets." She opened the door and handed Fu to him. "Here, darling. Hold Fu for a moment while I get organized. I'm dying to see your shop. How much time do I have before the show?"

Bill smiled. "About half an hour."

"Half an hour!" Mother shrieked. Her yell, combined with his fear of strangers, was too much for Fu. He struggled in Bill's arms for a moment, realized he was trapped, and began peeing in terror. Bill didn't notice, but Mother did. "Oh, my God. Here, Bill, let me take him." As Bill handed Fu over, the pee sprayed over everything like a fountain. I wanted to crawl under the car. Bill was too shocked to react. Mother quickly took charge, grabbed a balled-up, well-used Kleenex out of her purse, and began dabbing at the wet spots on Bill's jacket and pants. It didn't do any good. "Oh, well," she said, "don't worry. It'll come out at the cleaners."

Bill took it in stride and began laughing. "Our wedding all over again. Remember when your monkey relieved himself all over my suit?"

"It wasn't my monkey, it was Mother's," she answered with mock seriousness, "and I warned you not to give him a whole bottle of beer. Goddamn monkey!"

The next half hour should have been a chaotic scramble to get ready, but because of Bill's excellent preparations, everything went smoothly. He had rented the Taboo restaurant, eight doors down the street from his shop, for the lecture and converted his office into a dressing room for Mother. He even had a woman standing by with an iron and ironing board to press her dress. After getting Mother's things and the kittens out of the car, he dropped me off at the restaurant to set up the show while he went home to change.

The Taboo was a pleasant contrast to the nightclubs I was used to. It was clean, sedate, and elegant. Bill had rented a projector, tape recorder, and screen, all of which had been installed before I arrived. It took me just ten minutes to thread the film and tape and test them.

Guests had begun to arrive and were congregating in the cocktail lounge. Bill, knowing we would be a bit late in starting, had arranged for drinks to be served. I peeked around the corner to check out the audience. It was a different breed from our usual audience: silver-haired men wearing semiformal resort wear, accompanied by women who were dressed to the teeth in jewels and furs. One look and I decided to run back to Bill's shop and change for the show.

Mother was feeding the kittens when I arrived. She was made up and, aside from putting on her dress, ready to go. While I changed, I asked her if she had looked around the shop. "Quickly," she answered. "El crappo! Every bit of it. Bill has such good taste, too. But I guess it sells, and that's what counts." Needless to say, I was relieved.

Our entrance at the Taboo was electric. Bill took us through the front door into the cocktail lounge, and we were immediately surrounded. Bill's group may have dressed differently from Mother's usual audience, but they made the same comments. One gray-haired man of sixty even said, "I used to skip high school to see your show." Mother hated that line and answered sharply, "Honey, I wasn't even born when you were in high school." Then one foolish woman tried to pet Fu, and he snapped at her. He didn't draw blood, but Bill took it as his cue to break up the crowd and start the show. He knew where Fu's displeasure could lead.

It was hard to gauge the reaction to the show. The film broke twice and the tape once, but Bill had announced that it was still a work in progress and the audience was quite patient. I felt the laughs were few and the squirming constant, but during the question-and-answer period at the end, everyone was complimentary, and at dinner that night, Frank Hale — owner of the prestigious Palm Beach Playhouse — offered to play the show once Mother had finished it. She even got a good review from the local critic.

Though pleased by the response, Mother was not convinced. She knew too well that all but the most severe critics soft-pedal their opinions when face to face with a work's creator. Only a special kind of friend can be trusted to tell the truth. As it happened, Mother had such a friend living not far off our route home, and we left Palm Beach early the next day to visit him.

Judged by any criterion, Colonel Elliott White Springs was an extraordinary person. As a pilot during World War I, he had destroyed eleven enemy planes and was the United States' third ranked flying ace. After the war, he did some barnstorming before moving to Paris, where he wrote eight novels based on his wartime experiences. Although his writing was successful — he used to say that the two hundred and fifty thousand dollars he made off his books was the only money he had ever *earned* — after ten years he returned to South Carolina to manage his family's five separate textile concerns. When his father died, he consolidated, modernized, and expanded them until Springs Cotton Mills was the seventh largest textile company in the country and the world's largest manufacturer of sheets and pillow cases.

During his lifetime, he spent over ten million dollars improving his workers' living conditions, providing them with low-cost housing, excellent schools, recreation parks, bowling alleys, swimming pools, a hospital, and a golf course.

But for all his success and generosity, it was his humor and *joie de vivre* that set him far above the average and earned him, in the *New*

York Times, the title of the "world's champion fun-loving business-man." One of his favorite projects was writing and designing all of Springmaid's ads, always trying to see just how risqué he could make them without having them rejected by the staid women's magazines. In the forties, they featured drawings of barely covered, shapely women with copy lines like "How to put the broad in broadcloth." In 1950, after meeting Mother at an American Legion benefit, he decided she would be a perfect spokesperson, given his penchant for the double entendre, and she had been doing at least two ads a year ever since. One of the most notorious, in 1954, had a photograph of Mother lying seductively on her bed in a negligee. The copy read: " 'My favorite night spot is a Springmaid sheet,' says Miss Gypsy Rose Lee, prominent hostess of New York and Paris. Like so many aristocrats, Miss Lee finds Springmaid a must for her guests. Those favorite leaders of fashion who share her hospitality are treated to the very finest of bedroom appointments."

It was six hundred and fifty miles from Palm Beach to Colonel Springs's home, far more than Mother liked to drive in one day, but with a little urging from me she pushed through. We were both eager to arrive. Visiting Colonel Springs was like visiting a private amusement park. There were all those normal things one expects of the wealthy — good food, servants, lovely surroundings — and so much more. He gave me the run of his special gadget room, which was always filled with the latest and best technological marvels. There were Minox cameras, remote-control cars and planes, electronic gyroscopes, miniature walkie-talkies, star-gazing telescopes — things I had never imagined, and others I couldn't understand.

Mother's favorite spot was the nataborium, a huge greenhouse three stories tall, fifty feet wide, and one hundred and fifty feet long that was attached to the house. It enclosed a large, irregularly shaped swimming pool completely lined with mosaic tiles in various designs and surrounded on three sides by dense tropical foliage. The fourth side, next to the house, had a bar, tables and chairs, and a whirlpool bath that Mother could sit in for hours. Because of the high glass ceiling, there was no feeling of being indoors. On the contrary, the fragrant plants and the warm, moist air made it seem like a tropical paradise, especially after stepping in from the cold winter weather outside.

We would have been delighted to spend the day around the house, but Colonel Springs had laid on a special surprise for us. Another of his business toys was the Lancaster and Chester Railway. It was only a small feeder line used to move supplies and finished goods between the mills and the main line of the Southern Railway System, but he ran it, tongue in cheek, as if it were the New York Central. On the back of the railroad's stationery was a map showing every foot of train track in South Carolina, Georgia, Florida, and Alabama. Printed in large letters at the bottom was "The Lancaster and Chester Railway System." Below, and very small, was "and connecting lines."

In the official Railway Guide, and on the letterhead, he listed twenty-nine vice-presidents, one for each mile of track. Mother, appropriately, was the Vice-President in Charge of Unveiling. As our arrival coincided with the delivery of the first of a new line of freight cars, he had arranged a little inaugural celebration. It began with Mother breaking a jeroboam of vintage champagne over the baby blue and beige freight car as Colonel Springs looked on, wearing his derby hat and Inverness. Then the three of us climbed into the cab of a full-size diesel loco-motive and took turns at the controls as we piloted the car to the other end of the line. There, we had an elegant lunch in the line's "regional office" — an antique private railroad car that had been built in 1905 for Charles Schwab, the founder of Bethlehem Steel. Colonel Springs had discovered it in a junkyard and had had it completely restored. It was a wonderful day. Mother liked the lunch, I liked driving the train, and Colonel Springs — as always — enjoyed all of it.

That night after dinner, I ran the projector and Mother gave a private performance of *Curious Evening* for Colonel Springs. He liked the concept, but he told her that the film and the narration needed a lot of work. He didn't feel either came close to capturing the essence of Mother's wit. She recognized the truth and was relieved to hear it. It confirmed her own opinion and helped her gain perspective. We left for New York the following morning. Mother had a big job ahead of her.

CHAPTER FOUR

FOR NEW YORK, it was a typically miserable March day: damp and cold with snow flurries whipped around by a biting wind. I had my head down to shield my face and would have missed Charles had he not seen me.

"Erik!" he shouted. "Erik! Over here!" I looked up. "Come help us. Hurry." He was struggling vainly against the wind to hold an umbrella over the dressmaker's dummy that Alice, his seamstress, was easing out of the back seat of a taxi. Charles was tiny and delicate, a birdlike man who fluttered constantly, regardless of what else he was doing. He wore no coat, but was fastidiously dressed in a blue blazer, gray slacks, pale blue striped shirt, and regimental tie. Even with the wind I could smell his cologne, but it was not offensive. For a moment, it looked as if a gust of wind would carry him away, but he held fast to the side of the taxi. I went to help him, but he stopped me. "No, no. Help Alice with the gown. For godsakes, be careful."

Alice was holding the dummy by the neck, so I went around to the side. Slowly we continued sliding it out of the cab. The dummy had a dress pinned to it that was protected by a sheet. At one point, the sheet caught on the window handle of the door. Charles yelled "Stop!" so urgently that we froze. He released it with loving care, insuring the dress underneath was unharmed before he allowed us to continue removing the dummy from the cab. Each of his gowns was unique and represented weeks of work; they were his children.

Charles James was Mother's couturier. Since the thirties he had been designing for the crème of society. Millicent Rogers, Lady Diana Duff-Cooper, and Mrs. Vincent Astor were among his clients, two or more of whom were always on the list of best-dressed women in New York. He and Mother had been friends for years, but he only began making dresses for her after she managed to convince him that the publicity he would derive from her wearing his clothes would make up for the money he'd lose by selling them at cost.

Charles was never truly satisfied with the arrangement. He felt that he was a genius whose creations were well worth the thousand dollars and more that he normally charged. And he was particularly annoyed that Mother, while demanding "enormous" sacrifices on his part, was totally unwilling to make any herself. That day, for example, he complained for the entire elevator ride up to Mother's room: "Mrs. Rockefeller comes to my salon for fittings. She understands how much more sensible it is for one person to get into a taxi than it is for two people to transport themselves and a mannequin all the way up-town. . . .

"I don't know why I go to all this trouble for your mother, Erik. I really don't. I don't do it for anyone else, you know? All my other clients come to my salon."

I could have told him that he did it because she insisted, and he was afraid to confront her, but I only nodded sympathetically. I was used to Mother's friends complaining to me about things they'd never dare mention to her face. By the time we arrived upstairs, he was out of his snit. But not for long.

While Alice and I lifted the mannequin out of the elevator, he knocked on her door and announced himself. "It's Charles, Gypsy. I have your new ballgown. It's finished."

"Go away," she called through the door. "I can't see you now." Charles was stunned and stood there, looking at the door. No one ever dared be abrupt with him; he was too much the prima donna. And that day, of all days, it was the last thing he expected. The following evening, she was going to a Friar's Club testimonial dinner at the Waldorf in honor of Mike Todd, and for weeks she had been pressing him to have the gown ready on time.

Charles regained his composure. As if she hadn't understood, he knocked again and said, "It's Charles, Gypsy. I have your new gown with me."

"I can't see you today." The tone of her voice was sharp and final; it left no room for argument.

Charles was furious, but he controlled it. Pulling himself as tall as his five-and-a-half-foot frame would permit, he marched into the el-evator. "Take the gown, Alice. We're leaving." He said nothing more as we found a taxi and reloaded the mannequin. Then, just before the taxi pulled away from the curb, he leaned out the window and said, "Tell your mother that I'm very angry with her. If she wants her gown, she can collect it at my salon."

I didn't answer. My mind was upstairs with Mother. I knew something was wrong. I ran up to her room and knocked on her door. "Mother, it's me, Erik. May I come in? I'm alone."

She unlocked the door but didn't open it. I waited until I realized that she wouldn't, then entered. She was pacing the floor in the center of the room, wearing a threadbare cotton bathrobe. She had on no makeup, her hair was stringy and disheveled, as if she had been pulling at it, and her eyes were red from crying. She looked at me with the saddest expression I ever saw her wear.

"He's dead, Erik."

"Who?"

She started to answer but couldn't form the words. Instead, she handed me a crumpled telegram that had been balled up in her fist. It was wet with tears and sweat and tore as I straightened it out, but I could still see that it was the invitation to the dinner in honor of Mike Todd. I looked at her. She dried her eyes with a Kleenex. "In a plane crash . . ." She began before crying again.

"Is there anything I can do?"

She shook her head. "Just leave me alone. And answer the phone if it rings. I couldn't bear talking to anyone."

I kissed her on the cheek and left. She locked the door behind me. She had spoken highly of Mike, and I knew they had been friends, but her grief surprised me. When Boyd came home that evening, I went downstairs to discuss it with him.

He wasn't at all surprised. "But of course she's upset. Mike was the great love of her life."

"You're kidding," I said. Aside from her marriage to Julio, I had never seen her with a man. It had never occurred to me that she might have had flaming love affairs in her youth.

"There were even rumors that he was your father."

"Really?" I was immediately intrigued. The idea seemed so romantic and mysterious.

"Of course, it's not true," Boyd added quickly. Too quickly, I thought. I knew he had sensed my interest and I felt he might be trying to cover up a slip.

"Are you sure?" I persisted.

"Positive."

"Then how did the rumors get started?"

"Oh, you know how people love to gossip. It means nothing." He changed the subject, but my curiosity had been aroused, and I made a point of learning all I could about Mike and Mother. It took me years to piece together their story, and it still amazes me that a woman as levelheaded and direct as Mother could have behaved so foolishly.

Mother was never successful with men. Her first great passion was Rags Ragland, the burlesque comic. He was infamous for his treatment of women, but she was in her teens and naive enough to think it would be different with her. It wasn't. He made his conquest and moved on. Her second lover was the opposite: gentle, kind, generous, and honest. Eddie never made a secret of his being married, but he truly loved her and did the best he could under the circumstances. He gave her diamonds and promised to see that she was cared for as long as she lived. The night before they were to meet a lawyer in Chicago who was drawing up a special trust for her, Eddie died. On the rebound, she married her first husband, Bob Mizzy, a dental supplies manufacturer. Bob wanted her to give up show business, live in the suburbs, and raise a family. She tried, but it was doomed from the start. Mother was simply not the suburban sort. They were divorced in 1938.

In 1940, she met Mike when he hired her to star with Abbott and Costello in *Streets of Paris*, a show he was producing at the New York World's Fair, then in its second year.

They were perfectly matched. Mike, like Mother, had been raised poor. He was hustling shoeshines and living in the Jewish ghettos of Chicago and Minneapolis while she was trouping in vaudeville and living in tents. Both were self-educated and well read but hid their knowledge behind a Runyonesque facade. Their careers, too, were on a par. For each, the World's Fair represented a new level of success. In Mother's case, it marked the full recovery from her disastrous year under contract to 20th Century–Fox. Her show was the most popular at the fair, and the forty-foot-high photograph of her on the front of the Hall of Music could be seen from everywhere in the park. "My picture," she used to quip, "was larger than Stalin's."

As for Mike, in its second year the entire fair seemed like a Mike Todd production. In addition to Mother's show, he had built a ten-acre replica of the New Orleans French Quarter, complete with a duplicate Original Absinthe House. He called it Gay New Orleans and gave the customer three full-length shows and a number of smaller attractions for a quarter. He also ran the Dancing Campus, where as many as twelve thousand people a night danced to the music of Harry

James and Les Brown. He replaced the Shakespeare Theatre, which had died during the fair's first year, with the Old Op'ry House. It sold out every night. He owned Gay New Orleans and Mother's show but only managed the rest. Still, his name was on them all, and it was impossible to walk down the midway without seeing "Michael Todd Presents" at every turn. Not bad for a guy who had produced his first successful Broadway show only a year earlier.

They hit it off almost immediately. The day after *Streets of Paris* opened, between the 11 A.M. and 1 P.M. shows, Mike came to her dressing room and pounded on the door. "What's the matter in there? Can't you read?"

Mother opened the door. "Of course I can read."

He pointed to a huge sign on the notice board. It read, "No Cooking Backstage."

"I always cook in my dressing room. It saves money. On my salary, I can't afford to eat out."

"On your salary, I can't afford to have you stinking up the theater." He looked past her into the dressing room. "What the hell you making in there anyway? I could smell it all the way out in the lobby."

"Knockwurst."

He walked around her into the room. "They better be good. I'm a maven." After lunch, he tore the sign off the notice board. Hypocrisy was not among his faults.

They shared lunch often after that, dinner too, but it was strictly a friendly partnership. Mike was married and had a girlfriend as well; he didn't need more trouble. Mother, by then, was wary of men and especially of Mike. She sensed his ambition and knew she had a role to play in his plans, and she intended to be paid for it . . . in cash.

Gypsy Rose Lee was the perfect personality at the perfect time for him, but it would be unfair to imply that his success over the next few years was due entirely to her. He was, without question, one of the smartest and most talented theatrical figures of his day. If it hadn't been her, it would have been someone else; but it is a measure of his savvy that he used her as well as he did.

Like many slum kids, Mike used to dream of returning home in triumph; unlike most, he did. On Christmas Day 1940, three months after the fair closed, he opened Michael Todd's Theatre Cafe in Chicago. It was the largest nightclub in the world, eight thousand seats, and he filled it by catering to "your average working-class Joe" instead of "rich snobs." There was no cover or minimum, the first show was at five in the afternoon, dinner cost seventy-five cents, champagne cocktails were a quarter, and friendly waitresses replaced the usual arrogant waiters. It had a sixty-foot stage with a dance floor suspended above it, two dance bands working in shifts, a four-hundred-foot bar, and a spectacular show. *The Gay New Orleans Review*, "straight from 2500 performances at the New York World's Fair," featured the comedy team of Willy West and McGinty, a Ben Hur chariot race, and starred Gypsy Rose Lee.

It was a smash. The first night's attendance was sixteen thousand and an equal number were turned away. For three months, Mike made money hand over fist. Then the Mafia moved in and generously offered him a partnership in his own club. Mike considered the offer. With the mob's backing, he could easily have become one of the top men in show business. But just as easily, he figured, he could end up dead. So he sold them the club for one dollar and took his name off it. Mother left with him. Two weeks later, the club was raided and put out of business. He hardly noticed; he had a more pressing problem: all his life, he would spend money just a little faster than he made it, and right then he was broke.

Mother came to his rescue — and did pretty well herself — by taking *The Gay New Orleans Review* on tour around the country. It was the same show Mike had produced for the nightclub minus the chariot race, which was too expensive to transport. It was a grueling summer for Mother, but a productive one. She did three shows a day, six days a week, and wrote her second murder mystery during her free time.

She and Mike were still only friends, but rumors concerning them had begun to circulate and had reached Mike's wife, Bertha, who had sensed for some time that her marriage was in trouble. Determined to salvage it, she followed Mike when he came to Syracuse in August to check on the show, burst into Mother's dressing room while they were talking, and threatened to cause a horrible scandal unless they ended their affair immediately. Mother quickly convinced her that there was no affair, and Bertha apologized. Mike, however, realized that the ice was getting a bit thin and broke off with his girlfriend.

The tour ended in September, and Mother returned home to New York. *The G-String Murders* was published in October and transformed her from America's most successful stripper into the darling of New York's literary set. She was invited to all the right parties and began giving some herself. Regular visitors to her cold-water flat on East 57th Street included writers such as Carson McCullers, Janet Flanner, Carl Van Doren, Christopher Isherwood and the artists Max Ernst, Pavel

Tchelitchew, Marcel Vertès. She couldn't appear on stage in New York because all the burlesque theaters had been closed, but she didn't mind. She had finished her second book, begun a play, and was writing articles for *The New Yorker* and *American Mercury*. The only thing missing in her life was romance, but it was on its way, along with her biggest success as a performer.

By January 1942, Mike's career was in serious trouble. Since returning from Chicago, he had been unable to get anything off the ground, and he needed a show. In similar circumstances the average producer would seek out the safest, easiest project available, but Mike was anything but average. He decided to revive burlesque as a big, splashy, expensive Broadway musical starring Gypsy Rose Lee.

His friends and associates all warned him against it. Who, they asked, was going to pay $4.40 to see the same crap that was selling last year for fifty cents? And what about Mayor La Guardia, who finally managed to get burlesque out of New York? He'll close the show opening night. Provided, of course, you can find someone crazy enough to give you the money to produce it. Even Mother wasn't terribly keen on going back to "the old grind." But Mike always had an answer. He figured the average theatergoer had never seen burlesque and would gladly pay to see a stage full of pretty girls and risqué comics. The mayor had managed to purge New York of burlesque only by enforcing the building codes against the old theaters; he wouldn't dare try the same tactic with the Music Box, one of Broadway's most prestigious theaters. As for Mother, he reminded her that starring in her own Broadway show was a far cry from "her old grind." Then he clinched the deal by gradually involving her in all facets of the production.

He had her take him to every burlesque theater on the East Coast to see the acts and agreed to her suggestion that he use Bobby Clark, the male lead from her *Ziegfeld Follies*, and Georgia Sothern, her best friend from Minsky's, as her co-stars. They wrote the show together, too. At night, Mother and Georgia would run through all the old burlesque comedy skits for Mike; and after Georgia went home, they would stay up half the night selecting those they wanted in the show and perfecting them.

There is an excitement that comes with creating, an almost sexual thrill that rushes through the body whenever a difficult problem is solved. In a collaboration, the thrill is intensified by a euphoric feeling of camaraderie that for Mother was an awakening. She had never been close enough to anyone to share even an honest feeling, let alone an intense one, and she reacted in a perfectly normal fashion — she fell in love with Mike, threw caution to the wind, and began having an affair with him.

It was a heady time for her. She was in love and with her lover all the time, producing their very own Broadway show. There were problems, of course. With Mike there were always problems, and as usual one of the problems was money. As opening day approached, Mike was still twenty-five thousand dollars short. He could have trimmed costs, but he had a policy of never scrimping on the lavish quality of his productions. Instead, he performed major surgery: he canceled the pre-Broadway tour and limited the number of previews to one. Hassard Short, the director, was furious. "When," he wanted to know, "am I supposed to work the kinks out of the show?"

"Don't put any in," Mike answered. "We can't afford 'em."

It was a funny joke until the preview bombed on the night before the scheduled opening. The show needed at least a week's work, but Mike didn't have the money to postpone the opening, and he'd run out of backers. Rather than open a show he knew would flop, he decided to close it immediately and went to Mother's dressing room to give her the bad news. Mother, however, wouldn't accept it. She had too great an emotional investment in the show.

"How much do you need?" she asked.

"Forty thou."

"You just got yourself a new backer. Have Bill [their lawyer] draw up a contract. I'll bring the money to his office in the morning."

Mike didn't believe she had it, let alone that she'd invest it in something as risky as a show. She already had a reputation for being tight. "Come on, Gyps. Where are you going to get that kind of money?"

"From the bank, where else."

She was late arriving at the lawyer's office the next day. She never kept more than five thousand dollars in any one bank — the maximum insured by the government at the time — and it had taken her longer than expected to visit her various accounts. It also took longer than expected to get the contract signed. When it came to numbers, fractions, and percentages, she was never able to overcome her lack of a formal education, and she just couldn't understand the complicated figures. Finally, in frustration, she pleaded, "Can't you just give me a pie?"

"A pie?" Mike's lawyer asked.

"For chrissakes!" Mike yelled at him. "The dame wants a pie, give her a goddamn pie." The lawyer still didn't get it, so Mike drew a pie with appropriately sized slices representing the various investors' shares, they attached it to the back of the contract, and everyone was happy. A week later, on June 24, *Star and Garter* opened to rave reviews and endless lines at the box office.

Once the show settled into a routine, the creative excitement was over, and Mother began thinking of the future. She asked Mike to get a divorce and marry her. Mike knew it was impossible. Bertha had made that perfectly clear. Worse, she had threatened to keep him from his son if he even tried. Mike loved his son above all else in the world; he would never risk jeopardizing their relationship. Mother should have realized it, and Mike should have told her. Instead, Mother kept demanding, and Mike kept postponing. The ensuing fights were a legend backstage at the Music Box.

It was after one of these fights that Mother went alone to a party given by Carl Van Doren, a Pulitzer Prize–winning biographer and one of America's most distinguished literary critics. At the party, she was introduced to a handsome young actor then playing the romantic lead in *Junior Miss* on Broadway. Alexander Kirkland was the opposite of Mike — tall and fair, from a good family, considerate, and single. He was also totally captivated by Mother. Unlike the society women he was used to, she was open, honest, outspoken, and earthy.

Mother enjoyed Bill's company. She liked his manner, and she was flattered by his attention. Most of all, however, she saw him as leverage against Mike. The message was clear: Marry me, or I'll find someone else. Mike didn't respond to the threat. The more Mother nudged, the more he resisted; simultaneously, Bill was pressing Mother to marry him. It all came to a head the night of Bobby Clark's fortieth anniversary in show business. There was a party after the show to celebrate. Before the show, Mother told Mike that if he didn't promise to marry her, she was going to marry Bill. Mike didn't believe her and called her bluff. Later at the party, after all the toasts to Bobby Clark, Mother stood on an old beer crate and announced that she and Bill were getting married. Mike turned white, got up, and left the party without saying goodnight to anyone. The next day, he left for California "on business."

Bill was delighted. He knew nothing of the reasons behind Mother's decision; all he knew was that his "princess" had agreed to marry him. Mother, certain that Mike would stop her, went ahead with plans for the wedding. They read like a burlesque skit. The ring bearer was to be a chimpanzee, and the ceremony was to take place at midnight after the reception. Mother had an ulterior motive in reversing the normal sequence of events; she wanted Mike to have ample time to arrive and prevent the ceremony.

The day of the wedding, the guests, bride, and groom assembled at Mother's country house at four in the afternoon to start the festivities. *Life* magazine was in attendance with a reporter and a photographer, Georgia Sothern was the maid of honor, and Carl Van Doren the best man. As midnight approached with no sign of Mike, Mother stationed Georgia by a window facing the driveway to keep watch. She wanted to know the moment Mike arrived.

Midnight came without sign of Mike. Mother hid in her room, ostensibly fixing her makeup but actually staring out the window. She waited until twelve-thirty, then she could wait no longer. The minister was falling asleep, and Mike obviously wasn't going to show. Thus, she and Bill were married.

If the wedding was crazy, the wedding night was bizarre. Because both were in Broadway shows and had to be at work the following evening, it would be their only honeymoon. Bill tried to make the best of it and planned as romantic a night as he could: a room with a huge fireplace and a four-poster at a small country inn, chilled champagne, caviar, flowers. . . . He could have saved himself the trouble. When he came out of the bath in his new silk pajamas and robe, Mother was sitting in front of the fire wearing a long flannel nightgown and rubbing Vicks on her chest.

Bill thought she was sick and asked if he could do anything. "It's just a cold. I'll be all right in the morning." He opened the champagne, but Mother didn't want any. Finally he headed for the bed and asked if she were joining him. "Not right away, dear," she answered, tapping the book on her lap with her fingernail. "I have this wonderful book, and I think I'll read for a while. You go ahead." He hadn't the slightest idea of what to say, and the smell of the Vicks combined with the smell of his cologne had made him slightly nauseous, so he did.

In spite of this inauspicious beginning, Mother tried to make the marriage work, but after three months she gave up. Bill sadly agreed to a separation, and she went back to Mike on his terms. There was no more talk of divorce.

Mother was making so much money off her share of *Star and Garter* she couldn't spend it. For years, Mike had urged her to buy real estate, but Mother didn't believe in gambling with her money and invested in three life insurance annuities instead. Once these were paid off, however, Mike insisted she buy a house on East 63rd Street which he had found for her. As much as she loved the house, she still wasn't sure. The price of $12,500 was cheap even then, but it was in terrible condition. The basement was under five feet of water, the elevator cables were missing (God knows who took them or what for), all the water pipes were rotted, the old coal-fired furnace was beyond repair, and because of the war, no building supplies were available. Mike told her not to worry. "The store room in the basement of the theater is full of stuff. Use it." It wasn't his to give, but she used it anyway, and she even conned the stagehands into doing the work for her.

Then in March 1943, Mike agreed to produce the play Mother had written, *The Naked Genius*. All of her writing was semiautobiographical, and the play was no exception. It told the story of a stripper, Honey Bee Carol, who achieved fame and fortune by writing a murder mystery. Under the circumstances, Mother was positive that Mike would cast her in the lead, and it came as a great disappointment when he hired Joan Blondell for the part. Mother consoled herself with the thought that the presence of a movie star in the play would greatly enhance its chances for success and, in turn, her chances for a sizable royalty.

There was no disappointment in Mike's choice of a director. George S. Kaufman was one of Broadway's glittering stars at the time. Moreover, he had a reputation for quietly rewriting those plays he directed, often transforming a flop into a hit in the process, and Mother was not too proud to accept help from a pro. In fact, she looked forward to the collaboration. But there wasn't one; Kaufman rewrote by himself, and whatever she might have felt about his work, she didn't feel it was her place to criticize a man of his stature.

She questioned that decision when the play opened in Boston on September 13 to unanimously bad reviews. The critics said Blondell was great, the direction brisk and lively, but the play was awful. "Not outrageous, not funny, not even witty." Mike told her not to worry. He would go to Boston and stick with the show until it arrived in New York. He promised that he'd bring it in a smash.

The reviews from Baltimore were equally bad, and when it opened in Pittsburgh on October 12, they were worse. Unable to stay away any longer, she went to see the show. She hated it, and in talking to Kaufman discovered that he hated it, too. Together they urged Mike to close it out of town. He refused. The film rights had been sold, but it would have to run in New York for at least three weeks for him to get the standard producer's share of the price.

Finally, on October 21, the show opened in New York. John Chapman wrote: "Maybe *The Naked Genius* could be funny, but they'd have to throw it away and start all-over again." Louis Kronenberger said, "I can sort of understand why Gypsy Rose Lee and George Kaufman wanted *The Naked Genius* to close last week in Pittsburgh. In fact, what I can't understand is that they didn't take steps in the matter — didn't get out an injunction, or mutilate the scenery, or shanghai the cast. For the whole thing is an appalling mess, a silly and vulgar and embarrassing hodge-podge that wastes the time and withers the talent of a great many actors."

The reviews, however, were the least of Mother's disappointments that opening night. She expected them. She didn't expect what happened later. Mike took her to "21," gave her a gold compact from Cartier as an opening night gift, and told her that he had convinced Bertha to give him a divorce and was going to marry Joan Blondell. Mother didn't make a scene; she left quietly and quickly. In her haste, or perhaps deliberately, she left the compact. The next day, the huge Victorian nude by Bouguereau arrived at the house with a note. "You won't leave this on the table at '21.' Love, Mike."

It was years before she and Mike spoke again, and for the rest of her life she got upset if Joan Blondell's name was mentioned in her presence.

Mother remained locked in her room, mourning Mike's death for three days. Shortly after I returned from school on the last day, she buzzed me on the intercom and asked me to come to her room. The door was unlocked, and she was in bed, propped up on fresh white pillows. She had just taken a bath and the room was filled with the fragrance of her bath oil. She was wearing one of her prettier lace-trimmed flannel nightgowns, looked alert, clear eyed, and if not cheerful, certainly not depressed either.

I kissed her on the cheek and asked how she was feeling, but she dismissed the question with a wave of her hand, and instead tried to make small talk by asking me about school. The subject was quickly exhausted, and we lapsed into silence. I started to leave, but she stopped me. "Esther will be bringing dinner in a little while. Sit here with me until it comes." She didn't say please, but it was in her voice.

I sat and we waited quietly for dinner. It was a very pleasant interlude. I had missed her. I had also missed being in her room. It was the most pleasant in the house. This was, at least during the winter, partly a function of temperature. Mother hated spending money on oil for the furnace; to conserve it, she turned the thermostat off at night and kept it at a spartan 62° during the day. Her room, on the other hand, was maintained at a toasty 80° by an antique Franklin stove in which she burned coal day and night throughout the winter. Her room was the place to go when frostbite began to set in.

Mother's room also exuded a psychic warmth, embracing and secure, that made me feel safely isolated from the outside world. It was bright, cluttered, and filled with roses. The light came through two south-facing windows which, because the room was on the third floor, received sun all day. The roses weren't real, the sense of them came from the wallpaper which had a design of large American Beauty roses set less than a foot apart, floor to ceiling. The clutter was Mother's huge collection of Victoriana. In keeping with the period style of the room, each wall had its focal point. One was the tall, double-sized, black, wrought-iron bed with a white organdy canopy trimmed in lace. Another was the Franklin stove which was shaped like a Victorian mansion loaded with gingerbread. Next to it, on the same wall, stood a wind-up Victrola with a large, horn-type speaker painted with flowers. Between the two windows was an étagère that held her collections of antique parasols and beaded purses. Against the fourth wall, between the doors to her bath and the hall, was a chinoiserie desk with a mother-of-pearl inlaid pâpier-maché chair. Crammed into whatever space remained, and there wasn't much, were occasional tables whose tops overflowed with tiny objets d'art she had collected since her childhood: rare Victorian lamps with handmade silk shades, a wind-up music box that played tin "records," and a nature scene of stuffed birds under a glass bell. There was also a freestanding, mother-of-pearl inlaid pâpier-maché sewing box, green crushed-velvet overstuffed chairs with equally overstuffed ottomans, and a chaise longue.

Her room reflected a part of Mother's character seen nowhere else in her life. It was the realized fantasy of a little girl raised in seedy hotels and grubby dressing rooms, a little girl who read Brontë and Browning, George Sand and Lytton Strachey to escape, a little girl who grew up and, the moment she could afford it, created for herself a Victorian schoolgirl's dream of a boudoir.

We sat in peace for half an hour until Esther arrived with the dinner tray, ate quietly, sat a bit longer, and said goodnight. The next morning, she was up at six and back to work on *Curious Evening*. In the years that followed, Mike's name would come up many times. Whenever it did, she said only, "Mike was the most exciting, most vital man I've ever known."

CHAPTER FIVE

I HAD barely entered my room after getting home from school when the intercom buzzed. I picked up the phone; it was Mother. "Erik, where have you been? she demanded. "It's almost four o'clock."

"It was so beautiful out, I walked home through the park," I answered. It had been the first nice day of spring.

"Two hours to walk crosstown? Crawled is more like it. I do wish you'd remember to check with me when you know you're going to be late. Suppose I'd needed you to help me with the film today? Oh, never mind. Now that you're here, please come up to my room. I have something important to discuss with you."

"I'll be right there, just give me a sec to go to the bathroom."

"Well, don't dawdle. I've been waiting for you long enough as it is." She hung up.

I hurried into my bathroom to sneak a quick cigarette and to try to collect my thoughts. Mother's "important" discussions always made me nervous, usually because I was guilty about something. That day I was afraid she had missed the twenty-dollar bill that I had stolen from her purse earlier in the week. She hadn't sounded angry, however, and that was a good sign. The phone buzzed again. I knew it was Mother wanting to know what was taking me so long, so I flushed the butt down the toilet, and ran up the stairs to her room without bothering to answer it.

When I entered, she was lying on the right side of her bed, propped up with half a dozen pillows, dressed in her at-home work uniform of a denim skirt, unpressed blouse, and heavy wool socks. She wore no makeup, and her hair was tied up out of the way with an old scarf. She had the phone receiver cradled between her right ear and shoulder, her half-glasses perched on the tip of her nose, a cigarette in one hand, and a pencil in the other.

Clearly she had been working from her bed all day. It was strewn with old checkbooks and crumpled sheets from the yellow legal pad on her lap. The ever-present tea tray sat on the bed to her left, and the adding machine and an overflowing ashtray were on the bedside table to her right.

"There you are, darling," she said, hanging up the phone and offering her cheek to me for a kiss. "I had just about given you up for lost."

I took a step toward her. Fu Manchu, who was curled up at her waist, uncurled just enough to give me a dirty look and to growl menacingly. I paused.

"That will be enough of that," she said, slapping him lightly on the rump. "It's only Erik."

Still, he continued to growl, and she had to hold him while I kissed her. Fu was that way with anyone who got within a few feet of her. She always made a big show of finding it annoying, but I knew she was really flattered by his loyalty and attachment. Often I would make a snide comment about him — motivated by subconscious jealousy no doubt — but I held myself in check that day. I could tell from her tone of voice that I wasn't in trouble, and I didn't want to risk irritating her. The evidence around her bed suggested that she had money on her mind, and when that was the case it was wise to tread lightly.

"Sorry I'm late," I began politely. "It hasn't ruined your day, I hope."

She dismissed the possibility with a wave of her hand. "I was shot out of my cannon at the shriek of dawn, and it's been downhill ever since." That was her way of saying that she had awakened very early worrying about something and was still worried about it.

"Can I do anything to help?"

"We'll see. I hope so." She held out the legal pad. "Look this over." I took it and sat down in my favorite chair across the room. In the meantime, she continued. "I've spent my whole day going over our budget for the rest of the year, and I must say it's pretty bleak. Whatever I do, it boils down to the same dismal reality: without the act, we simply cannot afford to maintain our old standard of living.

"Now what I've done there," she pointed at the pad, "is list all of our expenses for last year, and next to each one I've put down what it's going to cost us this year . . . if we don't do something. As you

67

can see, at the rate we're going, we'll spend more money this year than last, which is clearly out of the question. Last year I had the book and the two films, so I was able to make ends meet. This year I haven't earned one red cent, and on top of that there's been the constant drain of *Curious Evening* . . ."

The phone rang, interrupting. She answered it. "Hello . . . Speaking . . . Put him on." She turned back to me. "It's Hilly [one of her agents] about the summer. While I talk with him, look over the list and see if you can find anyplace where we can cut down.

"Hilly, darling, how are you? . . . I've been better, to be perfectly frank, but never mind that. Have you spoken with the *Happy Hunting* people? . . . And? . . . Fifteen hundred is out of the question. By the time I pay my expenses and your commission I'll be working for free. . . . What about my dresser? . . . I suppose I should be thankful for small favors. . . . Of course I'm not happy. The money's terrible, and the whole idea of doing a musical leaves me cold. But what can I do? You haven't come up with anything better, and if I turn this down, I could end up sitting on my fat ass all summer, and I sure as hell can't afford that. . . . Tell them it's okay for two thousand. If they won't go to two, take seventeen-fifty, but not a penny less. . . . Absolutely not! I won't do it for fifteen hundred, and that's final. But don't blow the deal without checking with me first. . . . All right, darling, get back to me in the morning."

She hung up the phone and turned her attention back to me. "You heard. That ought to give you some idea of what we're facing." She shook her head. "Ten weeks, working my ass off, and we'll be lucky to break even. We simply must economize, that's all there is to it."

She paused to pour herself a cup of tea and light a cigarette. "You've looked it over. Any suggestions?"

I had glanced at the list while she was on the phone, but to me it was little more than a blur of figures with the astronomical total of $28,000. Only one item had stood out: my school. Since third grade, I had attended the Professional Children's School, a small private school designed for children in the performing arts. Mother had chosen it for me because it permitted students to complete their lessons by correspondence whenever they had to be out of town, which made it possible for me to accompany her when she went on tour. However, she recently had decided it was time for a change. I would begin high school in September, and she wanted me to go to a school that would help me get into a good college. Also, she felt it was time to start loosening the ties between us. So, she had enrolled me as a boarding student at the Riverdale Country School for Boys in the Bronx for the coming academic year. It had a beautiful campus and an excellent reputation for college admissions, and because it was in New York City, I would be able to come home every weekend. Mother had done her best to make it sound exciting, but I had serious doubts, and when I saw the difference in cost, I clutched at it as a way out.

"Why don't I stay at PCS," I suggested. "That would save over two thousand dollars, and I really don't —"

"It's too late for that," she interrupted. "You're already enrolled at Riverdale. Besides, that would be a foolish economy. It's better for getting into college, and even more important, you'll make contacts that will come in handy for the rest of your life. No, I was expecting you to find some economies we could make here, around the house. For my part, I've already canceled the morning paper, cut Mrs. Mitchell down to once a week, and stopped my masseuse altogether."

She paused, and I knew she was waiting for me to volunteer a cut in my allowance. Instead, I shook my head earnestly and said, "I don't know . . ."

"Well, for example, could you get another year out of your good suit?"

Oh, no, I thought. Next to my allowance, clothes were the area I had most dreaded discussing. Earlier in the week I had made a tentative thirteen-year-old's pass at a girl in my class, and she had rebuffed me sharply. One of my friends later ascribed my failure to my appearance. "Girls like guys who look sharp, and you look like a slob," was the way he had put it. I had never given much thought to my appearance at school. Mother bought me corduroy or cotton pants and sport shirts, and I wore them, unpressed, right out of the dryer. But my friend's comment had hit home, and ever since I had been rehearsing my request for some new clothes, a request I had decided to postpone indefinitely only moments earlier.

Now that she had raised the subject, however, I had to reconsider that decision. If I accepted cuts in the budget for my clothing now, she would use it to refuse any requests I might make later. On the other hand, this was obviously the wrong time to ask for anything. In desperation, I tried avoiding the subject when I answered her question about my suit.

"I don't know," I said apologetically, "it's getting pretty short in the sleeves."

"Oh, that's nothing. We'll take it to the tailor up the street and have him let them out. Hand me the pad." I took it to her, and she made a note on it. "That knocks fifty dollars off the budget right there. You see how easy it is?"

I could avoid it no longer. I held my breath and plunged right in. "That's great for the suit, but I'm going to need some new clothes for Riverdale."

"How can that be?" she asked sharply, as if I had touched a raw nerve. "I just bought you some new things."

"In September, and then it was only some socks and underpants."

"Well, it will have to do." Impatiently she put out her cigarette. "Sometimes, Erik, I just don't understand you. I just spent damn near an hour explaining what desperate financial straits we're in, and then instead of helping me, you ask me to spend money that you know we don't have on clothes to wear to school." She paused to light another cigarette. "I really don't understand . . ."

"I'm sorry, Mother. It's just —"

She waved her hand impatiently. "I don't want to hear another word. It can't be done, and that's simply all there is to it."

There was a knock on the door, and Esther entered with our dinner on a tray.

"Let's talk about something pleasant now," Mother said. "Dinner's here, and my appetite's been damn near ruined as it is. Be a dear and help Esther with the tray."

Dinner was a dismal affair filled with polite chitchat that did nothing to hide the strained feelings between us. I was miserable. Not only had I failed to get any new clothes or even to present my case, I had irritated Mother and incurred her displeasure as well. The last was the most upsetting. I hated having Mother annoyed with me, and I was angry with myself for causing it, especially as I had known better. It didn't occur to me that she might have been at least partially responsible for our disagreement. I may have wished, fleetingly, that she had let me explain, but I knew it wouldn't have made a difference. No. I should have gone along with whatever she suggested. When it came to money, that was the only way to handle her.

As soon as we finished eating, I started to excuse myself, but she stopped me. "There's something else I've been meaning to discuss with you," she said, "and this seems as good a time as any. Better, in fact, because I think what I have to say will provide a solution to your problem." She paused dramatically and lit a cigarette. Her tone, her manner, everything suggested good news.

"I've been thinking for quite a while that it's time you began earning some money of your own," she continued. "You'll never appreciate the value of a dollar so long as you are given all the money you want whenever you ask for it. So, I've decided to start paying you when you work for me."

She paused for me to comment, but I waited. So far, there was nothing new in what she had said.

"You don't seem terribly excited," she finally remarked.

"Well, I'm not sure I understand," I replied, cautiously. "You've always paid me for doing jobs around the house." Diplomatically, I didn't add that the only way she'd ever given me money beyond my allowance was when I worked for it.

"No, no, no. You've misunderstood me. I didn't mean around the house. I meant professionally."

"Like when I help you with the film?" I asked with fingers crossed. Since our return from Palm Beach, she had been working almost nonstop on *Curious Evening*, and I had been helping her after school, in the evenings, and on weekends. We had finished it twice during the four months, each time only to screen it for some of her friends and have her decide that it still needed some more work. I suspected it would need a lot more work before it was really finished, and if she was going to start paying me I stood to make a good deal of money.

"Well, that's the general idea," she said, "but I don't think it's fair of you to expect a salary for your work on the film. Let's keep in mind that I'm spending even more of my time and a great deal of money to boot with no guarantee that I'll ever get any of it back. And even if it does pay off, whatever I earn will be going to support the family which is, after all, just the two of us.

"No. I was thinking specifically of this summer. If I do this *Happy Hunting* tour, I'll need a dresser, and I can't think of anyone better qualified for the job than you."

That sounded good to me. If the past was any indication, I'd be doing the job anyway; I might just as well get paid for it. "How much will I make?"

"Well, I wouldn't pay you as much as I would someone from outside — you do get free room and board — but I'd say the job should pay around thirty dollars a week."

"Wow! That's great!" And so it seemed. Thirty a week for ten weeks was three hundred dollars, more than I'd ever made.

"I thought you'd be pleased. Now, if I were you I'd save what I earned for something really important, but that's up to you. If you want to buy clothes with it, it will be your money to spend as you wish. I might even be persuaded to make a small advance . . . once Hilly's closed the deal, of course."

"Oh, Mother, thank you." I jumped up and ran over to give her a hug, but my excitement startled Fu, who held me at bay, barking furiously.

"That's all right, dear," Mother said to me as she calmed him. "Better stay where you are. You know how Fu hates to see you happy. Oh my God, look, it's almost time for the news. Do me a favor, darling, and turn on the set."

We spent the rest of the evening like a typical American family — watching television.

Happy Hunting was scheduled to open at the Valley Forge Music Fair on June 9. Mother drove down on the first to begin rehearsals. Normally, I would have gone with her, but I stayed home until the sixth to participate in my school's commencement exercises. As I had made it, barely, through the eighth grade, I was entitled to receive a diploma, and I wanted to be there for the ceremony. As soon as it was over, I took the train to Philadelphia.

My train arrived at 4:10. Mother had Ruth collect me at the station. Ruth was "her" apprentice at Valley Forge. Every summer theater has a few stagestruck youths, usually drama majors on vacation from college, who work without salary in order to get some theatrical experience. Mother had done stock tours before and knew the ropes. One of the first things she did on arriving at a new theater was to appropriate the most intelligent female apprentice as her personal assistant. There was nothing official about it. Mother would simply learn the girl's name, ask her to run errands, and lose her temper the first time the girl wasn't around when she wanted her. Once was all it ever took. After that, the girl always remained within calling distance unless she was off doing Mother's bidding. It sounds odious, but it was actually quite a plum. Mother's apprentices always learned more from their week or two with her than from the rest of the season altogether.

The Valley Forge Music Fair was a huge, circular amphitheater covered by a green and white striped circus tent. Inside, it reminded me of a meteor crater with seats. The stage was in the center, and the audience sat around it on three thousand green and white director's chairs that were arranged in concentric circles, each higher than the one in front.

The company was rehearsing the choreography for the title song when I arrived. It was a major production number that began and ended with Mother leading the chorus on a hunt. It required a mad gallop up and down the aisles and was very hard work because the aisles, which radiated from the stage like spokes from the hub of a wheel, were each over one hundred feet long, and the incline was quite steep. At one point they ran up the aisle where I was standing at the back of the tent. Mother was wet with sweat and out of breath when she reached me. Pausing briefly as the chorus changed direction, she put her hand on my shoulder and gasped, "Oh, God!" Then she was off again.

They continued rehearsing for another twenty minutes until Mother, pushed to her limit and panting furiously, stopped in the center of the stage halfway through the number. She struggled to catch her breath enough to speak, but the effort was too much. Instead, she just shook her head and collapsed into the nearest chair. The director got the hint and called a five-minute break.

I had never seen Mother do anything so physically demanding and was very impressed. "That was great!" I said when I reached her, leaning over to kiss her cheek.

She was still out of breath, but she managed a hoarse "Not there; tooth's flared up," as she held me off long enough to turn her head to accept the kiss on the other cheek.

"Oh, no," I sympathized. "Not again."

"Wouldn't you know it. On top of everything else." By now her breathing was almost back to normal; she fished around in her purse for a cigarette and lit it. "I can't tell you how relieved I am that you're here. I've really needed you." She paused to drag on her cigarette. "How was your graduation?"

"Okay," I answered, feeling guilty that I was waiting around for a silly piece of paper when I should have been at her side.

The director came over and, after Mother introduced us, asked her how she was feeling. "Like death warmed over. No more running in the aisles for a while, all right, honey? It's killing me."

"Sure, Gyp. How about we go over the duet?"

"I'd rather do the tango."

"Good idea." Most summer stock directors ended up taking direction from Mother instead of the other way around. The smart ones accepted their subservient status right away.

Mother stood up, crushing her cigarette out on the floor with the toe of her sandal. Seemingly as an afterthought, she reached into her purse for the motel room key. "Why don't you go over to the motel now, dear, and walk Diana. Poor thing, all cooped up. I haven't been able to give her a good walk all week." She handed me the key. "If you hurry, you may catch her before she floods out the room. Ruth will show you where it is." She glanced around for Ruth, didn't see her, and called impatiently, "Ruth!"

I didn't want to be the cause of any problems and quickly said, "Don't worry, Mother. I'll find her."

"But I want my ice pack," she said testily, looking nervously around the tent. "It's so annoying. She's supposed to be helping me, and she's never around when I want her."

Just then Ruth arrived with a thermos full of iced tea and Mother's ice pack. "There you are," Mother said reproachfully. "Show Erik where the motel is, will you, dear. But first make my ice pack."

"I have it right here," Ruth said, handing it to her.

Mother's mood changed completely. She thanked her with a genuine "You're a lifesaver." Holding the ice pack next to her jaw, she climbed on to the stage and began rehearsing.

The motel was within walking distance, but because of my suitcase, Ruth drove me. As often happened with Mother's apprentices, Ruth had developed a protective attitude toward Mother and was terribly concerned about her sore mouth. Mother hated it when those around her became too solicitous, so I explained that she was used to problems with her teeth. They had bothered her all her life.

As a child and adolescent, they had been very crooked. Then, shortly after she began playing at Minsky's, she was introduced at a party to Waxy Gordon, an important New Jersey gangster. It was no more than an introduction, but the next day a strange man called her on the phone and said that Mr. Gordon had arranged for her to have her teeth fixed. He told her to be at the office of a Doctor Krauss, 1607 Broadway, that morning at ten-thirty. Her mother wouldn't let her go. "There's no telling what a man like that might expect in return."

That night at the theater Georgia Sothern, who was also on the bill, came over to her. "Gyps," she said confidentially, "Waxy's very hurt that you didn't see his dentist. He's got you another appointment for the same time tomorrow. You'd better go. Waxy's all right, but it don't pay to turn you nose up at him."

This time, she went. Doctor Krauss explained that he was from Waxy's old neighborhood and that because Waxy had put him through dental school, there would be no charge. Mother liked the price and hated her teeth; she told him to go ahead. He ground all her teeth down to stubs and covered them with jackets. It hurt like hell, but it was worth it. She thought they were the most beautiful teeth she had ever seen.

A few years later, Waxy tried collecting on his favor. He was in jail and asked Mother to come visit him because it impressed the other cons. She only went twice. "It made me uncomfortable," she explained later, "being on display that way. . . . Besides, that Doctor Krauss was a quack. He ruined my mouth." And so he had. Shortly after the work was finished, painful abscesses began to form around her lower left molar whenever she was run-down or under strain. First she had Dr. Krauss replace the offending jacket, then she paid another dentist to replace it, and finally she had her entire mouth redone, but the problem persisted. Now when it flared up, she gargled with salt water, took antibiotics, and suffered until it passed. The ice packs did very little to ease the pain, but since she refused to take painkillers when she worked, it was better than nothing.

Ruth loved the story and would have kept me talking all afternoon, but I reminded her that Mother was expecting her at the theater and suggested that she buy a copy of *Gypsy* if she was really interested. "Do you think she'd autograph it for me?" she asked naively.

"Sure. I'll ask for you if you'd like."

"Oh, thank you. I'd be too embarrassed. I'll stop by a bookstore and buy one tomorrow morning."

As I watched her drive away, I thought that I couldn't wait to tell Mother that I had made another sale. She appreciated things like that.

I never got the chance. When Mother returned to the motel room that night, she was in no mood to hear about books. "I'm so goddamned mad I could spit!" she said as she entered. Her voice sounded hoarse, and she was holding an ice pack against her jaw. "Every time I turn around these sons-of-bitches come at me with something else. As if I didn't have enough problems already. It's been one thing after another ever since I arrived."

She pulled the curtains apart and pointed to the theater's huge electric sign, which was visible through the window. The upper half announced the current show, *No Time for Sergeants*; the lower read "starting next week Gypsy Rose Lee in *Happy Hunting*."

"It took me three days to get my name on that friggin' sign. Three days. You'd think they were trying to keep me a secret." She continued talking as she went into the bathroom and filled a glass with warm water and salt. Fu was jumping up and down against her leg for attention, but she ignored him. "Until today, we had to drive to

75

Philadelphia for rehearsals. An hour-and-a-half commute each way, through rush-hour traffic no less. No wonder my tooth's acting up. It was all so unnecessary. We could have stayed in New York and rehearsed. Would have saved a hell of a lot of money, I'll tell you that."

She stood in the bathroom doorway, and I was struck by how tired she appeared. It was more than the bags under her eyes, the straggly hair, and the absence of makeup. She was stooped over, like an old woman. I felt very sorry for her. "Today," she continued, "the bastards hit me twice. This morning they told me they couldn't afford to give me anything for the use of my costumes. Half of what I wear in the goddamn show belongs to me, and not one red cent for wear and tear. It's really terribly unfair. I told them so, too."

She returned to the sink and gargled. When she came out, she sat on the edge of the bed, calm for the first time all evening. Fu jumped on her lap, but she gently pushed him aside. "Not now, sweetheart. I'll pet you in a moment." She lit a cigarette and looked at me before continuing. "The real blow came this afternoon when they told me that you can't help me with my changes. The union won't permit it. I tried everything. I threatened, I pleaded, I argued, the works. . . ." Her voice trailed off. She had spoken as if she were responsible and should apologize for having failed.

"Oh, no . . . well . . ." I tried to convey resigned disappointment, but I was actually pleased. The thought of a summer without work and responsibility was very appealing, and since I *couldn't* work, she would just have to give me the money for my clothes. Or so I thought.

"I'm sorry, dear . . ." She paused. When she began again, all traces of her apologetic tone had vanished. "Am I ever. After all, it will be hardest on me, breaking in someone new. But I know how much you were counting on your salary.

"So," she continued, with a growing sense of excitement, "I've thought of another way you can earn some money for school next year."

"Really?" I asked, trying to sound interested.

"You can set up a card table in front of the tent and sell copies of *Gypsy* before the show and during intermission. You'll have to buy the books, of course, but I'll advance you the money, and you can repay me as you sell them."

I didn't know what to say. The very thought made me shudder, but she was so enthusiastic. Somehow I had to say no without appearing to dismiss the idea out of hand. I ventured a tentative "I don't know . . ."

She looked and sounded crushed. "But I was sure you'd love the idea. I even called Erica and told her to get the books sent out right away." She paused to light a cigarette, and I knew she was reviewing the pro's and con's. "I really don't understand what you have against it," she said, a note of impatience edging into her voice. "I thought you wanted to earn some money this summer so you can buy new clothes for school. You do want some new clothes for school, don't you?"

"Well, yes, but . . ."

"Then this will be ideal. The more books you sell, the more you'll make. With a little effort, you'll do far better than you would as my dresser."

"I know, but . . . I'll be embarrassed."

"Oh, don't be ridiculous. People sell programs and things in front of theaters all the time."

"It's not the same."

"That's absurd." By now she had lost all patience with the conversation and with me. "Well, I'm sorry you don't like my idea, but it's the best I could come up with on such short notice. I do have other things on my mind. If you can suggest something better, I'm more than willing to listen, but you'll have to decide by tomorrow morning, before Erica orders the books. Now I can't talk about it any longer. I'm just too tired." Fu was at her feet, quivering and whining. "Yes, dear. I'll feed you in a moment."

"I'll do it," I offered quickly. Anything to reinstate myself in her good graces.

"Oh, thank you, darling."

"I'll walk him, too. When I take Diana out."

"That would be wonderful. I think I'll put on my nightgown then and go right to bed. Fighting the pain from this tooth has worn me out."

I fed the animals while she changed into her nightgown and brushed her teeth. It wasn't easy. The room was very small, and half the floor was filled with suitcases and animal paraphernalia. Mother and I shared what little space remained with the two cats, Fu, and my new dog, Diana, a full-grown Afghan hound that Mother had accepted in exchange for two of the kittens from Lichee's litter. Diana took up more room than the rest of us put together, and with her on the floor, eating, I had to climb on my bed in order to let Mother get out of the bathroom. I thought it was rather funny, but she didn't. In bed, as she rubbed cold cream on her face with a washcloth, she glanced around and said, "All this for ninety-eight dollars a week. No wonder I've been depressed every night."

No wonder at all. The motel was one of those cinderblock horrors that sprang up alongside the new interstate highway system during the late 1950s. Twenty-four attached cubicles and an office arranged in a horseshoe around a swimming pool. Our room was painted a sickly yellow-green. It was furnished with two skinny beds, a formica-veneered combination desk/bureau, a straight-backed chair, and a television set that gobbled quarters. Decorator touches were provided by the gilt-framed mirror above the desk, a hideous seascape that was screwed to the wall over the beds, and dark green curtains with hems that were shiny black from grime. For lighting, we had the choice of the overhead light and a lamp between the beds, or in other words, between glare and gloom.

"At least it's close to the theater," I said, stressing its only advantage.

Mother, however, had moved on. "Take a couple dollars out of my purse and get something for dinner at the coffee shop down the road. And while you're at it, get the thermos filled with ice. Just in case I need it for my jaw."

"I'll get it right now, when I walk the dogs," I offered as I put on their leashes.

"Oh, would you? What a dear."

I noticed that she had a mystery magazine on her lap. "Are you going to read for a while?"

"Just a few pages to unwind. We'd better say goodnight now."

"Okay." I walked over and started to kiss her on the cheek.

"Don't get too close, dear. I'm all greasy."

I grazed her cheek with my lips. "Goodnight, Mother."

"Goodnight, dear." She held on to me for a moment. "I can't tell you how glad I am that you're here."

I walked to the coffee shop, filled the thermos with ice, and sat beside the Interstate smoking a cigarette and watching the trucks roll past. I had never felt so confused and miserable. One moment, I hated Mother with an all-consuming passion. The books were the cause, or so I thought. I knew that I'd have to sell them; her mind was made up. How could she not understand? She just wanted to sell books and make money; she loved money more than me. Then, less than a heartbeat later, I loved her, understood her problems, felt sorry for her, and hated myself for having hated her a moment earlier.

It was, though I didn't know it, the onset of adolescence. Breaking

78

away is rarely easy; in my case it would involve an almost continuous, often painful, mutually destructive, five-year clash of wills between Mother and me. Fortunately, my affliction was still incipient in the early part of that summer. Mother barely survived the problems at hand.

When she awoke the next day, the abscess was much worse. The swelling pulled her mouth so out of shape, she could barely form words, let alone sing, and the pain was intense. It didn't stop her from arriving at the tent, ice pack in hand, promptly at eight to begin rehearsal, but it severely limited what she could do once they began. Finally, when they broke for three hours to let the current show play its Saturday matinee, she gave in and asked to see a dentist.

The theater had one on call who agreed to meet her at his office. He was an older man and very gentle. He let me hold her hand as he examined her, but then he took me into his waiting room and told me not to worry if I heard Mother yell. He explained that her gum was too inflamed to permit the use of novocaine, and that what he had to do was extremely painful, but it would help. I was glad he warned me. A few moments after he returned to his office, Mother let out an agonizing scream, and for what seemed an eternity she continued moaning.

After it was all over, he came out of his office and suggested that I take Mother home in a taxi and put her right to bed. Before he finished talking, she rushed through the waiting room and out the door. I caught up with her at the car. She was sitting behind the wheel, deathly pale, eyes closed, holding her stomach. I asked her if she wanted anything; she shook her head. I sat quietly in the seat next to her, careful not to fidget. Suddenly, she opened her door, leaned out, and retched. "I'm sorry, darling," she gasped, relaxing in her seat. "I know it's unpleasant. . . . What he did hurt me so. . . . It made me ill."

"It's all right," I said. She didn't respond. She was dozing.

Mother's recuperative powers were phenomenal. After napping for no more than ten minutes, she awoke with a start and said, "Oh, my God. I'll be late for rehearsal." She wasn't; she was right on time and worked straight through to seven-thirty. That night, she slept soundly, and the next morning she was able to eat her first solid food in three days.

Her tooth was just the beginning. As would happen throughout the tour, the elimination of one problem only served to reveal another. At dress rehearsal on Sunday afternoon, her mouth was sufficiently

79

recovered to allow her to sing the score in the tent for the first time. By the third number, she was barely audible in the fifth row. She finished the act speaking the songs in a near whisper. Opening night was less than thirty hours away.

I visited Mother in her dressing room during the intermission break. She came off stage drenched with sweat and out of breath. After giving the wardrobe mistress her wet costume, she dried herself with a towel, and dropped into the room's only seat, an uncomfortable folding metal office chair.

"How did it go?" I asked. I had been out front, but I wanted her opinion so I could adjust mine to it.

"Godawful. You were there. The lights were wrong, my mike didn't work, everyone was blowing their lines . . ." Her voice, I noted, sounded gravelly but strong. She leaned over, picked an old program up off the floor, and began fanning herself with it. "They really should install air conditioning. It's like an oven in here."

Working conditions that summer were even worse than we had expected. At Valley Forge, "backstage" was a large Quonset hut behind the tent. It was completely open inside, like an airplane hangar, except for a row of three adjoining dressing rooms that had been built out of steel dividers like those used for partitions in public toilets. Those on the ends of the row were large; the men in the cast used one, the women used the other. Mother had exclusive use of the smaller "star's" dressing room between them. Privacy was nonexistent. Curtains were used in place of doors, and voices carried from one end of the Quonset to the other. So did noise from the scenic, prop, and wardrobe departments that shared the open area, and at times it approached intolerable levels. But while sound traveled freely, air did not. In the summer sun, the metal roof became too hot to touch, and it in turn heated the interior like a huge radiator. There were no windows, and the only ventilation came from a small exhaust fan totally unequal to the task. The superheated air was trapped, stifling, and oppressive, exactly like an oven.

"Do you want me to open the curtain?" I asked. Mother's cubicle was opposite the Quonset's door, and at times a faint breeze stirred the air.

She shook her head. "I'd have to put on my robe. It's not worth it. Remind me to buy a small fan tomorrow."

"Gyp. You decent?" The director called from the other side of the curtain.

"Whatever it is, darling, can't it wait until after the break?"

"Chris is with me." Chris was the producer's representative.

"Oh, God," she muttered softly. "Now what?" She put on her robe, sat facing the mirror, and began brushing her hair. "Come in." The two men entered and waited for her to face them. She didn't; she established eye contact in the mirror and continued with her hair. "Yes?"

Chris hesitated, then began. "Ah . . . Well, frankly, Gyps, Hal and I are worried about your voice. We just got off the phone with New York. They'd like to send a specialist down. . . ." Mother stopped brushing and glared at him in the mirror. "Just to take a look," he continued quickly. "I mean, it can't hurt. Right?"

She turned in her chair to face him. "You had the nerve to call New York and complain about my voice?"

"Oh no, not complain. Let me ex——"

"How dare you!" Mother never used body language to express anger; she projected it with a deep, powerful tone of voice that was overwhelming. And very loud.

Chris held his hands up in front of him, as if to ward off a blow. "Miss Lee, please. You've misunderstood."

She threw her head back and laughed derisively. "I'm not exactly new to this game, you know. You're scared. I would be too, after that rehearsal. I've never seen such chaos and confusion in all my life. But don't think for one minute that you're smart enough — either of you — to leave me holding the bag."

"It wasn't like that," Hal began earnestly. "Believe me. Listen. We'll cancel the guy. I'll call New York right now and tell them it was a mistake. I'll say Chris and I got our wires crossed —"

"And have me appear uncooperative as well?! Not on your life. Let him come. But while you're at it, you'd better send for a specialist to fix my mike, and another one to run the lights, and anyone else you can think of to help get this show on the road. Because one thing I can promise you, gentlemen: if we have the same problems tomorrow night that we've had today, I'll have a few things to tell New York myself.

"Now leave me alone. I've wasted half my break arguing with you two, and I need my rest."

"Don't worry about the break, Gyp," Hall offered quickly. "I've got a few things to work on with the rest of the cast." Mother didn't answer; she turned her back on them and began brushing her hair. Chris covered their retreat. "Yes, well. Don't you worry now. It'll all work out. The show's going to be great."

81

She gave them a few minutes to walk away, then stopped brushing her hair and said softly, "Well, that's a relief."

"What do you mean?"

"I was going to call Dr. Hodas [our family physician] later and have him arrange for me to see a doctor in Philadelphia tomorrow. They've just saved me the drive and the expense." And given her a chance to read them the riot act. It did the trick, too. Out of nowhere, someone arrived to fix Mother's microphone, a first-rate electrician came to run the lights, and act two went very smoothly.

The next day was the first in two weeks that Mother didn't have to rehearse. We slept late, went grocery shopping, bought a couple of inner tubes at a gas station, and spent the afternoon lounging on them in the pool. The doctor arrived around two. He looked at her throat, said that she had been straining it, gave her two sprays, and left. Mother wondered why he hadn't just sent the sprays and his bill and saved himself the trip.

At six, after cooking our dinner in the room, Mother left for the theater. She liked to give herself plenty of time, especially on opening nights. I stayed at the motel to wash the dishes, feed and walk the animals, and change for my job. The books had arrived and Mother thought that my dark suit pants and white dinner jacket would be a perfect outfit for selling them. I thought I looked like the host in a Howard Johnson's.

At seven forty-five, three-quarters of an hour before the curtain, I displayed the books nicely on a card table by the main entrance and waited. I knew I should have been hawking them, but I couldn't bring myself to do it. I sold one book, to Ruth who had been unable to find it at the local bookstore. When I heard the overture, I packed up and stood at the back of the tent to watch the show. There wasn't an empty seat in the house.

Mother had accepted the *Happy Hunting* tour for the money, but that didn't affect her attitude toward the job. Others might walk through stock tours, take the cash, and run; not her. She was, above all else, a trouper. I never saw her give an audience less than her best. Sometimes it wasn't good enough, but usually it was, and occasionally it was wonderful.

That night, her best produced a triumph of vitality over talent. She didn't sing a note, but she punched out the songs in her deep, melodic speaking voice with such energy that they filled the tent with excitement. Indeed, her enthusiasm carried the show. She ad-libbed, flirted with the men in the audience as she ran up and down the aisles, and generally acted as if she were having the time of her life. It was infectious. The audience gave her a rousing, standing ovation at the end of the show. The next day, the reviews were excellent; and by the end of the week Valley Forge and Camden, the next stop on the tour, were sold out.

Success, however, didn't make the show any easier to play. It was a grueling job, running up and down the aisles, screaming her lungs out, eight times a week. As the summer wore on, the heat compounded the difficulty. In Camden, even Mother's seemingly inexhaustible supply of energy ran out. The first matinee day was blisteringly hot, and humid as well. Inside the tent, it was worse. It was a testimony to Mother's appeal that no one left, but many of the men removed their jackets and ties, and all the women were fanning themselves with programs. Onstage, under the hot lights, and running through the aisles, it was murder.

She made it through the show, but on her way to the dressing trailer (Camden didn't even have a Quonset), she fainted. The wardrobe mistress revived her with smelling salts and suggested salt tablets. Mother began taking them immediately, but they didn't work quickly enough. That night, she collapsed on stage seven minutes before the finale. The chorus carried her to her dressing room, a doctor in the audience revived her, and the stage manager offered to send in her understudy. She wouldn't hear of it. "When I'm dead you can send in my understudy." Ten minutes later, she was back on stage and finished the show. It was front-page news in the local papers the next day.

The heat was indirectly responsible for her next problem, too. To keep cool while she got some sun, she spent her days in the motel pool, sitting in an inner tube and reading mysteries. When she began getting cramps, she ascribed them to the heat and increased her consumption of salt tablets. It never occurred to her that soaking her bottom in the cold pool all day could be the cause. Finally she couldn't get out of bed one morning because of the pain and let me call a doctor. He diagnosed a urinary infection, prescribed pills, and told her to keep her bottom out of the pool. Three days later, she was fine.

In Westbury, Long Island, I became the problem. The books weren't selling. I had never been able to bring myself to hawk them, but it reached the point where I recoiled even from standing in front of the tent with them. I just couldn't do it. Mother was furious. It wasn't the books, it was the principle. She couldn't stand having someone around her who wasn't working and being productive. She gave me a choice. "I don't want you hanging around, doing nothing. Either you sell the books, or I'm sending you to camp where I won't have to worry about you having something to do. It's up to you." Going to camp might not sound like a terrible fate, but it meant banishment both from Mother's presence and from her good graces. Nevertheless, I chose it over selling the books. Mother arranged for me to take Diana with me; she wanted to eliminate as many annoyances as possible.

Her first letter from Atlanta was full of good news. Again, the critics had loved the show and the date was sold out. The working conditions were no better, but she was stronger and more able to cope. "I'm getting muscle from all the running around," she wrote, "and my endurance has really improved." The second letter arrived four days later. Her mood had changed completely. She was preoccupied with a rumor that the final date on the tour, three weeks in Houston, would be canceled because the theater was going out of business. "It's so unfair," she wrote this time. "I've worked so hard and now this. I don't know what I'll do if it does close. We need that $5,400. Desperately!"

Mother never told me the date had been canceled. She didn't have to. When the wire arrived, I knew. It read: "Hurry home. New act opens Reno September first. Love, Mother."

Later I learned that she had made the decision in Atlanta. Immediately after hearing that Houston was off, she called Charlie Mapes, owner of the Mapes Hotel in Reno where she had played many times in the past, and made a deal for two weeks. Then she called her agent to book her a break-in week somewhere around New York. Next, she called a writer. And then, I was proud to note, she wired me. My banishment was over.

Preparations for the new act were in full swing when I arrived home from camp. The center of activity, as usual, was the dining room. All the film and editing equipment had been shoved into a corner, and the dining room table was piled high with costumes. Mother, dressed in her at-home work uniform, was sitting at the table hemming a new petticoat, on her left the ever-present tea service and overflowing ash tray. Gene Wood, the writer she had hired to help her with the new act, sat two chairs around the table to her right. He had a legal pad in front of him and was struggling to write down her suggestions. It wasn't easy to keep up with her rapid delivery, even though she was dictating notes to Erica with every other breath as well as throwing an occasional comment to Esther, who was ironing by the window.

I stood in the doorway and soaked up the sight. Home. Mother looked up and saw me. "Oh, darling, there you are." She opened her arms, and we hugged. "It's so good to have you home. Why don't you run up to your room and change. I've lots for you to do. Hilly [her agent] has booked us a week in Wildwood to break in the act. We open in ten days."

The next six weeks were a joy. It was as if we had stepped back in time to the days before Fort Lauderdale, new careers, serious financial worries, or summer stock musicals. Mother wasn't at all melancholy about her decision to do the act again. On the contrary, she was very relieved to be going back to work for good money, knowing it would be physically easy and successful.

There were the inevitable crises, but they were familiar friends. We knew we'd be ready to open in Wildwood on time; we'd never missed a date in our lives. And while the first performance was a disaster, Mother knew that the new act would work. She had replaced the second part with an audience participation routine and added some new business to the strip, but it remained basically the same act she had been doing for thirty years.

In Reno, we were even spared the crises. Everything was perfect. We had a lovely two-bedroom suite with a full kitchen in the hotel, the act worked, and we both enjoyed ourselves. Mother sunbathed and I went horseback riding in the mornings, in the afternoons we'd play games or sit around and talk, Mother cooked dinner every evening at six, and at night we'd do two shows.

After Reno, Mother stored all the costumes in an easily accessible place. She never did the act again, but she needed to know that she could.

CHAPTER SIX

THE SENSE of having stepped back in time that began with the new act continued after our return home from Reno. Prior to writing *Gypsy*, Mother would work until the checking account reached an acceptable level and then vacation until it dropped to the point where financial worries forced her back to work. Since beginning the book, however, she had not allowed herself a moment's pause. It had been a strenuous two and a half years; she needed a vacation and with the bank account full and the new act stored neatly in the closet, she felt she could afford one.

Mother never vacationed in the accepted sense of the word. We always stayed home, and because her nervous energy made inactivity a torture, she always got involved with a hobby, usually driving herself as hard as when she worked. These hobbies, in fact, could only be distinguished from her other projects by their lack of money-earning potential; although occasionally, as with her home movies, she managed to switch horses in midstream.

While rarely profitable, her hobbies were always productive. She wanted to have something to show for her time; but aside from that, anything was fair game. "My" stamp collection and train layout were both hobbies of hers. Sewing was a favorite. For example, very early in the spring of 1955, Mr. John, one of her dearest friends and the top milliner in New York at the time, showed her his spring collection before it was unveiled to the public. Mother bought one of the hats, took it apart to see how it was made, and then made a dozen copies, which she gave to her friends as Easter gifts. When John saw one of the copies walk past his shop, he immediately called Mother to complain, but she didn't give him the chance. "Oh, John darling, I'm so glad you called. I made a few copies of your marvelous hat, and I need some labels. The hats look so naked without them." A few days later, the labels arrived. They read: "A Mr. John design stolen by Gypsy Rose Lee." Mother put one inside each hat. During the Second World War, it was knitting. She made hundreds of toe socks for the wounded soldiers in leg casts whose toes used to get cold. Then another year, she reupholstered every piece of furniture in the house.

A week after Reno, she started quilting. We were on our way to Bloomingdale's to buy curtains and a bedspread for my dorm room at Riverdale. As we passed one of the many thrift shops that lined our route down Third Avenue, she stopped short. "Look at that, Erik. My God, isn't it beautiful!"

All I could see through the filthy window was a dusty heap of mismatched crockery, rusty toasters, and chipped crystal goblets. "What?"

"The quilt." She pointed. "See the edge of it sticking out from under that stack of plates?"

I finally saw what she meant — the corner of an old, faded patchwork quilt. It didn't impress me in the least, but then I had never shared her interest in antiques. "Oh, yes," I said unenthusiastically.

She headed for the door. "I must have it."

No lights were on inside the shop, and the faint daylight that filtered through the dirty front window only added to the gloom. A little bell attached to the door jingled as we entered, but it was hardly necessary. Mother was well known in the neighborhood thrift shops, and the proprietress, an overweight woman with a pasty complexion, pounced on her before I was even into the shop.

"Good morning, dearie. What can I do for you today? Some nice china? That lovely set came in just last week."

"Just browsing," lied Mother. She was an old hand at these stores and knew better than to seem to interested.

"Help yourself, dearie. Look all you like."

She stayed right at Mother's elbow, and the three of us formed an odd, snakelike procession as we wound our way through the crowded shop. The aisles were narrow and didn't connect, so at the end of each one there was a confused dance as the snake turned back and passed itself. After two of these turns, I went back to the front of the shop and waited by the door. There was nothing I wanted to see, and I was only in the way.

At last, on her second pass by the window, Mother noticed the quilt. She had already noticed, examined, priced, and rejected — all for form's sake — a lamp and a hideous pair of cut-glass candle holders.

"May I see that please?" Mother asked, pointing.

"You have an eye for quality," the woman remarked, shifting around Mother to reach the window. "This ain't no ordinary quilt," she continued as she reorganized the window to reach it, "it's a genuine antique and handmade, every bit of it."

She finally handed it over to Mother, who examined it in the light from the window. Even from where I stood, separated by an aisle of junk, it was clearly a remarkable piece of workmanship, with hundreds of types and shapes of material joined by intricate embroidery. Mother put on her glasses and examined it very carefully, looking at all the different stitches and searching for every flaw.

"It's worth every bit of fifty dollars," the woman volunteered, "but seeing as you're a regular customer and all, I could let it go to you for thirty-five."

Mother didn't answer right away. She continued looking at the quilt for a minute or two, then she took off her glasses and said, "Thank you. It's quite lovely, but far too worn to be worth thirty-five dollars."

"Thirty," the woman shot back.

"No. I've decided against it. Thank you." Mother turned and started for the door.

"Twenty-five's as low as I can go."

Mother ignored her and left the store with a polite "Good day."

"Why didn't you bargain with her?" I asked when we were safely down the street; usually she liked nothing better than a good haggle.

"Because I'm going to make one myself," she answered, adding very self-righteously, "Twenty-five dollars, indeed. What does she take me for?" But for a change, it really wasn't a question of money. The quilt had aroused her creative instinct.

Mother was an excellent seamstress. As a child she made the costumes for the vaudeville act; in burlesque she supplemented her income by making costumes for the other strippers on the bill; and until 1949 she made every costume used in her act. Since then, the originals had been designed and executed by Charles James or the Parisian designer Serge Kogan. However, when they wore out, she carefully took them apart and used the worn fabric as a pattern to make the replacements. But this was drudgery endured only to save money, and she used to belittle her skill, saying, "I do it all with one stitch, my Abyssinian blanket stitch." The quilt then presented both a challenge and an opportunity to try something new. For Mother it was an irresistible combination.

At Bloomingdale's that morning, we spent ten minutes taking care of my dormitory needs and an hour in the notions department, where she bought a sack full of different colored embroidery thread, an envelope of needles, an embroidery hoop, and a book on basic embroidery stitches. She rummaged through closets looking for scraps of material in the afternoon, practiced a few stitches before dinner, and started the quilt that night.

Mother began every project with a similar burst of enthusiasm, but her interest rarely survived the third week, and nothing was ever quite finished. Over the years, she had made every curtain in the house; they were all hemmed with pins. Likewise, the edging on the furniture she reupholstered was either glued in place rather than sewn or missing altogether. In contrast, her patience with the quilt seemed infinite. After five weeks she had completed only one-sixteenth of it — a vaguely rectangular section fifteen inches by eighteen inches — but her zeal remained undiminished.

She was motivated largely by the satisfaction she received from creating something beautiful. In that first section, there were thirty-four pieces of material, each a different color, and all chosen and placed with an aesthetic eye. The embroidery was exceptional. On one piece of lavender silk, she had embroidered a grandfather clock; on a piece of pale blue velvet, an oriental fan in navy with beige decoration. The stitches connecting the pieces were varied and delicate. They weren't perfect, like those in the book, but their irregularity contributed to the old-fashioned charm of the piece. If all sixteen sections turned out as well, the quilt would be magnificent.

For all the work involved, quilting was less restrictive than most of her hobbies. She had to concentrate only when learning a new stitch or deciding on the placement of fabrics. While embroidering, which took most of the time, she could do anything that didn't involve the use of her hands: watch television, dictate letters, talk on the telephone, or visit with friends. That turned out to be one of its greatest advantages.

Just as the pressure of the past two and a half years had allowed her little time for relaxation, so they had also prevented her from having any social life. For the most part, she considered this a blessing, being a recluse at heart. She loved the serenity of her home, hated the noisy chaos on the streets, and for years had used work as an excuse to decline invitations. But she wasn't a hermit; she had a few friends that she actually wanted to see. With the men, such as Mr. John, interior designers George Thomas and David Barrett, or the theatrical producer

Leonard Sillman, she simply invited herself over for dinner, arrived with her sewing bag, and quilted as they talked their way through the evening. For her women friends, however, she came up with something far more interesting: a quilting bee.

The idea came to her from a book about antique quilts. In colonial times, many were made as a community effort. All the women of a rural area would gather in one of their homes and stay for as long as it took to complete a quilt for that household. The following month, they would meet again in another house, and so on until everyone in the group had a quilt. Then they'd begin the circle all over again. It was a social occasion: a way for the women to visit, gossip, and pass the long New England winters.

Mother updated it a bit. Her group met once a week for a few hours, and everyone worked on their own project, if they had one at all. Conversation was the real attraction, and it sparkled. Many of the women were in show business, most had careers, and all were intelligent, witty, and talented. The list, which varied from week to week, included actresses Imogene Coca, Faye Emerson, Arlene Francis, Hermione Gingold, Celeste Holm, Georgia Sothern, Nancy Walker, and Mother's sister June Havoc. Jane Ashley, an interior decorator who rented an apartment in the front of the house, and Bonnie Cashin, the fashion designer, were regulars; and Hedda Hopper, the Hollywood columnist, stopped by whenever she was in New York.

What Hedda got out of those afternoons made enough copy to fill her column for a week, but she also contributed. Mother, who was always trying to find new pieces of material for her quilt, asked everyone to bring whatever they could find around their houses, especially old silk ties. She loved the colorful patterns, and the material was virtually unworn except for an occasional stain which she worked around or embroidered over. One day Hedda arrived from California with a whole bag full of ties; Mother couldn't have been more delighted or surprised. "Oh, Hedda, you're a darling!" she exclaimed. "But where did you get them? I thought you were divorced."

"Of course I'm divorced," Hedda quipped, "but they all leave something behind."

Considering the sophistication of the women, their get-togethers were surprisingly old-fashioned. They sat around the dining room table, drank tea, gossiped, and played at quilting. Mother insisted everyone take a stab at sewing, but she was the only one to work seriously on a quilt. Georgia Sothern, however, made two pillows and Hermione made a patchwork tie that was as hilarious as it was ugly.

In the meantime, David Merrick had been doing a brilliant job producing the musical of *Gypsy*. He had enlisted Leland Hayward as his partner, and they had signed Ethel Merman to star as Rose, Mother's mother; Arthur Laurents to write the libretto; Stephen Sondheim, the lyrics; Jule Styne, the music; and Jerome Robbins to direct and choreograph. Mother was ecstatic; her life could not have been in more talented, capable hands. Laurents, Sondheim, and Robbins had performed similar tasks on *West Side Story*, the previous year's major hit, Jule Styne was one of the foremost composers on the street, and Ethel Merman was . . . Merman! Success in the theater is never guaranteed, but with these ingredients it seemed highly probable.

Then in January 1959, Arthur Laurents delivered the first draft of the play. He had distilled Mother's book into a powerful backstage drama. In act one, Rose leaves home with her two young daughters, determined to make June — the youngest, who could dance on her toes at two and a half — a star. She succeeds, and "Baby June" headlines on all the major vaudeville circuits, but in the process Rose smothers June with too much love and attention while totally ignoring Louise, who is pudgy and untalented. When, at fourteen, June escapes her mother's overpowering domination by running away with one of the boys in the act, Rose immediately turns to Louise and promises to do for her what she did for June. "I made her! And I can make you. . . . And I will. . . ." In act two, however, they quickly go broke. Louise truly is untalented, but it hardly matters because the Depression and radio have killed vaudeville. Desperate, they begin working in burlesque theaters. When the star stripper fails to turn up for a performance, Rose pushes Louise on in her place. ". . . you — are — going — to — be — a — star!" And she is, as Gypsy Rose Lee. But she, too, wants a life of her own and rejects Rose. Deserted now by both of her daughters, Rose vents her rage in a dynamic musical soliloquy. At the end, she and Louise make up, and the curtain falls as they walk off stage, arm in arm. It was a wonderful script. Everyone loved it.

Everyone, that is, but June, Mother's sister. She had been terribly hurt by Mother's book. She felt that Mother had exploited *their* childhood for her own gain and, worse, had often altered the truth to get a laugh or make a point, and in so doing had made her appear as a willful, spoiled, and not overly talented brat. She could have objected, even gone to court, but she knew how hard Mother had worked on it and — almost as a gift, sister to sister — had let it slide. Although her characterization in the play was basically the same, she felt the situation was entirely different. David Merrick and the others weren't family, they were *strangers,* and she saw no reason to let them exploit her childhood and embarrass her as well. She had her lawyer call David and tell him that she would not allow herself to be portrayed unless changes were made in the script and she was given a royalty.

The royalty wasn't a problem, but June's script demands seriously jeopardized the show. Arthur Laurents had spent months crafting the libretto, and Baby June played a pivotal role. He couldn't cut her out, but in good conscience, he couldn't make some of the changes she wanted either. He was convinced they would ruin the show.

Mother mediated a compromise, but she was a far from disinterested party. Not only did she love Arthur's script, she desperately wanted to see the show produced. Its success would mean a few years of financial security and enough time to find that elusive new career. Its cancellation would leave her with nothing but the new act and *Curious Evening,* which was still piled in a corner of the dining room. She never actually lied to June, but she implied that certain of her objections would be eliminated by casting or in the direction and promised to protect her interests. June accepted her word and signed a limited release on January 14. On February 9, the show went into rehearsal.

The crisis, although averted, reminded Mother that the odds against the show's success were very high (roughly one show in ten runs a full season). All her old insecurities surfaced, she began looking for a job, and once again she curtailed expenses. It couldn't have come at a worse time for me. Riverdale required ties and jackets in classes and at meals, but because of my refusal to sell books over the summer Mother had refused to buy me any new clothes for school, and I had been making do since September with my one dark suit. Over Christmas vacation, however, she had finally relented and agreed to take me shopping "after the first of the year, when everything goes on sale." She kept her word, but not in the way I had expected. Instead of a store, she took me to Leonard Sillman's house. He was cleaning out his closets and welcomed her suggestion that he sell her some of his old suits for me. Leonard was my height but at least fifty pounds heavier, and his suits hung on me like potato sacks, but Mother assured me that with a little tailoring they would look perfect. In spite of my doubts, I let her talk me into four of his circa 1945 Brooks Brothers suits and his prewar British-tailored tuxedo. When the local tailor finished with them, they still hung on me like potato sacks — old-fashioned potato sacks, I might add. Mother, of course, insisted they looked terribly elegant, and rather than fight a losing battle I left them in the closet and wore my one dark suit for the rest of the year.

In February, she was offered two jobs: a weekly late-night television show on a local station, and eight consecutive weeks with the new act at Casa Cugat, a Manhattan nightclub. The money for the act was great, but nonetheless she turned it down because "It's wrong for me to be shaking the beads in a saloon while the myth is on Broadway. The original must live up to the story." Similarly, she accepted the TV show because she felt it would be an ideal way to plug the musical even though the salary was poor, the budget minuscule, and her time slot put her into direct competition with Jack Paar.

From its inception, the TV show presented her with nothing but problems. It did, however, have one beneficial side effect. She was knee-deep in preparations for taping the first show when June called on March 13 to tell her that she was suing to stop the musical. Both of Mother's lawyers were on vacation, and there was nothing she could do until they returned but worry. At least she had the TV show to occupy her mind.

While Mother was frantic, David Merrick took it in stride. He changed Baby June's name to Baby Claire, billed the show as a musical fable, and promised to keep June so tied up with lawyers that she'd be unable to stop the show. Mother had been right when she chose to sell him her book; he was just like Mike Todd — nothing stopped him.

On March 30, the same day that Mother was scheduled to tape her first TV show, June called at twelve-thirty in the morning. They spoke until three, and June finally agreed to withdraw the suit in exchange for two minor, face-saving changes. Coincidentally, just as the TV show helped Mother cope with June's threatened suit, so the settlement of the suit helped her cope with her disappointment in the first show. Everything went wrong during the taping, and she knew it was dreadful. When it premiered on April 7, the critics agreed, and the show was canceled.

It was seven weeks before *Gypsy*'s Broadway opening, and with each passing day Mother became more excited and nervous. She tried to work on *Curious Evening* but couldn't concentrate. Quilting in front of the television set got her through the evenings, but she needed something more active for the days. She began by updating the scrapbooks, which took three weeks; for the final month, she worked on the patio.

For years, the patio had been an unending source of frustration to Mother. Every spring she'd put in new plants, and halfway through the summer they'd be dead. The problem was a lack of light. Because the patio was enclosed on all four sides, there was sun for less than an hour a day. This year, she decided to try something new and built a rock garden planted with moss and other deep-forest vegetation around the fountain. Boyd helped her break down the existing pool around the fountain with a sledgehammer, but she did everything else herself: she lugged attractive rocks in from the country, cemented them in place, went back to the country to collect moss from around trees, and then placed it on the rocks with loving care. It was an ideal project for this period in her life. After a day of lugging rocks, even her worries about the show couldn't keep her awake.

I didn't start worrying about *Gypsy*'s success until the Monday before it opened on Broadway. Mother had given me a note to bring to school asking that I be excused from classes on Friday, the day after opening night. I had expected some objection, but the principal couldn't have been more agreeable. After granting his permission, he even kept me in his office for a moment to discuss the show. When the bell rang, and I got up to leave for class, he asked if I thought the show was any good.

"Of course, sir. It's great!" I answered automatically. What did he expect me to say?

"Well," he said, in that skeptical tone insensitive teachers love to adopt, "we'll see about that on Friday when it's reviewed, won't we?"

I was halfway to class when his comment penetrated. Suddenly it dawned on me that *everyone* in the school was going to see the notices, and the thought of facing my friends — and worse, my enemies — if the show flopped made me ill. I spent that period in the bathroom being sick and the rest of the week trying to devise a way of never having to return to Riverdale if the show should fail.

By Thursday night, I was even more nervous than Mother, and when I saw myself in the mirror, dressed in Leonard Sillman's tuxedo, I decided I was simply too sick to go. I went upstairs to tell Mother, but she never gave me the chance; and before I knew it we were in the Rolls and on our way.

When we arrived at the theater, the excitement in the air was palpable. The audience was buzzing with anticipation, as though it knew that the show would be a smash. It was infectious, and Mother glowed as we walked down the aisle to our seats. She looked wonderful that night. She was wearing a long black silk taffeta skirt belted at the waist, a white silk blouse, her sable jacket, and antique diamond pendant earrings. It was a simple outfit, but stunning, and she was far more elegant than the overdressed and overjeweled matrons who stared at us as we passed.

While waiting for the house lights to dim, I noticed that people all over the theater were looking in our direction, and I realized that Mother was the most important person in the theater that night. She was the reason that everyone else was there. She *was* the show.

During the overture, which is a powerful and stirring piece of music, tiny lights above the stage flashed "Gypsy Rose Lee." I had often seen Mother's name in lights, but never like this. I got chills and thought, "All this is about *my* mother." I felt so proud. I grabbed her hand and squeezed it. She squeezed back, and we sat holding hands for much of the first act.

In the middle of the first act, Louise sits alone in a tight spotlight at the corner of the otherwise darkened stage and sings a song to a baby lamb she has just received for her birthday. It is a beautiful but melancholy song, filled with the loneliness of an adolescent girl. As I watched and listened, I remembered the many stories that Mother used to tell me to help her stay awake as we drove through the night from date to date. She had always tried to keep the stories light and funny, but her unhappiness as a young girl came through nonetheless, and occasionally we had even discussed how difficult it had been. I looked up at her and saw a tear rolling down her cheek. She, too, was remembering.

At intermission, Mother and I went into the lobby so she could have a cigarette. People kept congratulating her, and while she modestly directed their praise to the creators of the show, her eyes sparkled, and I knew how proud she felt.

When the play was over, the audience gave the cast a standing ovation and then began calling "Author, Author!" I thought they wanted Mother and nudged her, but she knew better.

She didn't need to take a bow. She had walked into the theater a famous personality; she was going to leave it a legend.

Boyd, who had volunteered to drive the Rolls that night, was waiting in front of the theater, dressed in a dark suit and wearing the chauffeur's cap he had purchased for the occasion. When he saw us, he began yelling, "Miss Lee! Oh, Miss Lee! Your Rolls is over here, Miss Lee!" His flamboyance was almost embarrassing, but it alerted everyone in front of the theater as to who we were, and the crowd parted for us as if we were royalty.

Back at the house, Mother was giving a small party. The guests were mostly close friends she had invited to hold her hand while she waited for the reviews. Leonard Sillman met us at the door and asked, "How did it go?"

"It's a hit!" I piped up.

Mother shushed me quickly but gently. "Let's wait for the reviews, darling." Then, to Leonard, she added tentatively, "I think it went very well." She wasn't about to risk inviting bad luck by being over-confident.

The party started quietly. It was a balmy, late spring evening, and everyone moved back and forth between the drawing room and patio, talking in subdued tones while waiting anxiously for the early editions of the newspapers to hit the stands. There was a brief break in the tension when Mother noticed a reporter for *Time* magazine, the only stranger in the group, sitting on the moss at the edge of the rock garden. "My God!" Mother shrieked. "Get up!"

The woman leaped to her feet. "What's wrong?"

Mother walked over and pointed to the moss. "I carried that moss back from the country with my own two hands. I don't want you killing it with your fat ass." It could have been a joke — everyone laughed — but I knew she was serious because when she passed me, she said quietly, "Dumb broad! Keep an eye on her, Erik."

Mother had stopped drinking many years earlier; but that night she began drinking Black Velvets, stout mixed 50–50 with champagne, as soon as she got in the door. When it came time to get the newspapers, she was already quite tight, which explains why she let me take the Rolls out of the garage to fetch them, although I had had only two driving lessons. I didn't know where to go, so the reporter from *Time* came along to direct me. Poor woman. First the moss and then my driving. No wonder she never wrote a story about the evening.

We made it back safely, and I gave Mother the *Herald-Tribune* first. Before she had finished reading aloud the first line, "Gypsy is the best damn musical I've seen in years!" she was laughing and crying so hard that Leonard had to finish reading it. All the notices were raves.

A few minutes later, the newspapers under her arm, she staggered into the elevator and went upstairs. After seeing everyone out and turning off the lights, I looked in on her. She was passed out on her bed, still in her clothes, with the newspapers clutched to her breast.

That night as I went to bed, all I could think about was going to school on Monday. It couldn't come soon enough.

PART TWO

CHAPTER SEVEN

GYPSY's success brought about a number of changes in Mother's life, the first and most notable being in her bank account. One week after the show opened, a $1500 check arrived from David Merrick's office. The lines at the box office guaranteed similar weekly arrivals for at least a year; and then there would be income from the touring companies, the movie sale, the original cast recording, stock and amateur rights. It seemed like a bottomless well of money, and her spirits rose with her bank balance. Never before had she earned so much without working for it. She put aside her worries about the future and a new career and concentrated instead on spending her newfound wealth.

Her first priorities were redecorating the house and taking a real vacation, and she decided to combine both by spending the summer antique hunting through Europe. We had been abroad before, but she planned this trip to be very special. Whereas our earlier tours had revolved around an engagement at some point along the route, this time there was to be no work whatsoever. Her only aim was to hit every antique and junk shop in eight countries. Without scrimping on cost, either. It was to be a European sojourn in the grand manner: a suite on the French Line's most intimate ship, *Flandre*, with the Rolls in the hold so we could motor from city to city; deluxe hotels at every stop, reserved before we left the States; and three-star restaurants lined up along our route.

A sudden influx of money, however, was simply not enough to change habits ingrained over forty-five years, and the trip bore only scant resemblance to its plans. Even the plans changed along the way. She dropped the idea of not working, for example, even before we left the States. When the Yugoslav embassy received our visa applications, they notified the Yugoslav Film Board, which invited Mother to be the guest of honor at the opening night of the First International Film Festival in Pula. At first she saw it as an opportunity to make some of the trip's expenses tax deductible, and that was reason enough to rearrange our itinerary in order to attend. Then it occurred to her that the film festival would be an ideal launching for *Curious Evening*, and offered to show it on opening night, out of competition. The Yugoslavs, obviously desperate for someone — anyone — from out of the country to attend and add an international flavor, were delighted.

Curious Evening, unfortunately, was in no shape to be shown out of competition or anywhere else, and we spent the two weeks prior to our departure locked in the dining room with the editing equipment, trying to put it into some semblance of order. We managed a pretty fair patch job. "Good enough," as Mother said, "for the Yugoslavs who won't be able to understand it anyway." But not good enough for her. Among the more glaring problems, she felt, was a lack of coverage of our previous trips to Europe; and while there was nothing she could do about it for the film festival, she decided to take a lot of film of this trip and use it to fill the gap on our return home. When she told me, I sensed the end of the vacation before it had even begun and reminded her that the summer was supposed to be "workless."

"Don't be silly, Erik," she answered. "How much work is it to take a few movies?" I didn't think of the answer until we got into the taxi to go to the pier. I was carrying two movie cameras (one loaded with black and white film, the other with color), extra lenses and filters for both, a still camera, a tape recorder, and a light meter. I felt like a pack horse but didn't dare complain. Mother only tolerated objections when she first made a suggestion and, even then, just barely.

Our departure was everything Mother could have wanted. The first reporter spotted us even before the taxi came to a stop. I noticed him when he pointed out the cab to his photographer, who was easily spotted by the huge Speed Graphic camera he carried. Mother noticed too and reached for her compact. She had expected the press and was dressed and made up accordingly. Still, she made a few last-minute swipes with her powder puff and touched up her lipstick as she rattled off final instructions with the precision of an officer sending his men into battle: "Boyd, take care of the luggage and meet us in the suite. Erik, I want you to get some shots of me with the reporters. Use the color camera. Leave everything else for Boyd." She paused and looked outside, judging the light. Although we carried a light meter, she never used it, preferring to trust her intuition. "Set the exposure at eight."

While I got the camera ready, she directed the driver to stop in the sunlight; then as he was pulling in to the curb, she turned back to me. "Hurry up now, Erik. Wave when you're in position. And for godsakes, hold it steady and don't cut off my legs." I managed to line up the shot and start rolling just in time to catch her stepping out of the taxi. She played it for laughs, first sticking out a shapely leg, then pausing for effect, and finally emerging with a broad smile into a burst of popping flashbulbs. "That's all you get today, boys. Remember, you're here to see me off . . . not to see me take it off."

That morning she posed at the taxi for the *Daily News* and the Associated Press, at the foot of the gangplank for the French Line's publicity people, at the top of the gangplank for the *Journal American*, and finally on deck for the *Mirror*, the *Post*, and the *Herald-Tribune*. The *Times* didn't go in for such things in those days.

It was too crowded around the gangplank for me to get any more footage, but I managed to make up for it on deck while she held an informal news conference.

"Gyps," the man from the *Mirror* began. "Is it true you're going to Europe to search out new ideas for your strip?"

Mother laughed softly. "Where have you been, honey? I stopped taking my clothes off in front of strangers long ago." She sat on a sea chest, crossed her legs, and lifted her dress to expose her calves. "I've gone legit."

He lined up the obligatory "leg shot" and tried for a shocked expression by commenting, "Too old?" The *Mirror* was never a very good paper.

Mother's expression didn't change. "I'll have you know I have everything I had twenty years ago." She paused for effect. "It's just a little lower, that's all." It was one of her favorite lines; she used it whenever she had the chance. "Actually, I'm going to Europe to show my film at the film festival in Yugoslavia. I'm the guest of honor, you know."

The reporter from the *Post* went next. "What do you think about the musical based on your life?"

"It's based on my book," she corrected him, "and I love it. It's paying for this trip."

"Well, how does it feel to see yourself portrayed on stage?"

She turned serious. "Very proud. And a little sad that my mother couldn't be here to see Ethel Merman play her. She would have loved that."

The reporter from the *Mirror* interjected another silly question.

"What do you think about the girl who plays you? How does she stack up against the original?"

"You mean Sandra Church? Why, if I had been that pretty, I wouldn't have had to take my clothes off."

"How about one with you and the boy?" asked the photographer from the *Post*.

"Erik, come here, darling." She put her arm around my shoulders, smiled, and without moving her mouth reminded me, softly, "Don't look at the camera, look at me. Now smile." I was used to posing for photographs, but I never learned how to be comfortable doing it. I always felt my smile was tight and forced, and I marveled at Mother's ability to break into a broad, open smile on cue. It was nothing like her real smile, of course, but then only I knew that.

"How does it feel to have such a famous mother?" asked the man from the *Tribune*, trying for an "original" angle.

"It's great."

"But don't you miss having a normal childhood?"

I shrugged. "For me, this is normal."

"Are you excited about going to Europe?"

"Sure," I answered nonchalantly.

"Oh, he's so blasé," Mother interjected in a lovingly exasperated tone. "We've been around the world twice, so he feels Europe is old hat."

"Does he travel with you often?"

"Always," Mother answered. "When he was six months old, I wrapped him in a blanket, put him next to me in the car, and drove to Cleveland where I was playing two weeks at the Latin Quarter. He's been with me ever since. I don't know how I would manage without him. Lately, he's been my cameraman. Shot over half the footage in my film, the one I'm showing at the film festival in Yugoslavia." Her first mention of the film festival had been missed, and she was trying again. The results, unfortunately, were the same.

"Let's get one of him taking a picture of you," suggested the *Tribune* reporter, motioning to his photographer.

I was posing with the camera when the warning whistle blew and the assistant purser circled the deck announcing our imminent departure. The reporters wanted to stay and hitch a ride back to shore on the pilot's tender, but Mother was firm. "Enough is enough, boys. I'm on vacation, remember."

Once rid of the press, we concentrated on getting in some serious

— Mother's version of serious, anyway — filmmaking. While posing for the photographers, she had noticed the French words for life-vests, "Brassiers de Sauvetage," stenciled on the sea chest that she was using for a seat. The first shot she wanted was a close-up of her pointing to them. When cut into *Curious Evening*, she would say "Brassieres for savages? Oh, my!" It was good for a small laugh.

Most of all, she wanted me to film her on deck, waving to imaginary throngs as the Statute of Liberty drifted past in the background. Every other passenger on the ship seemed to be on that side of the deck, Brownies in hand, waiting for the same shot, but that didn't faze Mother in the least. She quickly selected what she judged would be the best angle, pointed out where she wanted me to stand with the camera, and eased herself, with a number of polite "Excuse mes," between two blue-haired ladies. Then, just before Liberty Island passed behind us, she went into her routine.

"Oh, my God, Erik!" she shouted. "Here it comes. Get ready." I checked the viewfinder. "How does it look?"

"Okay, but both women are in the shot."

With an increasing sense of urgency, she gently but firmly pushed them aside. "Pardon me. Do you mind? How's that?"

"The one on your left is still there."

This time she wasn't gentle at all. "You're going to ruin everything if you don't move," she insisted, shoving the woman out of the way.

"Take one step to your right," I yelled.

"Hurry, Erik. We're going to miss it."

"I'm rolling."

"Warn me, for chrissakes! And don't cut off my legs," she shouted as she broke into her picture-taking smile and began waving.

Even after years of similar scenes, I found the shoving, yelling, and theatrical hysteria embarrassing, but I had to admit that it worked. There she was in the viewfinder, virtually alone, waving regally to the nonexistent crowd as the Statue of Liberty saluted in the background.

Mother wasn't at all embarrassed, which is not to say that she was unaware of having been impolite. As always in such instances, she made a joke out of it.

"The nerve of some people," she said loudly as we walked away. "Another second and I would have kicked that sweet little old lady right in her fat behind. How dare she get here ahead of me and take the perfect spot for my shot." She paused, then added, "Some people are so rude."

The *Flandre* was a small ship, but it took us a while to find our suite. There were only two, and they were tucked away, far from the rest of the first class cabins. Finally a ship's officer directed us to a narrow staircase behind the library. At the top, we were intercepted by a French version of an English butler, the same efficiency but much less polite. "Yes?" he demanded, blocking the corridor.

"I'm Gypsy Rose Lee, and I'm looking for my suite," Mother demanded in return.

His manner changed instantly. Somehow he managed to become deferential without giving up one iota of his arrogance. "Ah, yes, madame." He nodded his head in a curt bow. "I am Albert, your cabin steward. If there is anything —"

"Right now, all I want is my stateroom."

He pointed to the door at the end of the corridor. "Of course, madame."

I was very impressed. "You mean we get our own private cabin steward?" I whispered as we reached the door.

"I hope not," she answered. "Can you imagine the tip he'll expect."

Boyd was sitting in the parlor, staring out the large window at the New York skyline when we entered. "There you are," he greeted us. "I was beginning to worry. You missed all the excitement. . . ."

"That's what you think," I said, but he wasn't listening.

"The screaming and yelling, the horns, the streamers . . ." he continued.

Mother, however, was in no mood for idle chitchat. "Where are the suitcases?" she interrupted. "If I don't get out of this goddamn corset, I'm going to faint."

"I didn't know where you wanted everything, so I had the porter leave it all in the bedroom," Boyd answered. He always paid attention to Mother.

"Oh, God," she said when she opened the door. It was wall-to-wall suitcases. "Erik, darling, would you please climb around in there and get the robe out of my overnight case." As I went into the bedroom, she sat on the sofa and lit a cigarette, and Boyd resumed his enthusing. The view was "too much to be believed," the suite, "the living end," and the ship itself, "to die!"

It was to be expected. Boyd had never been outside of North America in his life. To go to Europe had always been his dream, and to be doing it in such style and with Mother as his guide was beyond anything he had ever imagined. I've always thought that was the principal reason she invited him. In certain respects she was very generous; she loved giving the perfect gift and then hearing all the "ohhs" and "ahhs" of appreciation. That is not to say she was being or even pretending to be altruistic. In this case she was very much looking forward to Boyd's company, and his eye, on her antique hunting expeditions; and having him along wasn't costing her a cent. The suite and the car expenses were the same for three as for two, and she expected him to pay for his share of meals and hotels. Boyd didn't care; he was just delighted to be there and would have raved all day had Mother not put a stop to it when I came out of the bedroom with her robe.

"Thank God!" she said, taking it. "Boyd, darling, would you please be a dear and stop talking long enough to find our cabin steward and order me some tea. Darjeeling or Lapsang Souchong."

"Why don't we just ring?" he suggested, reaching for the call buttons.

"I could have done that," she stopped him. "I want you to get out of here so I can get out of this friggin' corset."

"Oh, of course," Boyd mumbled apologetically, heading for the door. "What was that now, Darjeeling or . . . ?"

"Lapsang Souchong."

Mother didn't ask Boyd to leave for reasons of modesty. She had long ago mastered changing into her robe without revealing anything unseemly. No indeed. Sending Boyd after the steward was her way of establishing one of the ground rules for the trip: when she asked for something, she wanted her way, right away. The reminder wasn't necessary. Boyd had assumed he would have to do more than pay his share of expenses to earn his place on this trip. Doing Mother's bidding had always been the price he paid for her company, he hadn't expected it to change, and he didn't even mind it. It did, however, hurt his feelings that she had seen fit to remind him.

But it was easy to understand from her point of view. This was, above all else, *her* vacation; and while she was perfectly willing to share it, it had to be on her terms, and she wanted no misunderstandings about the nature of those terms.

To be fair, once in her robe with her feet up and her autocracy firmly established, she tempered it, at least superficially, with a touch of democracy. While we were waiting for Boyd to return from his errand, she asked me which dinner sitting I preferred. "The first is at six," she explained, "which is when I prefer to eat, as you know." She paused and then continued, thinking out loud. "But they do rush you out to make room for the second at eight."

"Let's take the second." I voted quickly while she was on a positive note. As far as I was concerned, only children ate at six. I was fourteen!

Mother pursed her lips, a sure sign of displeasure. Usually she did it when she felt she was being thwarted for no good reason. Just then, Boyd returned. "Let's see what Boyd would like," she suggested in a tone meant to imply evenhandedness. It was clear that she expected him to support her. To make sure, she gave him the same spiel she had given me but added that the second sitting meant black-tie every night.

"Whichever you want is fine with me, of course," he assured her, "but the second does sound much more elegant."

She pursed her lips again and appeared terribly annoyed, but after a moment's thought, she gave in. "Oh very well. I suppose it would be a shame to be rushed through dinner."

The arrival of the tea changed the subject but not her mood. "What's this?" she asked sharply as placed the tray on the coffee table in front of her.

"Vodka tonic, madam," he answered.

"I ordered myself a Bon Voyage cocktail," Boyd quickly explained.

"Vodka for breakfast. Bon voyage, indeed," she remarked. It was a half-humorous rebuke meant to be taken very seriously. Although she had been a heavy drinker in her early twenties and still drank occasionally, Mother really didn't approve of alcohol, especially hard liquor. At its worst, it could be terribly destructive; at its best, it was an expensive, overrated indulgence. One Boyd, who had a very limited budget, could ill afford, as she hastened to remind him the moment Albert left the suite.

"I hope you aren't planning to make a habit of that," she began with a nod toward his drink. He opened his mouth to answer, but she kept on going, forcing him to listen in silence. "Hard liquor is extremely costly in Europe, you know. It's a bit cheaper here on the ship, of course, but it's still extra; and if you're serious about conserving your funds —"

"Oh, but of course I am —" he started to explain in a tone of such abject servility that it sickened me.

"I'm going to explore the ship," I interrupted, heading for the door. "See you later." I left quickly, before either of them could stop me.

For years I had watched Mother demean people by lecturing them about things that were none of her business. It had always made me uncomfortable, but this time my reaction was almost violent. How dare she lecture my friend, I thought. But my greatest disappointment was with him. Why didn't he stand up to her, tell her that he was a grown man and could drink as he damn well pleased! I decided that

I would never allow myself to become such a spineless weakling. The next time she tried to trample on my rights, I was going to stand up to her. I would fight for my self-respect.

That night I had my chance. It came during dinner, which was the worst possible time aboard ship to annoy her. Dinner was the main reason she took the French Line to Europe. The First Class dining rooms on its ships were considered among the finest restaurants in the world, floating palaces filled with epicurean delights. Except for the first and last nights at sea and the night of the captain's dinner, when we were limited to what appeared on the menu, we could order whatever they had in their well-stocked larder prepared any way we wished. And because it was all included in the price of the ticket, money was no object, even for Mother.

Dinner began well enough. Boyd had caviar, which the waiter served from a ten-pound tin with a spoon the size of a soup ladle until Boyd told him to stop. He must have had half a pound on his plate. I know he had tears in his eyes. He kept repeating, "I can't believe it, I just can't believe it," until Mother shushed him. We weren't caviar fans and ordered the foie gras instead. It was served with equal largesse, and the three of us were stuffed after the first course.

The double consommé we had next was perfect for clearing the palate; it was also the last course of the evening that we were to enjoy. I was not the first to draw Mother's fire, however. That distinction went to our waiter, who was very slow in clearing the empty bowls. It wasn't deliberate; we shared him with a table for six and he was busy serving their entrées. Mother, who was a very fast eater, hated having dirty dishes in front of her. The longer she waited, the angrier she became. By the time the waiter got around to us, she was furious.

"I will not stand for this!" She let him have it, sharply but quietly, as soon as he was within range.

"Madame?" He leaned over as if anxious to hear her and be of service. It was a typical waiter's pose, and she was having none of it.

"You left us sitting here, staring at these dirty plates for entirely too long. I know you expect that table to give you a larger tip because there are more of them, but that is no excuse for ignoring us, and I will not put up with it! I expect our plates to be removed the moment we finish eating. Is that understood?"

"Yes, madame." He said it very politely but with an arrogant smirk.

Mother, fortunately, wasn't looking at him. "Very well. Now take these away," she ordered, waving her hand in the general direction of the plates.

The tension began to ease with the arrival of the entrée. Mother and Boyd were sharing a Chauteaubriand with béarnaise sauce, and I was having the roast duck Bigarade. We were all raving about how wonderful everything tasted when Mother offered me a bite of the steak off her fork. "Here, darling, you must try the béarnaise. It's magnificent."

For no particular reason, I declined with a polite "No, thank you."

"You'll love it. Believe me."

I looked at the piece of meat covered with the yellow sauce and didn't believe her at all. I tried to explain that the eggy béarnaise was the last flavor I wanted in my mouth on top of the sweet/tart duck, but she wouldn't let me.

"Erik, I insist," she interrupted.

All the feelings of the afternoon, greatly magnified, swept over me like a wave. I knew I should taste it, if only to keep peace in the family, but I just couldn't bring myself to do it. "I don't want any. Thank you." Even my attempt at being polite failed; my anger came through and I ended up sounding insolent.

"I don't want an argument, Erik. Just take it." Her patience was stretched to its limit.

"No." I said it quietly, trying desperately to keep my voice steady. Never before had I dared defy her so openly or abruptly. I was very frightened. But I was even more curious. What would she do? What could she do?

She could outmaneuver me, and did. "But you promised," she said, the soul of reason.

"Never!" I blurted indignantly. I couldn't imagine what she was talking about.

"Oh!" She looked at the ceiling, mugging indignation. "How can you say that? Don't you remember? It was in a dining room just like this, our first night out on the old *DeGrasse*. You gave me your solemn word of honor that you would try everything at least once."

I wanted to scream. Instead of fighting me like an equal, she made jokes and dug up a promise I had made when I was six years old. I began to argue that it had only applied to that trip, but it sounded petty even before I said it. Furious, I grabbed her fork, shoved the meat in my mouth, and swallowed it whole.

"There," I said defiantly, already regretting my action. It had been childish and silly and I knew it. Worse, I realized I had put myself in the wrong and thus forfeited the entire contest.

So did she, and she pressed her advantage to the limit. "Erik, I will not tolerate that kind of behavior on this trip. If you want to act like a child, you can go to camp; if you want to stay with us, I'll expect you to behave accordingly. Is that clear?"

I wanted to push the table over into her lap, but I didn't want to go to camp. "Yes, Mother," I agreed docilely.

"Very well, then," she said, offering me her fork again. "Now take a proper taste."

I did, and we managed to get through the rest of dinner without further incident. It was an uneasy truce, however. We both sensed that our fight had been but the opening salvo in what would be a long, long war.

But there were no more battles for a while, and the rest of the crossing was actually quite pleasant. Except for dinner, Mother left the suite only on the night of the Captain's Gala Ball when she served as emcee and managed to get the other first-class passengers to donate over eight thousand dollars to the Seamen's Relief Fund. She spent her days on our private sun deck getting a tan, working on the narration for *Curious Evening,* and reading. She would alternate between murder mysteries and books on antiques. At night, she'd collapse into bed right after dinner.

Boyd and I collapsed after dinner, too, but only for a nap. By one, we were up and off in our separate directions: Boyd to the tourist class section of the ship where he found the cruising better, and I to the First Class nightclub where I'd join the daughter of the couple who were traveling in the ship's other suite. We became a constant twosome, dancing, drinking, and partying until dawn when I'd leave her at her cabin door after a chaste kiss on the cheek. Try as I might, I couldn't work up the courage to suggest she invite me in for the night. At the time I excused my cowardice because she was an older woman — all of eighteen — and wouldn't want to sleep with a mere child of fourteen. Probably true, but I'll never know because I was just too shy to ask.

With such an active night life, I slept all morning. For once Mother didn't disturb me. She had decided at the start of the voyage to sleep on the sofa in the living room and let Boyd and me have the bedroom with its own entrance so that we wouldn't disturb her when we came in late at night. It worked perfectly, for all three of us.

I had one moment of panic during the crossing. The night before we arrived in Southhampton, I received my bar bill for the trip. One hundred and fifty dollars!!! It was a disaster. My five-dollar-a-week allowance was already overdrawn, Mother was keeping an eagle eye on her purse so I couldn't steal from it, and Boyd was nursing his meager resources.

The next day, I watched my girlfriend and the other England-bound passengers disembark and brooded over my problems. We were arriving in Le Havre the next day; I had to pay the bill that night. The thought of asking Mother for the money made me physically ill. Finally, Boyd took pity on me and lent me the cash. When I went to pay the bill, however, I discovered that my girlfriend's father had paid it for me. I never had a chance to thank him for his generosity, but I've never forgotten it.

CHAPTER EIGHT

OUR ARRIVAL in France did not bode well for the rest of the trip. Mother's insurance man had failed to provide her with a "green card"— the one form necessary for her to drive in Europe. It took four hours to straighten out the problem. Four hours of Boyd and me sitting with the luggage on the dock, staring through the windows of the customs shed at Mother as she argued, begged, paced, chain-smoked, and got increasingly annoyed over the bureaucratic foul-up. There was nothing wrong with the insurance, just the form.

I knew, just from watching her, that the rest of the day was ruined. She would be tense, irritable, and short-tempered all the way to Paris. True to my expectations, she was snappish during the loading of the car, cursed her insurance man for our first five minutes on the road, complained loudly about the cost and poor quality of French gasoline when we filled the tank, and made life very difficult for the poor restaurateur who, obviously against his better judgment, gave in to Mother's entreaties and agreed to seat us even though he had stopped serving lunch ten minutes earlier. But that was the end of it. Her mood changed completely once lunch was over and we were on our way with nothing to do but go. Or perhaps I should say, nothing to do but buy.

"Boyd, look!" she cried. "Do you see what I see?"

What she saw, and only a blind person could have missed, was an antique shop up ahead. It was the first of the trip; we were less than a mile from where we had had lunch. She slowed as we approached it and looked over the stuff on display in front. "Let's stop," she said, pulling in. It was impossible to miss the breathless excitement in her voice. Before getting out of the car, she turned to both of us and said, with almost exaggerated seriousness, "Now, don't let me buy anything.

Not yet. I want to get a good look around and see what's available before I start spending money."

She didn't need our help. She had planned this trip for too long and was too shrewd a shopper to buy rashly. But that didn't stop her from having a good time. She and Boyd picked their way, with much ohhing and ahhing, through more than a dozen shops during that drive to Paris, including one place that wasn't a shop at all but an old château with a crude, hand-painted sign reading "antiques" leaning next to its main-entrance gate. The caretakers, a husband and wife, who were selling the contents either on their employer's behalf or their own, seemed very impressed by the Rolls, and when Mother started making favorable comments about this and that, they offered us tea. Mother accepted without hesitation; we had been through at least seven shops by then and she was ready for a cup. For the next hour we sat in the château's formal garden drinking tea while the husband brought one thing after another to Mother for her inspection. Every time we made a move to go, the wife would arrive with another plate of cakes or sandwiches; and as Mother said when we finally got in the car, "It would have been terribly rude to leave without tasting them." Good manners, however, did not demand a purchase, and that she resisted. She wanted to look around some more.

Two shops more, as it turned out. At the third she found a toby jug in the shape of a pig for which the owner was asking "twelve dollars, American" — those were still the good old days. It was "to die," and when the owner agreed to take ten dollars, she decided that she "couldn't live without it."

That broke the ice. At the next stop it was a lovely old stereoscope, then a couple of antique picture frames, and at the last shop of the day, wrought-iron fencing. It was huge stuff, over ten feet high and in lengths ranging from three to ten feet, and extremely heavy, but that didn't stop her. She bought enough to cover the rear wall of the patio, plus a little extra because "you never know when it might come in handy," and blithely signed two more traveler's checks to cover the cost of having it delivered to the French Line in Le Havre. She had arranged for them to accept anything that arrived for her, store it, and place it in the hold of the ship we took home.

The shopping spree continued in Paris. She bought luggage at Vuitton, perfume at Grillot, and antiques wherever she could find them. She also ordered, for delivery in August, corsets from Cadolle, six pair of shoes from Ferragamo, a designer collar for Fu Manchu, and nine hundred dollars' worth of handmade silk flowers at Troussilier. On

Sunday, when every other place in Paris was closed, we went to the Flea Market where she bought fireplace tools with handles made from antique bayonets, a sack full of old silk scraps for her quilt, a porcelain *trompe l'oeil* ashtray in the shape of a sailor's hat, and too much more to list.

It was a stunning reversal of character. I had never seen Mother spend so much, so quickly, and with such unrestrained pleasure. Twice during our week in Paris she had to go to the local branch of her New York bank to buy more traveler's checks, but not once did she complain about how fast they were going. She was, in short, having the time of her life.

It was a good part of the trip for Boyd and me, too. He loved the shopping, of course, while I found it relentlessly boring, but we both enjoyed the evenings. One night after dinner Mother took us to Madame Arthur's, a nightclub that had recently opened and was quite the rage. The floorshow was straight burlesque but performed by female impersonators. Some of the boys were quite beautiful, but we found the acts — especially the strippers — very disappointing. They were neither provocative nor original. Still, we were glad we had gone. There certainly was nothing like it in the States in 1959.

The other nights in Paris, Boyd and I were alone. Mother went to bed right after dinner, usually around nine-thirty, in order to awake at six rested and ready for another grueling day in the shops. We would return to our room after saying goodnight, but only for half an hour or so to give her time to go to sleep. Then we'd sneak out and hit the streets.

Before leaving the States, Boyd had promised to get me laid in Paris, and the ostensible purpose of these evening excursions was to find the perfect hooker for my first time. Through the "velvet underground" he found streets literally lined with girls, some of whom were so beautiful that I can still recall them, but I couldn't work up enough courage to make an approach, and I refused to let him do it for me. So I didn't get laid, but I did have fun. Those nights walking the streets of Paris, stopping for drinks in sidewalk cafés, cruising the girls while Boyd cruised the boys, made up for all the boring days in all the boring shops ten times over. Like Mother, I was having the time of my life.

Good times never last, however, and ours barely made it through the week in Paris. There was a harbinger of the trouble to come on our last night in town, although neither Boyd nor I recognized it at the time. Fortunately Boyd and I had returned early from our nocturnal wanderings. We had been in our room less than fifteen minutes when

Mother knocked on our door. "Boyd . . . Erik? Let me in," she called in a loud whisper.

Mother never visited our room, and it was strewn with cigarette butts, dirty clothes, and wine bottles. Boyd was in the bathroom, so I jumped out of bed and scrambled to pick up. She heard me. "Hurry up and let me in. I don't want anyone to see me out here."

I opened the door and understood why. She had her ratty paisley robe on over a longer, equally ratty, cotton nightgown; her face was shiny with cold cream; and her hair was a stringy tangle. She looked as if she had just gotten out of bed, but she was wide awake and didn't miss a thing as she glanced around the room. I knew, with the certainty that comes from a guilty conscience, that we were in trouble.

"What are you two doing up?" she demanded in a tone that froze me.

Boyd came to the rescue. He entered from the bathroom with a towel around his middle and a concerned expression on his face. "What's wrong?"

She sat on the edge of my bed and continued her thought. "I wish I had known; I would have come over earlier." She held out her hand. "Look at that. I'm still shaking from it." Her hand was quivering. Our curiosity fully aroused, we waited for her to continue. Instead there was a pause while she reached for a cigarette, discovered that she didn't have any, and borrowed one of Boyd's. As she lit it, she looked around the room and, just to let us know that she was wise to our tricks, remarked, "No wonder you're both so tired every day, out gallivanting half the night. . . ."

"What happened?" I asked, only partially to change the subject.

"I had a nightmare. It was terrifying." She shuddered dramatically. "Terrifying."

"What was it about?" asked Boyd.

"I can't tell you. Not until after breakfast. It's bad luck to tell your dreams on an empty stomach. They might come true." She shuddered again. "God forbid."

She hadn't come over to talk; she just didn't want to be alone. For a while she paced the floor, chain-smoking, then she announced that she felt calm enough to return to her room. I offered to keep her company, but she turned me down. "I'll be all right, now," she assured me. "It won't come back."

The next morning, as always, we met in her room for breakfast. After her first bite of croissant, she began: "There wasn't much to it. You're both going to be disappointed, especially after all the hoopla last night. I can only tell you that I've never been so upset by a dream in all my life.

"I was on the Jack Paar show and I opened my mouth to say something and out poured this long, green thing . . ." She was bending at the waist and moving her hands as if to pull a long rope out of her mouth. ". . . like a snake, only there was no end to it. It just kept coming and coming. I felt like it was choking me to death." She took a bite of croissant and waited for our reaction.

"What do you think it means?" I asked.

"I think it means I'd better not eat before I do Jack's show next time." Her answer was not meant to be funny. The connection between the endless green snake of her dream and the endless river of greenbacks she had been spending seems obvious, but while Mother had read all of Freud's work, she accepted very little of it. For her, dreams were portents, windows looking into the future rather than on to the soul. In this case it certainly didn't matter; the dream, whatever its meaning, was forgotten in the chaos that always accompanied checking out of a hotel with Mother.

As planned, we left Paris that morning and headed southeast through the wine country toward Switzerland, stopping frequently at antique shops along the way. Aside from a slipping clutch, which was corrected by a gas-station mechanic while we had lunch in Fontainebleau, nothing happened the first day to interfere with Mother's fun or alleviate my boredom. The scenery changed on the second and third days, but everything else remained the same. I wanted to scream whenever we stopped, but I was staying on my best behavior. We were having a very special dinner on our third night out of Paris, and I wasn't about to risk being excluded from it.

From Paris Mother had telephoned her good friend Paulette Goddard, who lived in Ascona, Switzerland. It was almost on our route, and she was hoping for a quick visit. Her husband, novelist Erich Maria Remarque, answered the phone. Paulette was in the States. He and Mother had never met, but he knew of her from Paulette, and when he heard we were passing near by, he insisted we join him at his villa for dinner.

I had been excited ever since Mother told me about it. We had spent three weeks discussing his novel *All Quiet on the Western Front* in my English class at school, and I relished the prospect of telling my teacher that I had dined with its author. I knew he'd be very impressed. I was rather impressed myself.

Erich Remarque was warm, generous, and not the least bit condescending toward me. The latter quality alone would have made him tops in my book, but he went out of his way to make us feel welcome, and it was a wonderful evening.

He was a man of few but intense passions: his wife, whom he missed terribly and talked of at length; writing, which he hardly mentioned throughout the evening except to tell me, in response to my telling him about *All Quiet* being on my high-school curriculum, that he wrote it in six weeks, working nights; his wine cellar, which he both showed off and shared; and his collection of oriental carpets, which covered the floor of his living room, in layers.

As I've mentioned before, Mother didn't drink much, and with Erich bringing out one great wine after another, she quickly became tipsy. Then there was the port. And lastly the brandy. Then Mother threw up and had to be helped into the car and back to the hotel.

Nonetheless, I loved every minute of that evening.

It was ten-thirty before Mother knocked on our door the next morning, the latest we had slept since getting off the ship. The extra hours of sleep had cured Boyd and me, but she was still hungover and in a terrible mood besides. Too sick to manage more than a cup of tea, she rushed us through breakfast explaining that because of our detour to visit Erich and our late start, we were behind schedule and in grave danger of missing our hotel reservations in Rome. It didn't seem possible, but we didn't argue. It was always best to cooperate with Mother when she was in a hurry.

Much to our dismay, we could do nothing about the road which, the moment we crossed the border from the Swiss Alps to the Italian Alps, turned into a narrow, winding, mostly dirt ledge cut into the side of the mountain. Mother lasted twenty minutes. There wasn't room to pull off, so she just stopped the car, leaned out, vomited, and gave the wheel to Boyd.

Poor Boyd. It was typical of his luck throughout the trip that this would be the first time Mother asked him to drive. Under the best of conditions, he was nervous driving the Rolls; on the outside lane of a glorified goat path without guardrails, he was truly frightened. The best he could manage was a cautious crawl around the curves.

Then, not fifteen minutes after being sick, Mother announced that she was getting hungry and told us to keep our "eyes peeled for someplace to eat." There was hardly room on the road for another car, let alone a restaurant. Half an hour and ten miles' worth of rocks and dust later, she asked Boyd to drive faster. She didn't eat often and she didn't eat a lot, but when she was hungry, she had to eat quickly or she got stomach cramps and a headache. Not to mention irritable.

Boyd tried to go faster, but as soon as he glanced out his side window and saw the seemingly bottomless gorge just inches from the right tire, he slowed down. Mother reminded him twice, but he couldn't help himself. Finally, neither could she. "Stop the car, darling," she insisted, impatiently. "Let me drive. At the rate you're going it'll take us all day to find someplace to eat."

"But my God, if I went any faster we could all be kil——"

"Nonsense. You're being overcautious, and it's driving me crazy." She looked out the rear window. "Stop right here. There's no one coming."

So Mother took the wheel. As was her habit, she chose a speed and stuck with it. We careened down that mountain at exactly twenty-five miles per hour. From the back seat, where I was, it was only slightly terrifying. Boyd was in front and petrified, his knuckles white on the hand that was gripping the back of Mother's seat.

After an hour and the thousandth curve, a valley opened below us, and the bleached white of rock was suddenly broken by the green of trees and plants dotted, in the distance, with the orange of terra-cotta roofs. Civilization.

"Thank God!" Mother sighed. "I'm so hungry, I could faint."

Civilization was farther away than it looked. The road took twenty miles to wind its way down into the valley, tantalizing us, every second curve, with a peek of the town up ahead. It looked lovely and romantic at first, more a large village that had grown around a square with a fountain in its center than a town. But the closer we got, the less inviting it looked. On arrival, it was positively depressing.

It was, literally, a whistle-stop — a little town built around a railroad station where trains stop only on request. The station occupied one side of the square and the church the side opposite it. The pharmacy, two cafés, a butcher, and a patisserie lined the third, with another café, a grocery, and a hotel-restaurant opposite them. The buildings had been whitewashed once; now the colorful roofs sat on soot-streaked, cracked walls. The fountain in the center of the square clearly served as the square's litter bin; its bowl was half-full of paper and cigarette butts. So were the gutters. A singularly unattractive town, and not at all popular at four in the afternoon. All the cafés were shuttered and the streets were empty except for an occasional stray dog.

Mother stopped the car in front of the hotel; it looked as deserted as everyplace else. "Oh, God, I hope they're still serving lunch," she wished out loud. "You wait here," she told us, "I'll go inside and see if we can get something to eat."

The moment she disappeared into the hotel, Boyd turned to me. "Was I really driving that badly?" he asked. Poor Boyd, he was always so easily hurt by Mother's criticism.

"You know how she is when she's hungry," I reminded him.

"My God, yes!" he sighed dramatically. "Did you see the way she drove down that mountain?! Mary Miles Minter!! I knew my time had come. I may be overcautious but . . ." He stopped as soon as he saw her emerge from the hotel.

She opened the door and leaned in. "The dining room's closed and the chef's off duty, but the waiter said he'd make us some spaghetti. Let's wait on the veranda."

Veranda is hardly the word I would have chosen for the ramshackle wooden porch attached, obviously as an afterthought, to the front of the stucco-surfaced hotel. Whatever it was, there were three tables on it. We sat at the one with a tablecloth — very dirty — and waited. The town was quiet in the late afternoon heat. The only sounds were the buzzing of the flies and the tapping of Mother's fingernail against the ashtray. We waited. A train barreled through the station with a great deal of hooting and clanging, and then there was just the tapping and buzzing. I was thirsty and offered to go inside and get a bottle of water, but Mother wouldn't let me. She didn't want the waiter distracted from his cooking.

Even without distractions it took him close to an hour. Then the result was so overcooked that it had turned from spaghetti into a white blob covered with watery red goop. The waiter was even less appetizing than his cooking: dirty and unshaven, with his soiled, once-white waiter's jacket open to reveal an even less savory undershirt.

Mother was too hungry to care. She attacked her plate, almost shoving the food into her mouth. Fortunately for her, she didn't require a lot of food. After five or six bites, she sat back and pronounced herself full. Boyd and I picked at ours. I had decided to wait for dinner. Wherever we stopped for the night would have to have better food; how many places in Italy can ruin spaghetti?

But we were stopping right there for the night. After the waiter removed the plates, she announced, "I'm too tired to go on. Between the booze last night and that godawful road and the wait to eat today, I've had it. What do you say we stay here, go right to bed, and get a very early start in the morning."

As usual, she was soliciting agreement, not argument, but I couldn't help myself. "Here?! But why? It's not even six yet. We can make Genoa before dark. I thought we were behind schedule . . ."

"We are, but I can't help that," she snapped. "I've just finished explaining that I'm too tired to drive. It certainly can't hurt to see if there's room." She turned to Boyd.

"Well, if you can't go on . . ." he offered meekly. He never could stand up to her.

The hotel had nothing but empty rooms. Fifteen minutes later she had checked us in, said goodnight, and gone to bed. Her room was on the top floor and overlooked the square. It was, according to the waiter who doubled as the desk clerk, the best in the hotel and the only one with a private bath. Boyd and I had a twin, also overlooking the square, on the floor beneath hers. It was spartan, with only two beds, a table, and a sink, but it was surprisingly clean. In contrast, the communal toilet — a hole in the floor with steps on either side of it to stand on — was filthy. It was at one end of the hall, and we were at the other, but it smelled as if it were right next door.

Looking out the window I noticed that the cafés were opening. It was still light, too early for bed as far as I was concerned, and I suggested to Boyd that we go out for a drink.

"No thank you very much," he said firmly. "All she has to do is look out her window and see us. We'll never hear the end of it."

"Let's wait for her to go to sleep," I offered.

"Not tonight. To tell the truth I'm pretty tired myself. Watching her take those curves today was too much for me. I'm going to rinse out a few things and call it a night."

So by six-thirty we were all tucked in, nice and cozy, and ready for a good night's sleep.

At seven, every café on the square pushed its juke box on to the sidewalk and let it rip! The cacophony shook the hotel. Boyd and I looked out the window. It was a scene from a Fellini movie. People were streaming into the square, milling around, moving from café to café, shouting, talking, laughing. Young men slipped in and out of the crowd with their motor scooters and bicycles. An occasional truck, its bed full of men, lumbered up, discharged its passengers, and chugged out again. It was, Boyd and I realized, Saturday night and everyone from the town and the nearby farms was congregating in the square right outside our window.

Boyd and I rejoiced with malicious glee. Mother had stuck us in this godforsaken dump in order to sleep, but noise always kept her awake. We stood at the window and giggled like a couple of schoolboys at the poetic justice of it all.

At nine, it got better. The juke boxes were unplugged and the town's very own rock-and-roll band set up in the square. Their sound wasn't modern, more like Perry Como's hits of yesteryear than Elvis, but it was fully amplified. I thought of Mother trying to sleep and laughed out loud. Boyd grumpily asked what was so funny, and that made me laugh even more. He should have gone out with me.

But the best was yet to come, at least as far as I was concerned. At midnight, the band stopped playing, the cafés closed, and everyone went home. Within ten minutes the town was draped in peace and quiet. Even I drifted off. Until the first train charged through the station, its shrill whistle worse than an electric shock in the silence. The trains continued through the night; sometimes one an hour, sometimes one right after another. Each one woke me, so I knew they woke Mother. I felt, quite literally, like jumping for joy. That'll fix her, I thought. Oh, yes! Revenge did taste sweet.

But only briefly. Something happened to Mother that night. No doubt she had a lot of time to think as she tossed and turned, waiting for the noise to abate and for sleep to arrive. Perhaps she added up all the money she had spent and it got to her. Maybe she realized that the film festival was less than two weeks away, and panicked. Most likely it was a combination of both. One thing is certain: starting the next day her entire attitude toward the trip changed.

By the clock it was morning when she knocked on our door but it was still dark and felt like night. "Don't tell me you're sleeping in there," she called in to us. "No one could possibly sleep through all those goddamn trains."

Bleary-eyed, I pulled myself out of bed and opened the door. She was dressed and wide awake. "I haven't slept a wink all night," she announced, "and I couldn't lie there another second. Just as well. We'll have to push like hell to make Rome by tonight as it is.

"Well, I better get out of here so you can get dressed. I'm all packed and ready to go, so hurry. Come upstairs and get me when you're ready."

Half asleep, we pulled ourselves together. The clothes Boyd had rinsed out were still damp, and he was rearranging his suitcase to accommodate them when Mother returned. She was carrying her overnight case. "What in God's name is taking so long?!" she asked impatiently. Noticing Boyd, she said, "This is no time to be reorganizing your suitcase. We should have been on the road half an hour ago. I'm going downstairs to warm up the car." She didn't have to say hurry. Boyd stuffed the rest of his things in the bag, and we hurried after her.

It was barely dawn. The road was climbing out of the valley, and we could still see the town behind us when Boyd realized that he had left the pants of his dark suit in the room. Mother made no move to go back. "You really must learn to take better care of your things," she lectured him. "Well, perhaps this will be a lesson."

The pants were a vital part of Boyd's wardrobe. They not only matched his suit jacket, they were the only pair of dark pants he had on the trip. He started to explain, but she refused to listen. "You can call the hotel when we stop for breakfast," she interrupted. "They can send them to you. We simply can't afford to take the time to go back for them." Her tone of voice left no room for argument. Suddenly, she was in a hurry.

Mother drove that day like a woman possessed. The only time we stopped was when the car needed gas. Everything else — Boyd's attempt to phone the hotel (unsuccessful), meals, and answering the calls of nature — had to wait for a pit stop, and then had to be handled with dispatch. It was just like trouping with the act, so I found it easy to adapt, but Boyd spent the entire day rushing to catch up. He never finished a cup of coffee and only made it through lunch by eating the last half of his sandwich in the car. It was not a good day for him.

It turned out to be not so good for any of us. We did manage to get to Rome that evening, but only to discover that our hotel didn't have rooms for us. Mother had made a mistake in her date book or some such thing — her explanation was a bit vague — and our reservation was for the following night. All that rushing, just to arrive a day early! And, of course, to spend the next three hours driving all over Rome looking for a place to spend the night. We finally found a horrible commercial hotel on the outskirts of the city that could take us. By then it was after ten, and we decided to call it a night. We were, literally, too tired to eat.

Somehow, as only she could, Mother managed to find a bright side to the day. "Well, boys, just think," she said as we took the lift to our floor, "we're here in Rome — well, practically — and we'll be able to get an early start tomorrow and spend the entire day enjoying the city."

Enjoying the city, ha! The anxiety that had propelled Mother south to Rome continued to drive her at a frantic pace throughout our stay in Italy. Worse, she put away her checkbook and concentrated on sightseeing and movie-making instead. It was a nightmare, in double time. The first day in Rome, for example, we saw the Colosseum, the Trevi Fountain, the Spanish Steps, St. Peter's basilica, the Sistine Chapel, the Vatican museum and treasury, and the Villa d'Este gardens in Tivoli.

We could see so much because Mother employed what she called the "Ohhh, Eeee, Ahhh" method of sightseeing. Whatever the sight, she'd glance at it, say "Ohhh, Eeee, Ahhh," pose in front of it while I took a few feet of film, and then run like hell. It was a good way to cover a lot of ground and shoot a lot of film, but it sure wasn't much fun.

Except for the drive to Tivoli, we walked everywhere; and because we were filming Mother at all these places for *Curious Evening*, we walked carrying the two movie cameras, tape recorder, exposure meter, extra film, tripod, additional lenses and filters, and a still camera for souvenir snapshots. To be more accurate, Boyd and I carried the equipment. Mother never carried anything other than her purse because it would "get in the way."

We didn't exactly fight over the cameras. I told her that I felt like a pack horse. She explained, rather sharply, that taking the movies was part of how we earned our living and therefore must be tolerated. I didn't buy it and complained stridently and repeatedly about being tired. She got angry and insisted I do my part and do it cheerfully. Instead, I bristled, she lost her temper, and I took my only available option: I retreated into a more or less continual adolescent sulk. All of which did nothing to ease Mother's anxiety or improve the grim mood that hung over the three of us.

Neither did the phone call she received from the local English-language newspaper, the *Rome Daily American*, asking when she and Mr. Bennett were getting married. She explained that Boyd was "an old friend of the family, my son's traveling companion," which seemed to do the trick as nothing was printed.

She would have considered it beneath her dignity to be concerned by such a rumor and therefore never acknowledged a connection, but that night she added up Boyd's share of the meals and hotel rooms to date, and the next day she presented him with a bill for $518.72. He was devastated. He had only one thousand dollars for the entire trip; suddenly it was half gone and the summer had barely begun. Mother was sympathetic and helpful. She suggested he stretch what remained by staying apart from us in cheaper hotels. "After all, it doesn't make sense for you to live in such grand style when you can't afford it."

Rose Louise Hovick, 1925

Who would have believed this . . .

. . . would grow into this?

Gypsy Rose Lee, 1945

Maurice Seymour

Minsky's, 1931

The act didn't change
much over the years . . .

New York World's Fair, 1940

Nightclub act, 1953

. . . but Mother and the girls made a good living.

ON OUR STAGE
GYPSY ROSE LEE AND HER
ROYAL AMERICAN BEAUTIES

The Toronto Telegram

Robert Mizzy,
Grandma Rose

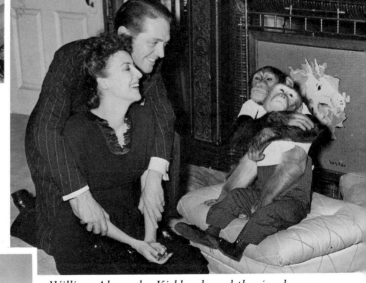

William Alexander Kirkland, and the ring bearer
at the wedding

Julio de Diego

Mother was married three times

With Mike Todd and George S. Kaufman during rehearsals for The Naked Genius

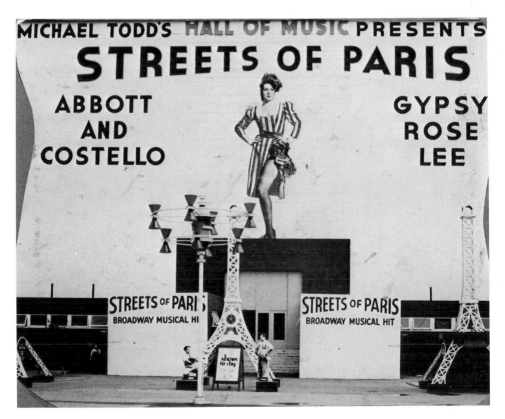

but the great love of her life was Mike Todd . . . who gave her a
picture "bigger than Stalin's" at the New York World's Fair

After Mother and Mike broke up, she went to Hollywood to make *Belle of the Yukon* — a few months later I was born.

With Dinah Shore

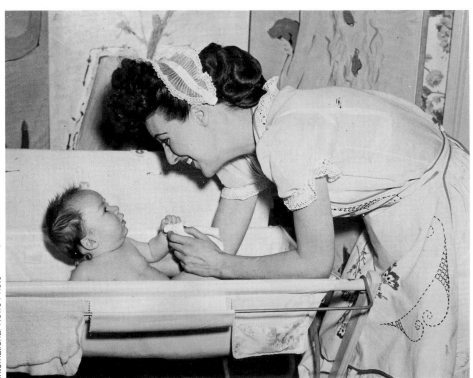

When I was little, Mother
dressed me up like a doll.

As soon as I was old enough, she put me to work.

The animals
got a free ride.

Mary Morris

In the drawing room during
Person to Person

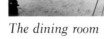

The dining room

We lived a palatial life
at home . . .

Mother's bedroom

JEFFERSON COUNTY UNION

. . . but on the road Mother didn't care where we lived as long as it was close to the club, cheap, and had a kitchen.

With Sandra Church and Ethel Merman

After *Gypsy* opened, Mother dated Billy Rose.

When *Gypsy* closed, Mother bought a house in Beverly Hills.

Her bedroom

The dining room with her Blind Earl tea set on the table

I joined the army, and Mother went to Vietnam to entertain the troops.

David Cox

Otto and Erik, 1977

Fathers and sons

Susanna Pashko

Erik and Christopher, 1984

Starting in Florence, he took her "advice," thus sparing his resources and her reputation. The new arrangement pleased everyone but me. I considered myself too old to share a room with my mother, and I hated the loss of freedom, but she felt a private room for a fourteen-year old boy was "ridiculous and extravagant." Her view, of course, prevailed.

I sulked some more. This was my only effective revenge against Mother. Not that she gave in to it — she never gave in to pressure — but it ruined her mood. Two hours of me looking sullenly out the window and answering her in monosyllables would reduce her to an exasperated bundle of raw nerves. It was self-defeating of me. The worse her mood, the less pleasant life was for all of us. But I didn't care. If I was going to be miserable, then everyone was going to be miserable.

My contributions were hardly necessary. By the time we crossed the border into Yugoslavia the atmosphere in the car was thick with tension, hurt feelings, and outright hostility. It was less than half a day's drive from Venice to Pula, the site of the film festival, but it seemed to drag on forever. I sat in back, feeling much abused, and sighed a lot; Boyd rode next to Mother and quietly worried about how he was going to make it through six more weeks and seven more countries with $450 and one pair of long pants; and she drove, nervously tapping the steering wheel with her fingernail, right into a motorcycle.

We were going up a gentle incline, heading into a curve along a new and virtually deserted road. Mother, lost in thought, had let the car drift into the left lane. To hear her tell it later, "the motorcycle came around the corner like a bat out of hell and smashed right into us." She always emphasized "smash" by clapping her hands dramatically, but the sound of the cycle climbing the bumper and imbedding its front wheel into the Rolls's right fender was much more a dull *thrump!* followed by a hideous shriek of metal against concrete as the car, its momentum barely checked by the collision, pushed the cycle back up the hill. Mother stepped on the brake. Through the windshield we watched in grim fascination as the two cyclists grasped desperately at the hood ornament, the cycle, the headlamp, and each other to keep from falling under the car.

They succeeded, thank God. Finally the car stopped. Mother set the handbrake, leaving the car in the center of the road, and jumped out to help, but there was nothing to do. The men paid us absolutely no attention as they disentangled themselves from the wreckage. There was no blood, but the passenger was limping and holding his groin.

Mother rushed over and used sign-language to offer to tie the cycle on to the roof of the car and take them to a doctor, but it was as if we weren't even there. Totally ignoring us, they yanked the cycle free of the car, pushed it into the woods alongside the road, and disappeared. Throughout the entire experience, neither of the men uttered a sound.

We had been told that Yugoslavian dictator Marshall Tito owned the only two Rollses in the entire country. That explained the cyclists' behavior, at least for Mother: "They obviously think I'm Tito's mistress," she announced as they fled. It wasn't very plausible, but it made a great punch line when she was next on the Paar show.

At the time, however, she was more concerned with practical matters. Once the cyclists had disappeared, she moved the car over to the right side of the road, artistically sprinkled some of the broken glass from the headlight here and there, and photographed the accident scene twice — with the still camera for the insurance company and with the movie camera for *Curious Evening*. Then it was time to get moving. Again, we were in a hurry. Mother had promised the festival officials in New York to arrive in Pula that afternoon, and she wanted to get there while it was still light enough to film the inevitable welcoming ceremonies.

But the bad luck wasn't over yet. It soon became clear that the accident had damaged the clutch. It was slipping badly in fourth, and she had to keep it in third. We stopped at the one gas station we passed, both for the clutch and to warn the festival officials that we were running late, but no one spoke English, so Mother decided to wait until Pula where "someone will be able to do something."

It was dark when we finally hit the outskirts of town, too late for movies. Nonetheless, Mother pulled over to the side of the road to prepare for the red-carpet reception she expected. There was no one about, so she put on a full makeup and did her hair by the light of the car's headlamps. Then she changed into her favorite "interview" dress, a tan jersey sheath covered with widely spaced, one-inch strands of small wooden beads that danced when she walked and shimmied when she posed for photographers. She was going all out for the film festival. "After all," she explained, "God knows who might be there. Maybe even Tito himself."

"Don't forget to ask him to lend you his mechanic," I reminded her in all seriousness.

CHAPTER NINE

PULA could have been a ghost town. Aside from the occasional streetlamp and a rare lit window, the city was dark. Every other building seemed to be under construction and the moldy odor of wet cement hung in the air. Not a soul was on the street. We drove around aimlessly searching for a hotel, restaurant, any sign of life at all. Eventually we came across a police station. Mother went inside alone; moments later she was back.

"No one speaks any English," she reported as she climbed into the car, "but they've sent for someone who does."

"What about the film festival?" I asked.

"How the hell should I know, Erik," she snapped. "I just finished telling you no one speaks English." We sat in silence and waited for the interpreter.

Yugoslavia had not been on our original itinerary for the summer. Mother had wanted to visit someplace new and different and had first applied for visas to Russia, but in those Cold War years there was a six-month waiting period. Yugoslavia was her second choice. We had never been there, she had been told it was beautiful and unspoiled, and like Russia it was Communist so we would get a chance to see how the "enemy" operated. Then the festival had come up as an added attraction, and we had been looking forward to our visit as a real adventure.

Well, we were getting our adventure all right, but it was hardly what we had expected.

After a long wait on the deserted street, a tall angular woman with badly bleached hair, wearing a loud green floral print dress, walked out of the shadows. She leaned in the car window and announced in a heavy German accent, "English I sprecht, you help." Our interpreter.

"Film festival?" Mother asked slowly, trying the basic approach.

The woman shook her head.

"Yes, here." Mother insisted. "Look." She took a letter from the festival out of her purse and pointed to the words of the letterhead as she read them aloud. "The First Yugoslav International Film Festival."

The woman shrugged. She didn't understand or she hadn't heard of it. Mother tried another tack.

"Hotel."

The woman shook her head again, this time holding up her wristwatch and pointing to it. *"Zut fur nicht."*

This news came as a real blow. There we were, in the middle of the night in the middle of nowhere, stranded with a car that hardly moved and an interpreter who didn't speak English.

But the despair written on Mother's face didn't need translation. The woman gestured for us to wait, went into the police station, and emerged a few minutes later, smiling. "Hotel, ya. I fix. Go now."

Without hesitation or invitation, she climbed in front next to Boyd and directed us with hand signals. Her body odor was staggering, and as nonchalantly as possible we opened our windows. Nonetheless, we were thankful to have her. It was impossible to tell where we were going. There were no landmarks or street signs, just block after block of identical gray buildings in various stages of construction. It was very strange.

The hotel was pretty weird, too. From the outside there was nothing to distinguish it from any of the other buildings. There was no sign, and it was dark as a tomb. Our interpreter rang a bell next to the door. Soon a light appeared behind it, and it was opened. She motioned for us to follow her and went inside.

Boyd and I looked to Mother. We weren't exactly frightened, more ill-at-ease with the situation, but Mother acted as if it were totally normal. "Might as well lock up and bring in the overnight bags," she said, turning off the ignition. "I guess this is it."

The lobby was a huge, high-ceilinged room crowded with large plaster columns and furnished with worn, overstuffed armchairs, a few spittoons, and a gray metal reception desk that belonged in a police station.

The desk clerk, who may have been the manager for all I know, looked right at home among the spittoons. He was short and dumpy, hadn't shaved in a while, and wore an armless T-shirt, very baggy pants, and dirty slippers. Like the woman, he considered himself fluent in English, but his five words were different from hers, and throughout the registration process — no minor formality in a police state — they kept arguing over whose English was correct. They agreed only when Mother asked about the film festival (neither had heard of it) and about something to eat (it was far too late).

Eventually the forms were completed and breakfast ordered for the morning. Very politely and excruciatingly slowly, our interpreter explained that she was not allowed upstairs, agreed to meet us in the lobby at nine, and said goodnight.

Without a word, the desk clerk took a huge key ring and walked toward the grand staircase that flowed upstairs from the side of the lobby opposite the front door. We got the hint, grabbed our bags, and followed him up the stairs and all the way to the end of the second-floor hallway. There he used one of his keys to open a room and motioned to Mother and me. We entered. He turned on the light switch by the door and closed us in. It was too abrupt. I opened the door and leaned out to say goodnight to Boyd, but the clerk had already led him more than halfway down the hall and gestured angrily for me to shut my door, so I did. The next day we learned that he had given Boyd a room as far from us as possible, on the fourth floor.

Given the surreal quality of everything else in Pula, our room seemed strikingly normal at first. Yellow walls, green shutters, twin beds covered with clean white knobby bedspreads, and the usual complement of hotel furniture. Then we opened the door to the bathroom. We saw gray concrete walls, exposed galvanized-iron pipes, and a wooden bathtub made of rough, half-rotted planks banded together like a large barrel. We were pretty ripe, and a bath would have been wonderful, but neither of us was willing to get into that tub.

Mother, for a change, didn't seem at all upset. "God only knows what exotic creatures call that home," she joked. "I, for one, am not about to find out." After a quick sponge bath, we got into bed. Her mood kept improving, which, in light of the day we had just spent, was as surreal as everything else. I drifted off listening to her make deliberately bad jokes about the microphones we suspected were hidden in the room.

We were awakened by a faint but insistent shuffling sound. We couldn't tell what it was or where it was coming from. Gradually it got louder and we knew it was outside. We opened the shutters and got our first look at Pula by daylight. Our window opened on a broad, straight avenue lined with half-finished buildings, most of which were still wrapped in cocoons of scaffolding. To our right the street was deserted, and the sun hung low in the sky. Beneath us and for a few hundred feet to the left, the street remained deserted; beyond that it turned abruptly into a living sea of blue-jacketed workmen flowing toward us on shuffling feet. No one laughed or even spoke. Like a tide coming in, they filled the avenue. Then almost as suddenly, as if the plug had been pulled, they drained into the construction sites, which soon bustled with activity.

We waited an hour for breakfast, ersatz coffee and inedible stale rolls. By then we were so hungry, we ate them anyway. Then we waited another hour for our interpreter, who arrived bearing nothing but bad news: there was going to be a film festival, but no one in town knew when. The film board's offices were in Belgrade, the capital, but she had been unable to get through. "Telephone kaputt!" she explained with a shrug.

Queries about the Rolls were also answered with shrugs. These ranged from disparaging at the very mention of Pula to mildly encouraging at the suggestion of Belgrade, but then she shook her head and said, "Wien." To make sure Mother understood, she had her get a map and pointed to Vienna.

Mother understood. Earlier we had consulted the list of approved service facilities that came with the Rolls. There was nothing in it for Yugoslavia. Nothing for Austria, either, but the manual was dated the same year as the car, 1949, and Mother was positive that Vienna had recovered from the war since then. All we had to do was drive 325 miles over some of the highest mountains in Europe without a clutch.

Impossible! But less impossible than staying in Pula. That was out of the question. I reminded Mother of the story told us by the salesman who had sold us the car. A new Rolls owner had taken his pride and joy to North Africa where he proceeded to run it without oil and ruin the crankshaft. A new crankshaft and mechanic were dispatched by private plane, and the car was "put to right within the week."

"Who do you think paid for it," Mother commented dryly. "It sure as hell wasn't Rolls-Royce. You can bet your bottom dollar on that."

A glance at the map showed Venice as the closest large city to Pula, but she didn't even consider it. That would have meant retracing our steps, and Mother never went backwards. No. We would head for Vienna by the shortest possible route and find help along the way. Somehow, we'd get there.

We said good-bye to our interpreter while getting into the car. Mother offered her money, but with a proud graciousness she refused it. She also refused the lipstick and two pair of nylons that Mother offered next, but this time her voice betrayed her desire, and Mother pressed them into her arms. The temptation was too great. Tears filled her eyes and she clutched the treasures to her chest. "Thank you for your great kindness," she said stiffly, but when Mother pulled away she loosened up, and ran next to the car shouting, "Gutt luck! Gutt luck!"

We were all touched, in a melancholy way, by this kind, unattractive woman who had proudly refused money only to accept frivolities. "Can you imagine what that poor thing is going to look like with lipstick smeared from ear to ear?" Boyd remarked.

"Her beau will love it," Mother said gaily. She had awakened in a wonderful mood, and none of the morning's bad news had dampened it. Neither did the unpleasant reminder we received on the way out of town of the car's precarious condition. We were on a slight incline, and the clutch began to slip in third gear. "Cross your fingers and pray for a good mechanic in Rijeka," she said lightly, shifting into second. Rijeka was the first sizable town along our route.

"And some decent food," I added.

"You're going to drive sixty miles in second gear?" Boyd asked gloomily from the back seat.

"Don't be negative," Mother chided him. "I can still use third on level ground and going downhill." She lit a cigarette and changed the subject.

"I know you two think it was my fault we missed the festival, but it wasn't. You can look at the letter in my purse if you don't believe me."

"I believe you," I said. I had peeked at it earlier.

"The stupid sons of bitches just gave me the wrong dates." She took a deep drag off her cigarette and exhaled with a sigh of relief. "Thank God! I'm so relieved to be out of it, I can't begin to tell you.

"It's been worrying me for weeks, ever since we left the boat. I'd lie in bed at night, run the film over and over in my mind and see all the things wrong with it. . . ."

"It's not that bad," Boyd offered.

"The critics would have torn me to shreds," she insisted. "And for what? The first Yugoslavian film festival? Ha. With those bathtubs, it'll probably be the last. . . . Who in hell is going to sit through a goddamn movie with an ass full of splinters!" That was her final word on the festival; she never mentioned it again.

If there was a part of this trip that Mother enjoyed more than any other, it was the rest of our stay in Yugoslavia. Pula excepted (and later we discovered that we had missed the beautiful old parts of town),

Yugoslavia was the kind of country that she loved to visit. The countryside was extraordinary and unspoiled, the cities and towns were old and exuded history, the people were friendly and welcoming, and the prices were dirt cheap.

We didn't find a mechanic in Rijeka, and we really needed one, but it didn't seem to faze her. After being politely turned away from the town's three garages, she parked the car and forgot about it. We went to a bookstore where she bought an English-Yugoslav dictionary, and then we set off in search of a restaurant, window shopping along the way. The central commercial area of the town was every bit as dreary as we expected it to be in a Communist country. The stores, clearly state owned, had very little merchandise in their windows and it was all overpriced, badly displayed, and poorly made. We passed a huge institutional-looking restaurant, but Mother refused to eat there. "I just know we're going to find someplace better," she insisted.

With the help of her new dictionary and a few basic gestures for eating, she managed to convey our need to an obliging passerby who pointed to a narrow street, held up three fingers, then indicated a right turn and held up two fingers. We followed the directions as we understood them, but instead of a restaurant we found a busy open-air market set in the square fronting a modest but active Byzantine Orthodox church.

For once I was glad Mother had insisted that I carry one of the movie cameras when we left the car; had she not, she would have sent me back for all of them. This was something I knew she wouldn't miss. Large peasant women with cheerful, toothless smiles wearing colorful dresses and babushkas were selling produce, eggs, live chickens, milk, cheeses, and sausages from all sorts of carts, wagons, and even wheelbarrows while the men played dominoes and cards as they watched the livestock that was tethered around the fountain in the center of the square.

"Oh, let's buy some groceries and have a picnic," she cried, her eyes bright with delight. She waded into the crowd, yelling back to me, "Set the camera for eleven and be ready to catch me with some of these women."

She paused first at a cart with an especially nice display of fruit that was being tended by an old woman with a deeply lined face. "How lovely," she exclaimed in a tone that overcame the language barrier. The woman smiled, revealing two teeth and lots of gum. Mother nodded to me, and while I filmed she picked out some fruit and bargained with the old lady over the price. She didn't try to use her dictionary for this; it wasn't necessary. She was in her element among these women, and they shared an affinity that permitted them to communicate very well with exclamations, facial expressions, and gestures. Mother's were exaggerated and hammy, but the women loved her all the more for it. Well, most of them did. A few looked at her as if she were crazy and kept their distance, but they were a minority. By the time she finished buying lunch, a crowd was following her from stall to stall.

That's when she spotted the woman selling goat's milk, right out of the goat.

"Erik! I can't leave without a shot of that."

There was a slight delay over a container, which the woman didn't supply and we didn't have, but the crowd immediately understood what Mother wanted and someone came up with a bottle and shyly presented it to her.

Mother waited until I had set up the shot, then she handed the woman the bottle and squatted next to the goat's head in order to be in the picture. I started filming, the woman started milking, Mother started hamming it up for the camera, and the goat decided enough was enough. Making full use of the slack in its tether, it butted Mother right onto her behind.

A collective shriek went up from the women in the crowd, and they rushed forward to help her. The avalanche of bodies was altogether too much for the goat. It shied away from its owner, kicked and broke the bottle, jerked its head, snapping its tether, and tore into the crowd butting at anyone and anything that got in its way. People, carts, cages full of squawking chickens, all went flying!

Forgotten in the pandemonium, Mother yelled at Boyd and me to follow her, and we beat a hasty retreat. Less than an hour later, we were parked by the side of the road calmly enjoying our lunch.

"You know," Mother remarked in a disapproving tone, "it's terribly irresponsible of that woman to bring that poor goat to such a crowded market. Why, the poor thing was terrified! . . ." She might have gone on, but Boyd and I were laughing too hard. Soon she was, too.

The drive from Rijeka to Ljubljana was very beautiful. We passed vineyards and fields well tended by farmers in lederhosen who, without exception, stopped what they were doing to wave to us. We also passed countless roadside shrines containing exceptional Byzantine-style paintings of Christ or the Virgin Mary. Bedecked with flowers and clearly revered, they were the last thing we expected to see. Back home all we ever heard about was "Godless Communism." So much for what we were hearing back home.

Meanwhile, the clutch continued to deteriorate, and with it, our speed. Nearing Ljubljana, we were unable to go above thirty miles per hour. Tedious, to say the least, but pretty. And lucky. If we had been going any faster, we would have missed the small arrow with "hotel" painted on it that pointed up a narrow dirt road heading in the general direction of a magnificent middle-European-style castle, complete with towers and turrets, that sat on top of a hill surrounded by trees.

"Well, boys, what do you say?" asked Mother, pulling over to the side of the road. "Shall we give it a try?"

"Oh, yes. Please," I said, excited at the prospect of spending the night in a real castle.

"Well, it's fine with me, of course," Boyd offered tentatively. "But what about the car? Wouldn't we be better off getting into Ljubljana while it's still running?" It was the largest city on our route to Vienna, and we were counting on getting the car at least patched up enough to get us through.

"There's no point in getting there in the middle of the night. Everything will be closed, and we'd have to search in the dark for a hotel. Again." She put the car in gear and turned up the road. "Anyway, it's certainly worth a look."

We were met at the castle's drawbridge by a middle-aged, portly man in his shirtsleeves. He didn't speak any English, but thanks to his patience and her dictionary, Mother was able to determine that the castle was a hotel and that there were two rooms available for the night.

The castle, aside from the tall towers on either side of the drawbridge, was two stories high and built entirely of stone around a central courtyard. Mother and I were given a room on the second floor. It was huge, and its size was accentuated by the very sparse furnishings: a lovely Regency-period double bed and a nightstand containing a chamber pot.

As in Pula, Boyd was given a room as far away from us as was physically possible. We assumed it was for reasons of propriety because we knew there were other rooms available, a castle full. In fact, we never saw another soul during our stay except for the portly man. He took our orders for dinner, served it (disappearing in between, presumably to cook it), brought our breakfast in the morning, and presented us with our bill as we were leaving. Our entire stay, including the meals, came to the equivalent of eight dollars. Mother was delighted.

The car was barely moving when we arrived in Ljubljana, but no one was complaining. That we made it at all was a miracle, and it was only the first of many that day.

Zalokar Zkenko was the second. He reminded me of the local sidekick who always helps the American hero in movies about the resistance fighters of World War II. Even his English could have been written by a Hollywood screenwriter. We found him at the seventh garage we tried, a ramshackle collection of shacks arranged around an unpaved yard. We would have skipped it had it not displayed a sign indicating that it was an approved Fiat service station. Fiat was a far cry from Rolls-Royce, but it was a lot closer than Skoda.

Zalokar wasn't the least intimidated by the car. A turn around the block and a glance under the chassis was all he needed to determine that the clutch had to be replaced and that he could do it.

"How long?" Mother wanted to know.

"Ah," he rubbed his chin in the best Hollywood manner. "Part from English, long time. Long time." Rubbing it some more, he added, "And very much dinar."

"But we can't wait. Surely you can help us," Mother said in her stranded-damsel voice.

"You want, I fix. Make part. One week."

"How much?"

"Dollars?" he asked. She nodded, and he said, "Fifty."

"Forty," she countered. He looked dubious. Quickly she added, "and two pair of stockings for your wife."

"No wife," he smiled, "but stockings good. Okay."

That left us without a car for a week. Ljubljana was an unattractive, industrial city with nothing to offer; staying there was out of the question. Getting anywhere else, however, would not be easy. Self-drive rental cars were not available, and we had far too much stuff to lug on and off of trains. Again, Zalokar came to the rescue. He suggested we go to Lake Bled, a nearby mountain resort, and he even had a friend with a car who could drive us.

It is a credit to Mother's intuition and to her faith in it that she never doubted Zalokar's good intentions. Without hesitation, she accepted his suggestion. Boyd was not so trusting. While Zalokar was off calling his friend, he took Mother aside and suggested that she at least send a wire home letting Erica know where we were going and with whom, but she cut him off with an abrupt, "Don't be ridiculous, darling. You can tell he's honest just by looking at him."

That was even more true of his friend who arrived driving a turquoise 1927 Packard touring car that was in perfect condition. He was a tiny, white-haired man with a thick, equally white, handlebar mustache, dressed to match the car in a pale blue duster and cap. Mother was enchanted and had me take over fifty feet of the two of them and the car during the drive.

Mother was also enchanted by Bled. It was extraordinarily beautiful. Set in a valley in the Julian Alps, the lake was surrounded by lushly wooded mountains. In its center was a large island, and on it an ancient fortress overlooked our hotel from atop a high granite bluff. The view from the terrace of our suite was a scene from a fairy tale, especially in the evenings when the air cooled and wisps of fog rose gently off the warm water of the lake.

Everything else about the resort, which catered to busloads of English tourists, was decidedly ordinary; but that was really all to the good. It made for low prices, which kept Mother happy, and a civilized approach to hygiene and comfort that I appreciated. Only Boyd found it disappointing. There was one bar in town and two nightclubs but all three closed, along with everything else, at eleven o'clock; even open he thought them "dull and middle class beyond belief." Still, a week later, after Zalokar had delivered the Rolls and we were once again on our way to Vienna, he admitted that the rest had done him a world of good.

Mother and I were rested as well. She even considered going down the Dalmatian Coast to Dubrovnik, but while the new clutch seemed to be working perfectly, she didn't fully trust it and felt we should go directly to Vienna where it could be inspected by an official Rolls-Royce mechanic.

We all were convinced that finding Zalokar had broken our string of bad luck, so it was terribly upsetting when everything went wrong in Vienna: the weather was overcast and depressing, there was no Rolls place, the only hotel room we could find was in a horrible third-class hotel, and the famous Royal Lipizzaner Stallions which Mother had especially wanted to see were away on tour. The thing that had the greatest impact on the rest of the trip, however, was waiting in the mail at the American Express office. Enclosed in a short note from one of Mother's bitchier friends was a Dorothy Kilgallen column from the *New York Journal American* that included the following blurb: "Gypsy Rose Lee is spending the summer in Europe with her 14-year-old son and 'his companion' the handsome 27-year-old actor Boyd Bennett."

The implication was clear, but Mother laughed it off with a disparaging comment about the author's receding chin and never mentioned it again. She had every reason to be concerned about her reputation and every right to tell Boyd to go home, but that would have meant admitting to him — and to herself — that she cared what people said about her, and she couldn't do that. She took far too much pride in living her life on her own terms without regard to social conventions or the opinions of others. Instead, and I am convinced she did it subconsciously, she began finding fault with Boyd over the most insignificant things.

It started the following afternoon with the small black canvas shoulder bag he had used throughout the trip to carry his passport, cigarettes, money, and other daily necessities. We had stopped at an outdoor café for a cup of coffee, and when the check arrived Boyd rummaged in it for his wallet in order to pay his share.

"Why must you insist on carrying that . . . purse with you every place you go," she snapped.

At first he took it as a joke and answered lightly, "For the same reason you carry yours, I suppose."

"Well, it looks ridiculous."

"You don't like it?" he asked, clearly stung by her criticism.

"It's terribly effeminate for one thing, and it's in very bad taste for another."

That was a low blow for Boyd because he always took great pains to appear masculine. "I don't know how you can say that," he said, holding up the bag. "Nothing could be less feminine . . . or more chic. Just look at all the men carrying purses, as you call them." As if on cue, a beefy sailor carrying a small clutch stood up from one of the tables. "Now you can't tell me that he looks effeminate."

"How *he* looks has nothing to do with it." She stood, closing the subject, and then sealed it by announcing, "I have a splitting headache. I think I'll go back to the hotel and lie down until dinner."

Every day after that was marred by another disagreement between them. Leaving Salzburg, for example, they fought over a hotel room key. Mother and I had been staying at the Golden Hirsch Hotel where the room keys were attached to heavy brass plates that had the room number on one side and the raised figure of a leaping stag on the other. While helping us check out, Boyd had noticed one in the door of an empty room and had stolen it as a souvenir. He showed off his trophy on our way out of town, and Mother blew up. She, too, had stolen a key from the door of an empty room; therefore, there would be two missing on the same day we checked out, and she was convinced the hotel would know who was responsible. It was all too embarrassing and, of course, all Boyd's fault. How dare he steal a key from *her* hotel. He thought she was overreacting and told her so, which only incensed her more. It was a stupid argument, but it ruined that day's drive.

In Munich they fought over a Beleek teapot that Boyd had found in an antique shop. She wanted it, but he refused to give it up until she reminded him that he couldn't afford it because he already owed her over two hundred dollars and would have to borrow more if he wanted to continue on the trip.

He gave in on the teapot, and he gave up on the trip. As we approached Paris two days later, he announced that he had run out of money and would be returning home on the first available flight. He told me later that he had hoped she would try to dissuade him. She didn't. She said, "Oh, what a shame. We will miss you. But it's probably for the best. London is so dreary this time of year . . . and so expensive."

The trip was barely half over when Boyd returned to New York. Mother and I still had six weeks in Paris, Brussels, and London ahead of us. Fortunately the second half of the trip bore no resemblance whatsoever to the first half, and we had a wonderful time.

The absence of external annoyances like the clutch and the film festival had something to do with the difference, but mainly it was due to Mother's approach to the trip, which changed completely on our arrival back in Paris. Instead of staying at the Ritz or another deluxe hotel, for example, we moved into the Terrace, where we had stayed on our first trip to Paris in 1951. In those days it was a run-down little hotel known in theatrical circles for its cheap rates, its lovely views, and the tiny kitchens in every room, which allowed tenants to take full advantage of its proximity to the Marche Lepic, one of the great retail food market areas in Paris.

The hotel had been renovated since our last visit, but it had lost none of its charm, and we both loved being there. Mother, for the prices and because she could come and go dressed as she pleased without worrying about whom she would meet in the lobby; I, for the romance. On the days when Mother had to go downtown to try on the corsets and shoes she had ordered earlier in the summer, I would buy some wine, cheese, and bread, sit in the room, and eat lunch while gazing out of the french windows of our suite at one of the most romantic views I had ever seen: in the foreground, the beautiful Montmartre Cemetery, overcrowded with weathered tombstones and ornate antique mausoleums; beyond it, all of Paris, capped by the Eiffel Tower in the distance.

Mother enjoyed saving the money on the hotel, but she wasn't on an economy binge, and we spent just as much time shopping as before. She did, however, try to make it more fun for me by injecting some humor whenever possible. One Sunday, for instance, after five hours of rummaging through the flea market, an American woman turned to her and said, "I know you. You're Gypsy Rose Lee. I recognize your voice." Mother pulled herself erect, stuck her nose in the air, and shot back a withering, "Madam, how dare you!" The woman was mortified and apologized profusely as she slunk away. We barely managed to suppress our laughter until she was out of earshot.

Even taking movies got to be fun. *Life* magazine wanted to do a photo-feature on Mother visiting the strip shows of Paris. She had long been a favorite of *Life*'s editors, and the publicity they had given her over the years was beyond value. Whenever possible, she tried to accommodate them, and this time she was delighted to do so, figuring it would give her an ideal opportunity to film the shows for *Curious Evening* while *Life* picked up the tab.

The Lido was scheduled for the first night. Mother and I arrived with one of *Life*'s staff photographers in good time for the first show. Ironically, the pro had only a small Leica while the amateurs were weighed down with the two movie cameras, extra lenses and film, and a tape recorder. But not for long. The manager took all of our equipment at the door and absolutely refused Mother permission to film. Some stills for *Life* were fine, but movies? Never!

I didn't mind. It meant there was nothing to distract my attention from the scores of naked breasts dancing before my eyes, but I was careful to maintain a blasé attitude for the photographer; the last thing Mother needed was a shot of me in *Life* with my eyes falling out of my head. Except for the topless showgirls, the show was straight vaudeville even down to a juggler, and Mother thought it was a bore. She was right, but I didn't care. All those naked breasts! It was an adolescent's dream.

The next day, *Life* canceled the story. Too many naked breasts in all the pictures. Mother, however, now had her heart set on some footage of Parisian strippers, so the following night we tried again, this time at the hottest new club in town, the Crazy Horse Saloon. Like the night before, we arrived loaded down with film equipment, and the manager made us check it at the door; unlike the night before, Mother was carrying her large Vuitton handbag and had the second camera hidden inside it. Two dollars to the headwaiter got us a table in an out-of-the-way corner with an unobstructed view of the stage, and the rest was easy. Mother kept one eye on the waiters, the other on the stage, and told me when to shoot. I kept both my eyes on the stage at all times. To this day, I have never seen as sexy a show. Even Mother admitted it was the best strip show she had ever seen. We got three minutes of excellent film, and I limped back to the hotel a very excited young man.

In addition to hotel keys, Mother had "liberated" ashtrays from hotels and restaurants all over the world. She didn't just slip them into her purse on the way out, either. She gave up that approach in '51 after being spotted as she left Maxim's in Paris. They made her empty her purse at the check room and pay for the ashtray. Ever since, her methods had become increasingly sophisticated, and she had never again been caught. However, Brussels presented her with a formidable challenge.

The night we arrived from Paris, we went to L'Epaule de Mouton for dinner. It was one of the great restaurants in Europe, and we had been there before, but since our last visit they had changed their ashtrays. The new ones were large, heavy, pewter things that included a holder for a box of matches and had the name of the restaurant in raised letters around the base. I could tell by the way Mother lovingly examined it that she wanted it, and by the way she glanced around the restaurant that she was working on getting it. The problem was twofold: there was the size, weight, and conspicuousness of the ashtray itself. Its absence from a table would be as obvious as its presence in a pocket. And then there was the size of the restaurant. It had only five tables, and the owner was in constant attendance because while the basic cooking was done in the kitchen, he prepared the heart of each dish, its sauce, at a small hot plate in the center of the dining room. I offered to hide the ashtray under my jacket when we left, but Mother shook her head. "We'll come back for lunch tomorrow," she said, "prepared."

The next day, she carried the same Vuitton handbag she had used at the Crazy Horse, and the moment the owner turned his back after seating us, Mother swept the ashtray off the table into it. Then, with barely a pause to close the zipper, she lit a cigarette and asked for an ashtray. The owner brought one immediately, we had a magnificent lunch, and she left with the prize of her collection.

As in Paris, Mother decided against a deluxe hotel in London, taking instead furnished rooms in Knightsbridge, one of the city's nicer areas. Here, too, comfort rather than economy was her motive. Mother had initially conceived of this trip to Europe as a three-month shopping spree, and in that regard it reached its zenith during our stay in London.

It began as soon as we were settled, when she telephoned Mr. Perkins at Hoffman's of Halifax. He had sold us our car, and because Halifax was too far to take it for the repairs it needed, she wanted him to recommend a place in London. She also wanted to tell him about the continual sloppy workmanship and price gouging she had encountered at the authorized Rolls service in New York and to enlist his help in improving the situation there. It was quite a tale of woe, and relating it didn't leave her particularly well disposed toward Rolls-Royce; but Mr. Perkins was to salesmen what his product was to motorcars, and I could tell from her tone of voice that he quickly mollified her. What I didn't learn until they had hung up was that he was driving two hundred and fifty miles from Halifax the next day in order to oversee the repairs on our car and, incidentally, to show her a 1956 Rolls with a special-built body that he had recently taken in trade.

Mr. Perkins arrived the following afternoon. He was just as I remembered him from eight years earlier: average height, ruddy complexion, gray eyes crinkly at the corners, salt-and-pepper hair, a quick smile, and possessed of that rare British manner which somehow managed to combine warmth and formality. We never learned his first name, for example, and he always called us Mrs. Lee and Master Erik, but there wasn't an iota of standoffishness about him.

His appreciation of Mother's taste in automobiles hadn't changed either. It was uncanny. The Rolls he drove down had none of the stylistic features Mother liked in our car. It didn't have the classic boxy shape, the running boards, the separate headlamps; it didn't even have a sun roof. But she loved it, and so did I. Everything about it was extraordinary. The hood, roof, trunk, and window frames were beige; the lower part of the car appeared to be navy blue until the sun hit it, releasing a mysterious, deep red undertone similar to aubergine. Instead of the stodgy, pedestrian look of the newer Rollses, its line was sleek and rakish, sweeping back from fenders that began as cowls over recessed headlamps. It looked fast and ready to pounce, totally unlike a Rolls-Royce except for the traditional grill. In fact, there was only one other car like it in the world, a sister car made at the same time by the same coachbuilder, Freestone & Webb.

As much as she liked the car, Mother was far from sold. Before she'd consider buying another used Rolls, she wanted to investigate having a new one made to *her* order. Rolls itself made only standard, stainless-steel bodies, and Freestone & Webb, like most of the independent coachbuilders, had gone out of business, so the next day Mr. Perkins took us to visit James Young, Ltd., one of the only two remaining.

The designer at Young's was very accommodating. After Mother explained that she wanted a car with lots of luggage space, perhaps even a station wagon, a sun roof or open top, and unique styling, he sketched a classic "shooting brake" — his term for a station wagon — complete with separate headlamps, running boards, and a special top over the front seat that would slide back, similar to a sun roof only larger. Young's could make such a car and incorporate most of Mother's other wishes, such as a place to make tea in the front seat, for approximately $17,000, but it would take at least eighteen months and probably two years.

The two years seemed excessive until we visited the shop and saw how the cars were made. Everything was done by hand with incredible care and attention to detail. There were five Rolls-Royce chassis on the floor. Two were exactly as they had been delivered from the factory: four wheels and an engine on a metal frame. A craftsman was building an oak frame on the third. He worked alone, measuring the four-by-fours, cutting them to size, sanding the joints, and finally screwing them into the whole, all by hand without any power tools. On the fourth, two men were wrapping the oak beams in sheets of aluminum; and on the last car, a craftsman and his apprentice were hanging one of the front doors. It was a very painstaking operation. Using a winch, the apprentice would place the door in the frame so the craftsman could examine the fit, then he would remove it, the craftsman would tap at the hinges with a very light hammer, and then they'd repeat the process, over and over again. No wonder the doors on special-built Rollses close so easily and yet so tightly.

Mother was tempted, but she didn't like having to depend on our car for another two years, and when word came from the garage that it would cost over $5,000 to repair the motorcycle damage and to put it right mechanically, she decided to buy Mr. Perkins's car.

She didn't tell him, though. First she wanted some assurances as to its condition, so Mr. Perkins arranged for us to bring it to the Rolls factory in Crewe for a "thorough examination." That turned out to be a man in a white jacket taking it for a quick spin around the block, but Mother pronounced herself satisfied, and on the drive back to London they made a deal. Our old car plus $12,000! "And of course you'll take care of the few little things that need tending to," she added as an afterthought. He agreed. "Of course."

Mother's "few little things" turned into quite a list of modifications and additions, and there was an upward adjustment to the price, but even after she and Mr. Perkins had agreed on who should pay for what, the Rolls-Royce Service Director in London made problems over certain of the changes. He could not "in good conscience" install power steering because it would put "too great a strain" on the car; he flatly refused to mount Mother's bud vase on the dash until she assured him that it was antique crystal; and they had a long debate over the heater. The one in our old car was terrible, and we had often been cold. Mother wanted the rear ducts in the new car permanently closed so that all the heat would come through those in the front. He was appalled. "But what about your passengers?" "Oh, never mind about them," Mother answered. "Anyone who rides in the back seat of my car deserves to freeze their ass off!" She meant it as a joke, but he had no sense of humor. "I assure you, madam," he said, nose high in the air, "that will not be necessary. The heater is more than adequate for the entire passenger compartment." She would have insisted had Mr. Perkins not mentioned that it would adversely affect the resale value of the car. She also lost on the trailer hitch, but Rolls did agree to install compartments in the front doors to hold her lunch box and thermos, to make seat covers to protect the leather from the animals, and to paint the initials GRL on the rear doors. Discreet ones, of course.

The new Rolls was Mother's most extravagant purchase in London, but by no means was it her only one. London abounds in shops that specialize in Victorian and Regency antiques, which were her favorites, and she spent a great deal of time and money in them. Three of her finds were truly magnificent: a round table commemorating the career of the Duke of Wellington, a scene from the battle of Waterloo painted in the center and around it scenes from all his other great victories; a Victorian lacquered pâpier-maché étagère inlaid with mother-of-pearl; and an exquisite Regency sofa. The rest of her antique purchases were, in comparison, quite modest, but they filled three crates and four packing cartons, and that didn't include the modern, but very expensive, tea set in the Blind Earl pattern. Created originally for a blind earl, with a raised design of leaves and flowers so he could appreciate it by feel, it was nonetheless beautiful to the eye, with extraordinary greens and pinks.

With all of this, Mother wasn't surprised by Erica's wire of September 6 telling her the bank account was empty. She wasn't even disturbed. The next day we were sailing for home, and the ship's hold would be filled with beautiful things. Her beautiful things. She couldn't wait to get home and play with them.

CHAPTER TEN

ALTHOUGH I had to go back to school when we returned from Europe, Mother's vacation was by no means over. *Gypsy* continued to refill her bank account as fast as she emptied it, and her sole interest was in preparing the house to accommodate all her new purchases. Still, when Jack Paar called late one afternoon, desperate for a guest for that evening's show due to a last minute cancellation, Mother didn't hesitate before accepting. She never thought of Jack's show as work, mainly because it paid barely enough to cover her cab fare to and from the studio, but it was widely seen, and she considered it vital to remain in the public eye. After all, she wouldn't be on vacation forever. Sooner or later *Gypsy* would close, and she would have to go back to work.

Doing that Paar show turned out to have a totally unexpected side effect as well. When Mother arrived at the studio and was introduced to the other guests, among them was Billy Rose, the multimillionaire showman and Wall Street investor. It could have been a touchy moment. They had known each other for over twenty-five years, but hadn't spoken for all but two weeks of them, and the story of their feud was something of a Broadway legend.

They met first in 1934, when Billy hired her away from Minsky's to appear at the Casino de Paris, the grandest nightclub in post-Prohibition New York. The money wasn't very good, but Mother wanted out of burlesque even then, and the featured spot in one of his shows seemed a step in the right direction. Or so it seemed until their second meeting, on the first day of rehearsals, when Billy announced that he expected her to appear nude in an "artistic" still-life tableau depicting Botticelli's *Birth of Venus*. Mother didn't care how artistic it was, nude was nude, and she refused. Billy was furious.

"You won't pose nude!" he stormed in front of the entire company. "You who were raided twice at Minsky's."

"I may have been raided, but I wasn't nude. I had my bows pinned on," she answered primly. "And, I was getting more money."

"Then your virtue is venal."

Mother knew better than most when a line couldn't be topped, and she took the lady's way out: she slapped his face, turned on her heel, and went back to Minsky's.

They didn't speak after that; however, it wasn't exactly intentional. At first, when the story of their fight was hot news, mutual friends and acquaintances carefully avoided inviting both to the same parties and openings. They became even more careful later when Billy, who considered the New York World's Fair his private domain by right of his lavish water ballet, the Aquacade, had a running feud with Mike Todd who eased into the fair during its first year and then, with Mother as his star, completely overshadowed it and Billy during its second. That was way back in 1940, but as so often happens, long after the reasons were forgotten, people still remembered that Billy and Mother didn't get along and kept them apart.

Although it was unnecessary, it did have its advantages. By the time they ran into each other on the Jack Paar show, each had a quarter-century's worth of anecdotes, gossip, and inside jokes that the other hadn't heard. They began reminiscing while waiting to appear, told the story of their fight as a joke on the show, and then went to Reuben's, where they continued talking over coffee and tea until early morning. The next night, Billy took her to dinner at El Morocco. Two nights later they went to the opening of *The Gang's All Here*, left after the first act, and had dinner at "21" where they bumped into Leonard Lyons who made their "blossoming romance" official by announcing it the next day in his column.

"Blossoming romance" was hardly accurate, but Leonard's exuberance was understandable. From a gossip columnist's point of view, there were no two more newsworthy people in all of New York at the time. Mother, of course, had always been good copy, but since *Gypsy* opened she was better than ever. *Life* magazine, for instance, had run two stories on her over the summer and was preparing another. As for Billy, he was as unique a figure on Broadway as she. Not as well known by the general public perhaps, but just as successful and a hell of a lot richer.

In fact, making money was Billy's greatest talent. At sixty he was the largest individual stockholder in AT&T, and he had enormous holdings in both the Pennsylvania and New York Central railroads as well. Not bad for a kid born in New York's poorest Jewish ghetto.

But Billy was much more than a self-made millionaire, and what set him apart were his other talents and the drive with which he exploited them. At nineteen, he was one of the fastest shorthand stenographers in the country, and there is little doubt he would have won the national title had he not gotten drunk (for the first time in his life) the night before the finals and collapsed with a hangover in the middle of the competition. He took it as an omen, gave up both shorthand and drinking, and turned to songwriting instead. During the next ten years, he wrote the lyrics to over four hundred songs, many of which were successful and some even classics such as "It's Only a Paper Moon," "Tonight You Belong to Me," "Me and My Shadow," "Barney Google," and the first commercial jingle ever written, "Does the Spearmint Lose Its Flavor on the Bedpost Overnight?"

With his profits from songwriting, he opened his first nightclub, where he gave an unknown singer named Helen Morgan her first job. Opening night the place was so crowded, he filled the stage with tables and made her sit on the piano when she sang. It became her trademark. There were other clubs, each grander than the last, including the Casino de Paris, until he got bored with them and moved on to producing Broadway shows, which is when he really hit his stride, mounting some of the most lavish extravaganzas in the history of the American theater. For *Billy Rose's Jumbo*, a "spectacular musical comedy" set in a circus, he tore the insides out of the old Hippodrome and put the stage in the center of the house with the seats around it, just like in a real circus. Then he collected a creative team that included Richard Rodgers, Lorenz Hart, Ben Hecht, and Charles MacArthur. And finally he used a real circus, complete with acrobats and animal acts, in the background to provide the proper atmosphere. It was a *tour de force*.

Billy could make history without being extravagant, too. After fourteen other producers had rejected it, he saw the value in Oscar Hammerstein's adaptation of Bizet's opera *Carmen*. Had he not, the landmark, all-black *Carmen Jones* might never have been produced. Later on, as the owner of the Billy Rose and Ziegfeld theatres and an occasional backer of shows, he helped support the production of *Kismet, Brigadoon, Who's Afraid of Virginia Woolf?*, and other plays. Somehow with all of this he also managed to write a syndicated newspaper column, do a short-lived television show, and assemble two extraordinary art collections.

Fortunately, Mother found this kind of energy and drive attractive in a man, because the last thing Billy would ever be was a lover. A squat 5'3" and unattractive enough to pass for ugly, he freely admitted to being "not so hot in the bed department." Sex just didn't interest him. What he enjoyed, above all else, was talk; and in that sense, he and Mother were ideally suited. She loved nothing more than stimulating conversation. After an evening on the town, they would often come back to the house, where Mother would make Billy a pot of coffee and herself a pot of tea. Then they would sit in her room, she on her bed with Fu Manchu next to her, he in an overstuffed armchair with my Afghan's head resting on his lap, and talk about books, plays, art, Hollywood, antiques, their friends and their enemies until three or four in the morning.

They had other traits in common too, but unfortunately these didn't mesh nearly so well. Like most successful people, both were opinionated, had a deep-seated faith in their own infallibility, and took it for granted that everyone with a modicum of intelligence would agree with them. This was fine as long as they agreed with each other, which they usually did; but it was inevitable that they would differ sooner or later.

The first of these collisions occurred in the middle of a formal sit-down dinner for forty that Billy gave at his house on East 93rd Street in Manhattan. The evening began well enough. Mother was serving as Billy's hostess, and his chauffeur called for her at six-thirty. I walked her to the door to say goodnight. She looked magnificent, dressed to the teeth in her Charles James maroon silk-taffeta ballgown and glowing with joie de vivre. The glow had been present since Billy had arrived on the scene. A recluse at heart, she hadn't been so active socially since Mike Todd, and she was finding all the going out, the opening nights, the fine restaurants, and the attention flattering and fun. She was even looking forward to this particular evening, although it was not the kind of party she usually enjoyed. The guest of honor was Nahum Goldman, head of the Jewish Agency, who had recently convinced Billy to donate his entire sculpture collection to the National Museum of Israel along with a million dollars to build a garden in which to display it. The guest list combined a lot of wealthy bores, whom Billy planned on hitting up for contributions to the museum, with a select group of New York luminaries whom he had invited to carry the conversation and to make the prospective donors feel honored at having been invited, people such as playwrights Paul Osborne and Moss Hart, publisher Bennett Cerf, the Broadway caricaturist Al Hirschfeld, and, of course, Mother.

It must have been a beautiful party. To this day, I have never seen a privately owned home to compare with Billy's in lavish opulence. It was made for entertaining. Black marble Doric columns flanked the inside entranceway to the large foyer, which was tiled in alternating squares of black and white marble. The living room was paneled in bleached oak, carved and signed by Chippendale. A large Gainsborough portrait looked down on a dining room table that was big enough for a palace. The sculpture was modern and dotted around the house like jewels on a beautiful woman: Robus' *Song* in the foyer, Rodin's larger-than-life bronze *Adam* and Maillol's *Chained Liberty* in the hall outside the living room, and figures by Lipchitz, Epstein, Daumier, Archipenko, and too many more to name, everywhere, even in the powder room!

Not having been invited, I don't know exactly what happened, but a little past nine I heard the front door slam. The next thing I heard was Mother yelling up for me to get some money out of her purse so she could pay for her cab. I took it downstairs, and we rode up to her room together in the elevator. She looked as lovely as when she left, but the glow of anticipation had been replaced with a flush of rage.

"How come you're home so early?" I asked. "Are you all right?"

"Madder than hell, but aside from that I'm fine."

"What happened?"

"He's simply insufferable!" She shuddered dramatically to make her point. "Typical man. Typical. Can't stand it if a woman has a mind of her own. I swear, Erik, for a nickel I would have slugged him right then and there."

"What did he do?" I asked excitedly, expecting something really juicy.

She shook her head in exasperation. "It's all so silly really. All evening long I'd had to fight to get a word in edgewise, and then when I did, he'd interrupt me halfway through my thought as if I hadn't even opened my mouth. I can't tell you how annoying it was. Finally I'd had it up to here, and the next time he tried it I stopped midsentence and told him to let me finish!" As she remembered, she gradually got more and more annoyed. "And then would you believe the son-of-a-bitch had the nerve — not to mention the bad manners — to tell me in front of the entire table that I shouldn't bother to finish because what I was saying was all wrong anyway!" She shuddered again, this time for real. "It was the last straw. I knew I just had to get away from him. If I'd stayed, I would have slugged him. Swear to God. I couldn't even trust myself to say anything, so I just got up from the table, went downstairs, got a taxi, and came home."

"Right in the middle of dinner?"

"The beginning, wouldn't you know, and I'm famished. I can't wait to get out of this dress and make myself something to eat."

Mother's departure must have put something of a damper on the party, but Billy either didn't mind or realized he was to blame, because he phoned Mother the next day, apologized, and invited us to his private island off the Connecticut coast for the weekend.

Friday night, Mother had me help her collect in the foyer the things she wanted to bring along. In addition to her overnight bag, which also contained my things as we would be sharing a room, there was an antique sewing bag with her quilting. Fu Manchu's carrier, a paper bag filled with his dishes and dog food, and a cardboard box containing some of her gardening implements. We weren't "weekend in the country" people, so I had no experience on which to base my opinion, but I knew the box was too much.

"Oh, Mother! You can't be serious. Fu's bad enough, but your gardening stuff too. What are you going to do with it? Billy must have his own gardener."

"Don't be a smart-aleck. Of course he has a gardener. But this way I won't have to disturb him when I collect some moss for the rock garden.

"But you might be right about Fu," she added as an afterthought. "Billy hates him even more than you do. . . . I'll give it a try and see if he says something. I hate to leave poor Fu here all alone."

Mother turned out to be right, as usual. Billy didn't even notice the box which the chauffeur put in the trunk, but when she climbed into the car with Fu in her arms, he put his foot down. No Fu. If Mother couldn't live without an animal for two days, she should bring my Afghan. He'd even enjoy having her around. But Fu, in his Rolls, never! Mother didn't argue. She put Fu back in the house and we went without animals.

Mother avoided arguing with Billy over anything that day, but it wasn't easy. He spent the entire drive talking about the sculpture garden he was donating to the National Museum of Israel in Jerusalem. He had just that week hired the famous landscape architect Isamu Noguchi to design it, and he was very excited. Mother couldn't have approved more of his generosity or of his taste in architects, but Billy had made it a condition of his gift that he be buried in the garden, and she felt that was in very poor taste. (The trustees of the museum must have shared her opinion because after his death they refused to accept his body.)

Mother's restraint was especially admirable considering that she hated riding in a car when someone else was driving, and on top of that Billy's chauffeur had a habit she found particularly nerve-wracking: he always cruised in the right lane, moving to the left only to pass and then going straight back to the right, even if there was another car immediately ahead that he knew he was going to pass. After forty-five minutes of this constant lane switching, Mother could contain herself no longer and asked him why he didn't just stay in the left lane. Billy answered for him, and very sharply too. "He drives the way I tell him to drive. It's stupid to drive on the left. That's where all the accidents happen because it's closer to the oncoming traffic." He said it as if it were an unassailable fact, which was pretty nervy for someone who didn't even know how to drive. I knew Mother couldn't have disagreed more strongly, but she held her tongue. She could be very diplomatic when it suited her.

We didn't get to spend the weekend on the island. When we arrived at the dock, Billy's caretaker met us with the boat and news that the electric cable from the mainland was out and couldn't be repaired until Monday. That meant no heat or hot water, no appliances for cooking, and no lights. Fortunately, Billy had to go over to get some papers, so at least I had an opportunity to see the place.

It was extraordinary: four acres of fairy-tale serenity; the place where Prince Charming and his bride live happily ever after. The moment the boat's engine was turned off, tranquility descended over everything like an eiderdown. It wasn't quiet, but all the sounds were comforting: the ocean washing over the rocky shore, the raucous caw of sea gulls mixed with the gentle music of songbirds, and the wind rushing through the leaves of trees and bushes. And standing on the gravel path to the house, next to a magnificent bronze by Malderelli entitled *Seated Woman*, a miniature deer kept a watchful eye on us as it nibbled the grass.

The main house had been built in 1710, and Billy had furnished it with antiques of the period. I found it dark and cold, a perception influenced, no doubt, by the lack of electricity.

While Billy collected his papers and discussed closing the island for the winter with his caretaker, I looked at the deer and the aviaries filled with exotic birds, chased the free-running peacocks in a futile attempt at frightening them into opening their tails, and aimlessly explored. Mother used the time to collect moss for her rock garden, lovingly placing large hunks of dirt that were covered with it in her cardboard box.

Billy finally noticed the box and teased her about the moss on the drive home, but he did it gently, obviously impressed with her willingness to work and get her hands dirty in order to get something she wanted. He was just as clearly annoyed, unfortunately, to discover on our arrival home that the box had leaked, soiling the carpet in the trunk of his Rolls. Mother's offer to pay for having it cleaned only partly mollified him, and the day ended on a sour note.

Billy didn't call for a few days after that, but he did send the cleaning bill, and Mother did pay it. She didn't seem in the least upset by his lack of attention, however. Since our return from Europe, she had spent her days working on the house, and she just expanded her efforts to include the evenings as well.

There was no lack of things to do. Since buying the house in 1943, she had worked on it a room here and a project there as time and money would allow. This time she had no such constraints and was determined to do everything to it that she had ever wanted. It was an enormous undertaking, but one she delighted in. She adored her house, she loved the things she had bought in Europe to put into it, and most of all she thrived on seeing her dreams for it realized.

She began by sending every painting, watercolor, and drawing in the house — except for the seven-foot-tall Bouguereau — to the framer for remounting in the antique frames she had purchased in Europe. Then, while the walls were empty, she repainted. The foyer, ground-floor hall, and all the woodwork in the stairwell up to the top floor, including the doors to the rooms and the elevator, were painted a pale blue-green. The dining room was done in sky blue, and the drawing room, a light gray. But these were only the base colors. Mother had far more in mind. To accomplish it, she needed a very special talent, and she found it in a recent émigré from Austria named Hedi Fisher.

Educated in Europe as an artist, Hedi knew all there was to know about paints, pigments, preparing surfaces, thinners, and so on. If it concerned painting, she knew it, and what's more, she knew how to do it. Under Mother's direction, she spent four months painting, in oil, a *trompe l'oeil* balustrade festooned with cascading roses around the walls of the foyer, clouds on the ceiling over the table in the dining room, and three murals depicting rustic Mediterranean village scenes on the wall facing the patio in the ground-floor hallway. She also antiqued the wainscoting in the drawing room and all the woodwork in the stairwell. And finally she gold-leafed a delicate scrollwork design that had as its centerpiece Mother's initials on all the interior doors in the foyer and stairwell.

All this ornate decorative painting could have been hideously baroque, but Hedi never got carried away. Her work was in perfect harmony with the neo-Italian Renaissance architecture of the house, and when she was finished the ground floor looked like many of the villas we had seen in Northern Italy during our summer travels. Mother had been collecting more than antiques in Europe, she had also been collecting ideas. But while the ideas were borrowed, the style and taste were uniquely hers, and it took no small amount of courage and imagination to have Hedi do the work she did. After all, whatever Mother had seen in Europe, she hadn't seen an Italian villa filled with Victorian and Regency furniture and contemporary paintings.

The painting was just the frame, so to speak. Mother also had much of the furniture in the foyer, her room, and the library reupholstered, made new curtains for the foyer and library, had the decorative ironwork she had bought in France installed in the patio and painted, and rearranged the furniture in the drawing room to accommodate the new Regency sofa and Wellington table. This rearrangement brought to light certain glaring deficiencies in the drawing room furniture, which necessitated the purchase of a few new tables and lamps; and while she was at it, she picked up some new furniture for the library as well. It was really the best time to do it, as she pointed out, because she got a discount from Jarvis House for buying in quantity.

My room was not neglected in all this. She transformed it from a child's room into one suitable for a well-brought-up young man, or prince royal, for that matter. All my old furniture and toys, including the train layout that had been Mother's favorite project when I was six and had occupied most of my room ever since, were given to charity. Then the room was painted and refurnished with antiques Mother had been keeping in storage for years, just waiting for me to grow into them: two overstuffed chairs and a marble-topped, low Victorian table for in front of the fireplace, a mahogany desk loaded with cubbyholes and secret compartments, a lovely marble and wood chest of drawers with a matching bedside table for either side of the bed, and the bed. What a bed! It had been President William Henry Harrison's while he lived in the White House, and it was, quite simply, magnificent: oversized, made of oak, with intricately carved birds, branches, and leaves all over the headboard, which reached within inches of the ceiling.

The house took months to finish, but Billy was over his snit about the car rug in less than a week, and when he called to ask Mother out, she accepted. It was more than just that she enjoyed his company; she was flattered by his attention. In spite of his looks, Billy was a catch. After all, how many forty-five-year-old women are courted by eligible, wordly, intelligent multimillionaires? And courted she was. At least four nights a week it was dinner followed by a theater opening or party, and it was always first class, as befitted a legend.

Through it all, Mother continued to insist on her independence, both in public and private. One night at Sardi's, for example, Leonard Lyons came over to their table, pad and pencil in hand, and remarked of Mother's sable jacket: "That's new, isn't it? A present from Billy?"

Mother fixed Leonard with an icy stare and lectured him sharply. "A, it isn't new, and B, it isn't a present from Billy or anyone else. You of all people should know that I write my own books, I catch my own fish, and I buy my own clothes."

All true. However, even Mother was not above accepting the right gift at the right time. Three weeks before Christmas, Billy came to the house with a jewelry designer and gave her a choice between a diamond ring or a gold pin for her Christmas present. She chose the pin. "The ring was too suggestive of an engagement ring," she told me after they had left, "and, besides, the pin is much more unusual." That it was — a hammered gold figure of a man with a square cut emerald, close to an inch on each side, surrounded by diamonds as the torso and a large, cabochon-cut ruby, also surrounded by diamonds, as the head. For the rest of her life it would be one of her favorite pieces of jewelry.

The same day, Billy asked her what he should buy me for Christmas. She told him I needed a new overcoat, so that's what he gave me. It was a handsome coat from Brooks Brothers, and I did need it, but I couldn't help wishing that Billy had asked me what I wanted. . . .

Billy's generosity to us decided Mother on her present to him. Because he was so enamored of my Afghan hound, she had been thinking for weeks about giving him one, but the high price had put her off. No longer. That weekend, she and I drove to a kennel in the country to select a dog. The season for puppies had passed, but there were a number of excellent, well-pedigreed young males and females from which to choose. She decided on a male even though he was more expensive than a female, rationalizing that he'd be more practical in the long run because we'd be able to mate him with my dog without having to pay a stud fee. That was Mother, always thinking ahead.

An hour later, we arrived at Billy's house with the dog. Jupah was beautiful and friendly and endeared himself to Billy right from the start by prancing into the house, jumping up, putting his paws on Billy's shoulders, and licking his face.

That night, however, there were the first signs of trouble. Billy had never owned a dog before and phoned Mother to ask her advice. Jupah, it seemed, wouldn't sit still. He kept wandering around. And he was so big and clumsy, he kept knocking things over. Mother told Billy not to worry. Of course the dog was wandering around; it was his first night in his new home, and he was exploring. He'd settle down as soon as he got his bearings. The clumsiness, she admitted, might take a bit longer. Jupah, she explained, was just going through his adolescence, which was an awkward age in boys and dogs. "Just be thankful it passes faster in animals than in humans," she added lightly, with a wink to me so I'd know she was kidding.

The crisis seemed to have passed the next morning when Billy phoned to report that Jupah had slept quietly on the floor next to his bed; but an hour later he called again, and this time he was furious. While Billy had been taking a bath, Jupah had chewed through the leg of an extremely valuable antique table. Mother commiserated with him over the loss and suggested he not leave Jupah alone among his valuable things until he finished teething and became more accustomed to the house. "Be patient, Bill," she said before hanging up, "animals take time, but they're worth it. Believe me."

That afternoon Billy had to go out for lunch, and he left Jupah in what he judged to be the most dog-proof room in the house — the billiard room. There was no carpet, the legs on the billiard table and bar stools were metal, and the sofa was so worn Billy didn't care what happened to it. Of course, no room in Billy's house was without something of value. In this case it was eight paintings by Salvador Dali, but they were on the walls, safely out of Jupah's reach.

The eight paintings had a facinating history. In 1944, Billy produced a lavish revue entitled *The Seven Lively Arts* at the Ziegfeld Theatre, which he owned. He refurbished the theater for the event, and as part of the face-lifting he commissioned Dali, who was virtually unknown at the time, to paint seven large canvases for the lobby, one for each of the seven arts depicted in the revue: Radio, Ballet, Musical Comedy, Opera, Jazz, Drama, and Modern Dance. He paid Dali $14,000 for the seven paintings. When the revue closed, Billy moved the paintings to his country house in Mount Kisco, New York, which subsequently burned to the ground destroying not only the Dalis, but Billy's entire collection, which included Rembrandts, Renoirs, Titians, and others. Dali heard of the tragedy and, in appreciation for Billy's early support, offered to recreate the paintings. Billy accepted. Money was not discussed. When the new paintings arrived there was an eighth painting depicting television, a new lively art, and a bill for $14,000, exactly what the original seven had cost.

Obviously these paintings had a tremendous sentimental value to Billy over their considerable market value, so when he returned from lunch and discovered Jupah standing on the sofa, chewing the corner off "Radio," it was the end of Jupah.

Billy called Mother and told her that if the dog wasn't out of the house within the hour, he'd have him destroyed. I heard her end of the conversation. She pretended to be indignant. "You should have known better than to leave him alone with those valuable paintings. How can you expect a puppy to know the value of a Dali? Of course I'll take him back. Erik will be right there."

I didn't see Billy when I went to collect the dog. His butler answered the bell, handed me Jupah on a lead and two packages, which I gathered from their sizes to be Billy's Christmas presents to Mother and me.

Poor Mother. When I got home with the dog she was clearly upset. She told me that Billy had called while I was on my way to his house to tell her that he had changed his plans for the holidays and would spend them at his house in Jamaica. We both knew the incident with the dog had precipitated this decision, and Mother was terribly guilty about it. "I felt the least I should do is offer to have the painting restored," she confided, "but I can't afford that kind of money, and Billy can."

On top of everything else, the kennel refused to take back Jupah. Just what we needed around the house, another dog. Another big dog at that.

But however badly Mother may have felt, she wasn't about to let it ruin her Christmas. Mother loved Christmas. She couldn't care less about other holidays, but Christmas was different. Most years we spent it on the road, opening our presents under a plastic tree in the hotel lobby. It wasn't as grim as it sounds; Mother always went out of her way to make it special. Of our hotel-lobby Christmases, my favorite was the one we spent at the Desert Inn in Las Vegas. It was 1950, and I had just turned six. Mother's gift to me was an electric train, and I awoke on Christmas morning to find the transformer under the tree in the lobby and track laid all through the ground floor of the hotel. For two days my train and I were the center of attention, then Wilbur Clark, the owner, made us take the train out of the lobby because it was drawing too much action away from the gambling tables.

Occasionally we managed to be home for the holidays, and then Mother was even more excited. She used to say it was one of the rare times when we could be like a normal family. Perhaps we could have behaved normally, but we didn't. Mother never did anything normally. But she did have fun. And of all our at-home Christmases, I think she had the most fun that Christmas after *Gypsy* opened.

She had begun planning for it even before we left for Europe by writing up a list of all the people for whom she wanted to find presents. Mother refused to give just any old thing; it had to be perfect. She could find it anywhere. For example, while in Paris we went to a restaurant called Le Mouton de Panurge. Supposedly "Rabelaisian," it was really just a tourist trap with waitresses in low-cut dresses, a live sheep running loose, the sommelier dressed like a monk with a cork-screw around his neck in place of a crucifix, and individual breads at every place shaped like penises complete with testicles. Mother put one of the breads in her purse and saved it. When we got home, she mounted it in a box, gilded it, and then gave it to Boyd for Christmas. He adored it.

Aside from collecting gifts, Mother didn't really start preparing for Christmas until November when she designed her Christmas card. She didn't always send out cards, but when she did, they had to be unique. This year they were a printed photograph of a dressing room makeup table on which lay a pair of long gloves and a single rose, two of her trademarks. Stuck in the frame of the mirror was a telegram. It was too small to read on the front of the card, but inside was a close-up. It said, "Merry Christmas, Gypsy and Erik."

After the cards went out, she spent the next few weeks wrapping presents. As far as she was concerned, the package was just as important as its contents, and often she spent more money on Christmas wrap-pings than on gifts. Every year had its theme; this year it was brightly colored paper bags, which had just been introduced, with contrasting colored tissue paper exploding from the top, tied off with gold cord, and garnished with a sprig of holly. Each package took at least ten minutes, and the awkwardly shaped ones often took much longer, but she never took short cuts. Spending time on such things was her way of telling her friends that she cared.

Next to Christmas Eve, when we opened our presents, the high point of a Christmas at home was the night we trimmed the Christmas tree. Sometimes Mother would invite a few of her close friends, have Esther cook a good dinner, and make a party out of it. Other times it would be the two of us with Boyd and perhaps a friend of his, with a light dinner served off a tray in the drawing room and a bottle of champagne "to keep the boys working." This year it was just Mother and me, and all the sweeter for the intimacy of it.

But first we had to buy the tree. This was one of those tasks Mother refused to delegate, and as with any project she undertook, it became something of a production. We ventured forth Saturday morning, right after breakfast, and because she always liked to kill two birds with one stone we brought both Afghans along to "give the poor dears a good outing." Don't for a moment, however, imagine an elegant, perfectly dressed and coiffed star accompanied by her equally well-dressed son with two regal Afghans leading the way. The dogs were regal, no doubt about it, but Mother and I were dressed for the bitter cold day: I in unpressed corduroy slacks, desert boots, and an old dirty car coat; Mother, without makeup, a heavy wool snood covering her hair, in rubber midcalf snow boots and her blanket coat.

A few words concerning this coat. While touring in vaudeville with the kiddy act, her mother had stolen blankets from the hotels they lived in and had Mother make them into overcoats for herself and the others in the act. They hadn't been chic, but they were warm and cheap. During World War II, when it had been impossible to get wool fabric, Mother had remembered these coats and made herself a new one. She never said where she got the blanket, but she swore it was the warmest coat she had ever owned. It certainly was the least attractive. Navy blue with half-inch-wide red and yellow stripes crisscrossing all over it, whatever shape it had once had was long gone, and it hung on her just like a . . . blanket. What with it, the rubber snow boots, and the two Afghans, it's no wonder people stopped to stare at us.

But Mother didn't care if people gawked. She had a job to do, and she was going to be comfortable doing it. Then, as now, Christmas trees were sold by street-corner entrepreneurs who would buy a truckful of trees in the country, bring them into the city, and set up shop on any unoccupied stretch of sidewalk. Three or more dealers per block were not unusual, and while there always seemed to be an unofficial agreement among them as to price, anyone willing to brave the cold, hunt through all the trees on display at a number of stands, and bargain hard could come away with a nice tree for a few dollars less than the going rate. Mother, needless to say, was willing.

More than willing, she loved every moment of it. We must have stopped at every Christmas tree stand within a ten-block radius of the house. She had decided to have a tall tree this year, which meant it would be expensive. Translated into her language this meant she had to find one with flaws that could be used to reduce the price and that could still be hidden at the back or with decorations. She came close to buying one across the street from Bloomingdale's when the guy agreed to knock five dollars off the price because it had a gap without branches, but then he insisted on two dollars for delivery and lost the sale.

Other trees were "lopsided and much too expensive," "scrawny and much too expensive," or just plain "much too expensive," but the effort wasn't wasted. After three hours she found a tree on Second Avenue that was close to perfect. The men who were running the stand took five bucks off without an argument, and one of them offered to follow us home with the tree for no charge. Best of all, he even put it in our stand for us when he got there. That was the kind of service Mother found irresistible. She tipped him five dollars and gave him a couple of beers to share with his partner. She was definitely in the Christmas spirit!

Mother always gave a tree twenty-four hours in the stand to assume its natural shape, so we waited until late Sunday afternoon to start the trimming. As Sunday was Esther's day off, she had left a stew in the refrigerator for us to heat for dinner, but Mother decided we should celebrate and sent me out for Chinese food.

Mother loved Chinese food, another legacy from her childhood in vaudeville when the local Chinese restaurant was inevitably the cheapest place in town to eat. In New York, there were three that she patronized. House of Chan on Seventh Avenue was her favorite for after the theater. During *Star and Garter* she had been such a regular they named a dish after her — See Gyp Good. Mother never actually went to Sheila Chang's on 63rd Street and Third Avenue; she felt it was far too chic and expensive for a Chinese restaurant, but as it was only half a block from the house, she would send me there for takeout when the weather was truly foul.

Her favorite Chinese restaurant in all of New York, however, didn't even have a name, just a neon sign announcing "Chop Suey" in its window. Located on the second floor of an old building on the corner of 59th Street and Third Avenue, right above a pizza parlor, it had white tile walls that had yellowed with age and dirt, old Chinese waiters who had been there for years but nonetheless could barely speak three words of English, great food, and the cheapest prices in town. Mother had been a regular since the late 1930s, and they never failed to put a little something extra in the bag for her, an order of soup or fried rice or, her favorite, four fortune cookies instead of the usual two. Moreover, since I had gotten my Afghan and been bringing her with me when I went to collect our orders, they had always given her a bone to gnaw while we waited. When I arrived this day with two Afghans, it seemed to be cause for a general celebration. Amid much petting and many oriental sounds of affection, both dogs got bones, I was given an order of spareribs, and Mother was sent two huge handfuls of fortune cookies.

Usually we ate in the drawing room while trimming the tree, hanging decorations between bites, but because the food was already a little cold from the trip home, we broke with tradition and ate off a tray in Mother's room as soon as I arrived. Then, after stuffing ourselves with won ton soup, spareribs, egg rolls, beef with snow peas, sweet and sour pork, and three fortune cookies each — Mother having decided to save the rest for another day — I went down to the basement and brought the ladder and boxes full of decorations up to the drawing room while Mother made herself a pot of tea.

It took me a number of trips to get everything. Mother hated throwing things away, and this was especially true of anything with the slightest bit of history or tradition attached to it, like Christmas ornaments. She saved everything off our tree — toys, balls, lights, geegaws, even the tinsel and garland. Every year there were a few new things, and the inevitable breakage, but we still had the engine and one car of a little tin train that had been on the tree in the lobby of the Orpheum Theatre in Saint Louis when she was ten, a string of the first commercially available Christmas tree lights (she had started with four strings and combined them as bulbs blew out), a Santa Claus doll made from an argyle sock she had knit for me when I was three, a net bag of foil-wrapped chocolate money that had hung on the tree at the Desert Inn, and enough other treasures to fill five large boxes. Even the green felt cloth that we put under the tree was traditional: it was left over from the tree she had at her country house in 1942, and it had the moth holes to prove it.

By the time I had all the boxes up, Mother had a fire going. We opened a bottle of champagne, toasted to a Merry Christmas — with Mother warning me as I drained my glass, "Easy does it. We don't want you falling off the ladder and breaking your neck. At least not until after you've finished trimming the tree" — and got to work.

Just as Mother's decorations were traditional, so too was her routine for decorating the tree. We'd begin with the lights, move on to the heavier toys, then the lighter ones, the fragile toys and balls, and finally the garland and tinsel. Boyd had taken down our last tree and put everything away very neatly, marking each box with its contents, which made it easy to get started. We simply opened the box marked "lights," checked the bulbs, and strung them up. Or, to put it more accurately, I checked the bulbs and strung the lights while Mother directed from the sofa. I didn't mind. That's the way it always was with her. Besides, after each string of lights, I had some more champagne. By the time all the lights were up, I was feeling no pain.

Mother's attitude toward my drinking had always been liberal. As early as six, I was allowed watered wine with meals. The watering didn't last long, and on the last trip to Europe she had made no effort to limit my consumption of wine or beer. Still, close to a whole bottle of champagne to myself was out of the ordinary, but I assumed it was due to the holiday, and I certainly wasn't going to question it. Just as well. Being slightly inebriated made what followed much easier to handle.

After the lights, I opened the box marked "heavy toys," and as I was reaching for the matador doll that Mother had purchased on our first trip to Spain, a water bug scurried out of the box, down its side, and across the marble floor. Our reaction was pretty average. Mother lifted her feet off the floor, shrieked in surprise, and grabbed hold of Fu Manchu, who had seen it and was ready to give chase. Meanwhile, I ran over and stepped on it.

"Eeech!" I shuddered involuntarily as the bug's back snapped with a crack.

Then the next one crawled out of the box. These were not everyday, little, skinny, half-inch-long, light brown, repulsive cockroaches. Oh, no. These were truly disgusting, dark brown fatties at least two inches long. As this second hideous monster ran down the side of the box, a third appeared and stopped on the flap of the box, antennae waving. I killed number two, but I didn't know what to do with number three. I couldn't step on him where he was. Stunned, I looked to Mother.

"What should I do?"

"Kill it!" she yelled, simultaneously looking around to make sure none was sneaking up on her.

I looked at my slipper, a rubber sole held on my foot with a single rubber thong. It hadn't seemed so bad for the first two, but now that I had time to think, I had visions of this huge creature crawling over my toes.

"I'm going upstairs to put on some real shoes," I said, heading for the door.

"No! Wait. What if it moves?" Mother asked in a half-scream.

"Step on it."

"Oh, no. Please, Erik. Don't leave me here alone with it."

We looked at each other and began laughing. The two of us were semihysterical, all because of three water bugs. Bravely, I took charge. As I couldn't kill the bug on the unsupported flap, I kicked it from underneath, flinging the bug into the air. For a moment both Mother and I lost track of it. She screamed, and I jumped back from the box at least three feet. Mother saw it first.

"There it is," she shouted, pointing.

It was heading for the sofa and safety. I ran over and caught it just in time. Stomp, crack!

"Thank God," Mother sighed in genuine relief.

"I'll be right back," I said, heading for the door. By now my skin was crawling, and I had to have heavier shoes.

"Please hurry," Mother begged weakly.

Her tone had changed by the time I returned wearing my riding boots. No more bugs had appeared, and she even saw fit to remark as I clomped across the floor, "Now don't you think that's carrying this thing just a bit far?"

I didn't bother to answer. I just kicked the box. Four more of the bugs scurried out. They were quick, and I had to do a pretty fast dance to get them all before they found sanctuary under the furniture.

Fu Manchu was, by this point, almost impossible to control, so Mother went upstairs to put him in her room. When she returned, she was wearing her heavy boots and had with her another bottle of champagne.

"I thought my great white hunter might need some more fortification," she said putting the bottle on the table. I hardly needed it, but it did take the edge of horror off the rest of the evening.

Countless bugs had set up housekeeping in our Christmas decorations. Every remaining box was infested. They had thrived on the chocolate money, candy canes, and other edibles, reproducing until there were, literally, hordes of them. Had the decorations not been so important to Mother, we would have tossed them right into the garbage; as that was impossible, we developed a routine for unpacking the boxes and killing the bugs:

After very gingerly opening a box, I'd kick it. An initial wave of ten or fifteen bugs would immediately abandon ship, and Mother and I would run around the room, stomping them. We'd repeat this until no more bugs emerged after a couple of kicks, and then we'd begin unpacking the box. If either Mother or I had had to put our hands into those boxes, I know we would have gone no further, but fortunately one of Mother's truly useless purchases finally came in handy. A few years earlier she had decided that we needed a pair of those tongs used by grocers to reach items on high shelves. They had sat, unused, in one of our storage closets ever since, but that evening they were invaluable because they allowed me to remove items from the boxes without risk of having one of the bugs crawl on me, a fate if not worse than death, certainly more repulsive.

So, using the tongs, I'd remove a decoration from the box and shake it. If a bug dropped off, Mother would step on it. If, as all too often happened, a number of bugs dropped off, I'd put down the tongs and help her get them before they could hide under the furniture. Then, after carefully inspecting the decoration to insure no exceptionally tenacious bugs were still hanging on, Mother would carefully place it on the tree wherever she felt it would look "just right."

Once we got used to the routine, it became quite funny, with Mother and I running around the room after the hideous things. We even made little games out of it, such as doing it to a beat. One-two-three, stomp, crack! One-two-three, stomp, crack! Thank God for champagne.

Finally, a little after midnight, the boxes were empty, the last bug was dead, and the tree was trimmed. It looked beautiful and reflected every bit of Mother's care and attention to detail. The floor, on the other hand, was so strewn with squashed brown carcasses and bug juice that it looked like the set of a horror movie. But aside from making sure all the bugs were completely dead, we left everything as it was and went to bed. Mrs. Mitchell was coming the next day, and we decided to leave the truly disgusting job for her. Sometimes it was so nice to have a maid.

Four nights later it was Christmas Eve. The next day we would take the Rolls and visit Mother's friends, dropping off presents and, I hoped, collecting some as well. But that night it was, once again, just the two of us.

Esther served us a wonderful dinner of baked ham with macaroni and cheese in the drawing room. All evidence of the bugs was long gone, the tree sparkled, Mother's colorfully wrapped gifts looked festive and joyous displayed underneath it, a cheerful fire raged in the fireplace, and the animals lounged in front of it enjoying the warmth. We ate, sipped champagne, and felt secure.

"How fortunate we are, Erik," Mother said wistfully. "There are times when I wake up at night, in the dark, and I'm almost afraid to turn on the light for fear it will all be gone." She glanced around the room, freshly painted, with the new frames on the art and all her new acquisitions in place. "All my life I've wanted to be surrounded by beautiful things, to have my eyes rest on something pleasing wherever I looked, and now . . ."

She was interrupted by a loud crack from the fire, which, with clockwork precision, set off the following train of events: Jupah, startled, jumped up and shied away from the fire, frightening Fu Manchu, who began yapping, which so upset Gaudi that he dashed madly for the nearest refuge — the Christmas tree. It started to list before he was even halfway to the top.

"Oh, my God!" Mother shouted. "Not the tree. Grab it, Erik, before it falls."

I was on my way, but so was the tree, and so, too, was Gaudi, who had already realized the precariousness of his perch. We met simultaneously. I caught the tree about thirty degrees short of impact with the floor, and Gaudi caught me with all of his claws after a death-defying leap through garland, tinsel, and a papier-mâché Santa Claus. Fortunately he caught mostly shirt and proceeded in his flight to safety with a hiss, a snarl, and another leap to the sofa, without doing me any damage.

The same was not true of the tree. Mother and I managed to get it upright and steady, but all the decorations had shifted, giving it a decidedly lopsided appearance. Only removing everything and re-decorating it from scratch would put it back to normal, but we didn't even consider it. Every year one of the cats knocked over the tree at least once, and we were used to it being slightly askew. As Mother remarked after we sat back down, "You know, Erik, I think it looks nicer like this. More lived in."

After all the excitement, opening our presents was almost anticlimactic. Mother began by apologizing. Now that I was past the toy age, she explained, she no longer knew what to get me, consequently she had only two gifts for me, and one of them was, in her words, "rather peculiar."

She was putting it mildly. It wasn't wrapped. She made me close my eyes, then she put it in my hands and made me try to guess what it was. It felt like an oval box, about the size of my palm, filled with clay in which two marbles had been imbedded. I was close. Only they weren't marbles, they were glass eyes, and when I looked down and saw them staring up at me, shivers ran down up and down my arms. They looked familiar. I didn't understand until I read Mother's card: "Remember, dear, Mother is *always* watching." Then I realized the glass eyes were exactly the same hazel color as Mother's.

She thought it was an hysterically funny gift. I thought it strange and unsettling, and I was beginning to regret having outgrown toys when I opened her second present. It was an antique gold pocket watch and chain that was the most beautiful thing I had ever owned.

Coincidentaly, I had two gifts for her. Every year I gave her the latest volume of Burns Mantle's Broadway anthology, *The Best Plays of the Year*, and this year was no exception; but I was especially pleased with her other gift which I had found in Europe over the summer: an antique inkwell in the shape of a shoe. She had a large collection of shoe-shaped antiques, including a buttonhook, a few paperweights, and a pin cushion, but no inkwell. She was thrilled with it, which made my night. Finding something for her, something really special, was so difficult.

The other packages under the tree were all from us to the people we'd be visiting the next day, except for Billy's presents, so we finished the evening by opening them. I went first, and only after I had modeled the overcoat for Mother did she open the package containing the pin. She hadn't seen it since the day the jeweler had brought it to the house, and her hands shook in anticipation. As she opened the case, tears came to her eyes.

"Oh, Erik. Isn't it the most magnificent piece of jewelry you've ever seen!"

She held it out for me to examine, but I had hardly glanced at it before she clutched it to her breast.

"I do wish Bill were here, so at least I could thank him." She glanced around the room, noticed the animals, looked at the lopsided tree, then turned back to me and added, "On second thought, I suppose it's better that he's not."

We shared the laugh and called it a night. It had been a lovely Christmas Eve at home, just like a normal family.

CHAPTER ELEVEN

MOTHER gave me one other present that Christmas. It wasn't a surprise, and I didn't actually get it until after the holidays, but it was by far my favorite gift that year: she let me move out of the dormitory and commute to school from home.

I hated Riverdale. After the laissez-faire atmosphere of Professional Children's School, Riverdale's strict discipline, emphasis on academic excellence and formality came as real shock. Somehow I managed to adjust to these; however, I was far less successful in adjusting to my new classmates. I had spent most of my life in the company of adults and the rest of it with socially precocious professional children, so I had nothing in common with the boys at Riverdale. They played sports; I had never thrown a football. Their parents were doctors, lawyers, and other upper-middle-class types; mine was an ex-stripper, and an eccentric one at that. They were raised in mainstream America; I came out of nightclubs, a backwater off the minor tributary of show business. To be fair, they were less conscious of the differences than I. I felt uncomfortable with them, not vice versa. Nonetheless, I felt like an outcast, and I reacted by adopting an attitude of aloof disdain. This worked well enough during the day when classes kept us busy, but in the dormitory I was limited to staying in my room alone or hanging out with one or two other misfits. Given the opportunity, I would have left the school and returned to PCS, but Mother would never have allowed that, and I was more than delighted just to be getting out of those long, isolated evenings in the dormitory.

There were also other advantages to living at home: I could sneak cigarettes with comparative ease, watch unlimited television, and stay up as late as I wished just to name a few of the minor ones. Above all, however, moving home felt to me as I'd imagine returning to

Versailles after a long exile felt to a courtier of the Sun King. That might seem a bit overstated, but it is altogether accurate. Mother ruled in her home like a monarch, and life at her court was certainly more exciting and dramatic than life at school.

This was especially true during the first half of 1960. She began the new year with only one resolution — to go back to work — and with *Gypsy* still paying all the bills, she resumed her search for that elusive new career with a lighthearted sense of daring and adventure. She considered every offer, and if it had potential for the future or even just for fun, she gave it a try. And living at home, whatever she did, I did too. It was an ideal time to be at court.

The first offer to catch her fancy came from Joseph E. Levine, the motion picture distributor. He had recently purchased the North American rights to an English B-picture entitled *Jack the Ripper*, and he asked Mother to help him sell it. It wasn't a bad movie, but it wasn't very good either. There was nothing new or special in its approach to the infamous Victorian murderer, it had no stars, and it wasn't even in color. Well, part of it was. In the film's final seconds, the character we suspect of being the Ripper is trapped beneath a descending elevator, and when it stops in the basement his blood spurts up between the elevator's floor boards in bright cherry red!

This was the film's big moment. Its only moment actually. Because of Levine, however, it still had a good chance of being successful. A showman in the Mike Todd tradition, Levine had built his reputation by selling second-rate films through massive advertising and publicity campaigns. The previous year, for example, he paid $120,000 for the North American rights to an Italian "epic" entitled *Ercole et la Regina de Lidia* starring an unknown American athlete named Steve Reeves. Then he dubbed it into English, changed the title to *Hercules*, and spent over $1.5 million on advertising and publicity. It was an unheard-of amount at the time, but it worked. The film grossed over $15 million, and he was chosen "Showman of the Year" by the National Association of Theatre Owners.

He planned a similar approach for *Jack the Ripper*. Again his advertising and publicity budget was well over a million dollars. There were going to be full-page ads in forty top national magazines and all major newspapers, saturation spots on radio and television, and countless gimmicks to generate talk and interest, such as 2500 electric clocks shaped like pocket watches with "Watch Out For Jack The Ripper" on the face and over ten thousand similarly inscribed rubber daggers that were to be given away to moviegoers around the country.

Mother's role in all this was relatively small. She wrote the liner notes for the sound track album, gave a formal dinner party and private screening at the house for select members of the press and other "opinion makers," and went on a four-city publicity tour as a member of Levine's "Potent Panel of World Famous Connoisseurs of Crime: Gypsy Rose Lee, she writes 'em. Peter Lorre, he slays 'em. Basil Rathbone, he solves 'em."

Aside from her salary, which was extravagant, the party was reason enough for her to take the job. Of her thirty guests, all but three were either important business contacts or close friends. At Levine's expense they enjoyed a lavish dinner that included champagne and caviar catered by one of New York's finest restaurants. Jule Styne gave a delightful two-hour impromptu concert after the screening, which made up for the film, and everyone had a wonderful time. Even me. I wasn't invited, but I got $25 for running the projector.

The party cost Levine close to $1500, but he didn't get much for his money beyond an enjoyable evening. Not only was his film projected on our prewar Bell and Howell with two interruptions for reel changes and unintelligible sound, as the film ended he discovered that the 16mm print which had been made expressly for the party — at an additional expense of $2000 — didn't have the blood colored red! It wasn't a total washout. Of the six stories written about the party, five kindly forgot to mention the film, and Louis Sobol in the sixth wrote what were probably the only nice words about it ever to appear in print: "It was exciting but not recommended for the weak hearted or those subject to nightmares."

In spite of Sobol's nice words and Levine's millions, the film faded into oblivion almost immediately after it opened. Its failure didn't hurt Levine, who eventually produced many modern film classics such as *The Graduate* and *Lion in Winter.* Nor did it bother Mother. She had enjoyed herself, given a great party for all her friends, and made some money.

Her next offer might have solved her money and career problems forever. I learned about it right after she did. Another advantage to living at home was being on the scene for all the news. It was late on a Saturday night. Mother was at a formal dinner with Billy — they had resumed dating upon his return from Jamaica — and I was in my room, smoking cigarettes and watching television. It must have been an engrossing show because I didn't realize that Mother had returned home until she knocked on my door.

"Erik, are you awake?"

"Yes, Mother." Frantically I put out my cigarette and hid the ashtray in my bureau.

"May I come in?"

"Just a second," I yelled, playing for time as I stood on my bed and tried to dispel the smoke by fanning the air with the *TV Guide*. And that's how she found me — standing on President Harrison's bed in my underwear, magazine in hand — when she got tired of waiting and entered.

"What in God's name is going on in here? Have you been smoking again?" I began to mumble a lie, but she spared us both the embarrassment. "Why you insist on doing something that you know is so bad for you is beyond me."

I could have asked her the same question, but I wouldn't have dared. Instead, I got down off the bed and tried to change the subject. "How was the party?"

"Awful, but for once Bill agreed with me, so we left early and went to El Morocco for dinner."

"How was it?"

"Overpriced and mediocre, as usual. It's shocking, actually. Tonight Bill asked for some vegetables with his steak. They brought him a dish this big . . ." She made a circle with her hands by touching her thumbs and forefingers. ". . . of frozen peas. Frozen, mind you. And then they had the nerve to charge him seven-fifty extra for them. Seven dollars and fifty cents for thirty-nine cents' worth of frozen peas! I really don't know why he puts up with it."

"Maybe he likes frozen peas," I suggested in a nervous attempt at levity.

She didn't respond, but she made no move to leave either. Something was on her mind, and after a brief pause she told me what it was.

"On the way home, Bill asked me to marry him."

I was caught completely off guard. Since her divorce from Julio, Mother had repeatedly said that "three husbands are enough for any girl," and neither her manner nor Bill's had suggested a romance. Yet she wouldn't have mentioned it unless she was considering it, and I felt called upon to react. This could mean a major change in our lives.

My first thought was money. If she married him, we would be *really* rich. Then I wondered if we would move into his house and felt uncomfortable with the idea. Where would I live? Then I realized that I'd probably be sent off to boarding school, but with an enormous allowance to soothe their guilt. The possibilities seemed infinite; to weigh them, make a choice, and then decide on the best reaction to affect that choice would take weeks. I had to react immediately, so I played it safe.

"What did you tell him?" I asked.

"That I was flattered and would need some time to think about it, but I could never marry him."

"How come?" I asked, feeling a twinge of disappointment.

"Sooner or later he'd expect it to become physical, and I couldn't bear that."

"Sooner or later?"

"People often get married who aren't physically attracted," she explained, as much, I thought, to herself as to me. "All Bill really wants is a hostess. And someone to keep him company at El Morocco."

"Couldn't you arrange that in advance?"

She laughed softly and shook her head. "Besides, I could never stand Bill's kind of life. One boring party after another. I'd go out of my mind." She paused, then added decisively, "No. It's out of the question."

Abruptly she changed the subject. "I'm going to get out of this corset and make myself a cup of tea. Keep me company?"

"Sure. Go on ahead. I'll get my robe and be right up."

"Don't be too long."

As soon as she left, I checked to make sure a fire wasn't smoldering in my underwear drawer. Then I put on my robe and joined her.

The subject of marriage never came up again, but I have often thought about her reaction to Billy's proposal and the reasons she gave for turning him down. She probably would have been bored as his wife, and the sexual angle certainly had something to do with it. As far as I've able to learn, she had very few affairs in her life and none whatsoever after her divorce from Julio. Sex was not one of her driving passions, and the prospect of making love to a man as unattractive as Billy could not have appealed to her.

Beyond these, however, I am convinced there were at least two more reasons why she wouldn't marry him. The first and most obvious is that she didn't want to give up her independence. She had been her own woman for most of her life and for all of the ten years since Julio. She was used to her freedom, and she enjoyed it. She also enjoyed being able to walk out on Billy whenever he became too insufferable. The second reason was put succinctly, albeit facetiously, by Louis Sobol when he asked in his column, "If Gypsy Rose Lee marries Billy Rose, will it be Gypsy Rose Rose or Billy Rose Lee?" Both Mother and Billy had spent their entire lives establishing their personas. Had they married, one of them would have had to sacrifice at least a part of that individuality to the other, and no doubt it would have been Mother doing the sacrificing. Selling would, perhaps, be a more accurate term, for in exchange she would have gained financial security for life. Yet as important as security was to her, she was not willing to forgo her identity or her independence for it, and that as much as anything else has come to define her strength of character for me.

Mother gave Billy her answer a few days later, and he stopped calling afterward. He could accept anything from her, it seems, but rejection.

She admitted to me that she missed him, but she didn't allow herself to brood over it. Instead, she accepted a last-minute offer to appear in a revival of Moss Hart's comedy *Light Up the Sky* at the Drury Lane Theatre in Chicago. Ironically, she played the part of Frances, the figure-skating wife of a pint-sized Broadway producer who had made a fortune collecting art and antiques. When the play first opened on Broadway in 1948, there were rumors that Billy, who was then married to swimming star Eleanor Holm, would sue. He didn't, but I doubt Mother would have played the part had she and Billy still been dating.

The play wasn't one of Hart's best, but it was a nice little comedy, and as with everything Mother did during this period, she learned from the experience. Unlike *Happy Hunting*, this show wasn't a musical and it wasn't being staged in the round, so there was no score to sing and no running up and down the aisles. Moreover, while she was billed as the star, the play was an ensemble piece with no one part overshadowing the others. She didn't have to carry the entire evening, and she had an easy time of it for a change. As a result, she was bored to distraction halfway into the first week. She complained about hard work, but she loved it, and she never again accepted a role that wasn't a challenge to both her talent and her fortitude.

I couldn't perform my usual job as Mother's dresser because I had to wait for spring vacation to join her and didn't get to Chicago until after the show had opened. She, of course, found another way to put my time there to good use, but for once I was delighted. She taught me how to drive. Twice before she had given me the wheel for a few minutes on a virtually deserted highway, but in Chicago the lessons were for real. She took me out for at least an hour every day, and she made sure I experienced every type of traffic and road condition including, thanks to Chicago's weather, driving in a snowstorm. It was one of our more successful collaborations. Mother was an excellent teacher; in spite of her generally nervous disposition, she never once lost her temper or gave any indication of being tense. For my part, I had wanted to drive for as long as I could remember, so I was determined to do well and make her feel comfortable with me behind the wheel. I succeeded, too. When we left after the show on closing night, she told me to drive, reclined her seat, and slept all the way to New York. Needless to say, I arrived home feeling like one hot-shot fifteen-year-old.

Mother had nothing to do after our return from Chicago. Billy was squiring his last ex-wife around town (he knew she would marry him, and eventually they did remarry), the few job offers coming in were for the summer, she had finished redecorating the house, it was too early in the year to work on the patio, and she had not been able to think of an approach to *Curious Evening* that would solve its many problems. So for want of something lucrative or productive to occupy her time, she turned to something frivolous: a party.

It was to be her first fun-only party in years; she invited no one who could possibly be of use to her, professionally speaking. And, because it would never occur to her to give an ordinary party, she billed it as a "musicale." Everyone was told to bring a musical instrument, and after dinner we would gather in the drawing room, make music, and have a good time. On the day of the party, *Curious Evening* as always in the back of her mind, she decided to take some footage of her friends playing away. Then, realizing that silent footage of a musical party would be useless, she hid a microphone and long-playing tape recorder behind the drawing room sofa. She started the recorder when we came in from dinner and let it run for the rest of the party, which was, I might add, a great success. Thus she ended up with a three-hour tape recording of Red Buttons, Faye Emerson, Jule Styne, Jane Kean, Hermione Gingold, Ben Grauer, and other famous and not-so-famous personalities singing songs, telling jokes, and exchanging juicy bits of gossip, all spiced with lively off-color language.

Mother read *Variety* every week; she knew comedy albums were among the hottest selling LPs at the time, and it didn't take much imagination to envision "A Party with Gypsy and Her Friends" up there on the charts with the others, just a little optimism. The next day she cut the dull, the libelous, and the truly obscene moments from the tape and arranged through her agent to play it for executives of RCA, Decca, and Columbia records. They all felt that the quality of the recording was too poor to be used; RCA, however, thought enough of the content to offer to finance another party which they would record in hi-fidelity stereo. They wouldn't guarantee to release it as a record, that would depend on the party, but Mother was willing, and she managed to convince her friends to go along. As she explained it, the possibilities in terms of exposure and royalties were just too good to pass up.

The second party took place six weeks after the first. The guest list, the food, and the booze was the same; but the atmosphere couldn't have been more different. The technicians with their huge console tape recorders and mixers were hidden in my room, but downstairs microphones and cables were everywhere. It was impossible to take three steps without almost bumping into the one or tripping over the other. Most of the guests were professionals long used to such things, so maybe it was the knowledge that they were being taped rather than the equipment, or perhaps it was being taped without the security of a script. Whatever the reason, everyone was stilted and ill-at-ease throughout the evening. No one told off-color jokes or risqué stories, and even the clean stuff was self-conscious, awkward, and unfunny. In short, the party was a bust and everyone knew it. By midnight, all the guests had left; and much later, when all the equipment had been packed up and moved out and the producer from RCA was leaving, I overheard him say to Mother, "Too bad. It seemed like a hell of a good idea, too."

She wasn't one to accept defeat that easily, and when RCA called the following week to confirm their producer's assessment, she insisted they were wrong and offered to prove it by editing the tapes herself. RCA had nothing to lose, and later that afternoon they sent over sixteen hours of tape — four hours from each of the four separate microphones. She spent most of the next six weeks trying to glean an album from them, but in spite of her hard work and optimistic tenacity she couldn't get it to work.

The frustration of struggling unsuccessfully with the album took the edge off her mood for the first time that year, and concern over her summer employment further dampened it. By May 1, she had been offered only a few weeks on the tent circuit with *Happy Hunting*, which she wasn't about to do again, and a fifteen-week tour with the L.A. Civic Light Opera as Parthy Ann in *Showboat*. She didn't like the part, and the money was terrible, but the company had an excellent reputation which would help her get work in the future, and she always figured any job was better than none, so she accepted.

She regretted her decision immediately. During the day she had visions of sitting in her dressing room, chewing her makeup towel while everyone else was getting all the laughs, and at night she had nightmares about it. One so upset her that she came down to my room and woke me up to keep her company. The next morning, after breakfast of course, she told me about it. It was opening night. When she went to put on her costume, she discovered the costumer had sent one for a different show, and it didn't even fit. But the worst part was that while she struggled to get into it, her cue came and went, and nobody even missed her.

Fortunately, before Mother became too dispirited, an offer arrived that turned everything around. John Kenley, who managed the Packard Music Hall in Warren, Ohio, asked her to star in *Auntie Mame*. It was only for a week, but the money was good, and the part was great! She grabbed it. Then she backed out of the *Showboat* deal and managed to book four more weeks with *Mame* in Detroit and Miami, so by the time we left for Warren, she had forgotten the album fiasco and was in a good mood indeed.

During our stay in Warren it only improved. We were there for two weeks, one rehearsing and one performing, and they constituted the most pleasant and most successful summer stock engagement of Mother's career. There were a number of reasons for this, but most of the credit belongs to John Kenley for hiring Mother to appear in a play and a part that were ideal for her. *Auntie Mame* is about an outrageously eccentric, warm woman and the nephew, Patrick, she inherits when her brother dies. Mame's character bore a marked similarity to Mother's; and her dialogue, which was sprinkled with four-letter words and quick witticisms, could have been lifted right out of Mother's everyday speech. Yet while the character was easy for her to assume, the part was taxing enough to challenge her and hold her interest for as long as she played it.

John's contributions went far beyond casting. Working for him was a joy. Everything about his operation was first class from the director and supporting cast he had assembled through the scenery, props, and costumes right down to the publicity and advertising. Moreover, he was attentive, supportive, and constantly on the lookout for ways to make Mother's life easier so that she could concentrate on her role and on giving a good performance.

A typical example of this occurred opening day. Mother had eighteen costume changes during the play. Most involved her entire outfit from shoes to wig (she wore seven different hairstyles and colors) and they all had to be made very quickly, some in less than a minute. I was her dresser. We had worked out a plan in which some of the changes were done in her dressing room, which was on the right side of the stage, and the rest were done in a cubicle that had been built in the wings on the left side of the stage. During the dress rehearsal, however, we discovered that she was late or barely made her cue after the changes in her dressing room because it was quite far offstage. John picked up on it, and after the rehearsal — without Mother's asking — he offered to have another cubicle built in the wings stage right. What's more, he had the thing built in plenty of time for a trial run before the show that night. It saved Mother no more than thirty seconds each time she used it, but he understood how important half a minute can be to an actor's performance.

There was only one minor drawback to having an ideal producer, a wonderful supporting cast, and an excellent part: it left the entire burden of the play's success on Mother's shoulders. As the opening night's performance approached she was feeling the strain. Which is one explanation for the misunderstanding with the hairdresser. There is also the psychological one that she needed a crisis to distract her from worrying about her performance, and therefore she subconsciously created it. It is even possible that he gave her the wrong instructions, as she later claimed. Whatever the true cause, there was a crisis. With Mother, there was always a crisis.

This one began with the only other problem she had encountered during the dress rehearsal — she had found it almost impossible to keep wisps of her own dark hair from showing beneath the front of the light colored wigs that she wore in the show. To solve the problem, a hairdresser was summoned to "lighten her bangs." He arrived after our runthrough with the new cubicle. Reluctantly — Mother had to insist, "It doesn't matter *how* my hair looks, darling. I'm in a wig throughout the show!" — he applied bleach to a one-and-a-half-inch-thick band of hair along her forehead. He wanted to stay and rinse it out, but Mother needed to be alone to collect her thoughts before the show and dismissed him after asking how long she should leave the bleach on. This is where the misunderstanding occurred. Later the hairdresser claimed that he told her to leave it on fifteen to twenty minutes at the most. She insisted he had said forty minutes. There were no witnesses, so the truth remains obscure; the result, however, was all too obvious: most of the bleached hair fell out, what remained had the color and texture of singed straw, and Mother's scalp had a bright red burn an inch and a half wide from ear to ear at her hairline.

She cursed the hairdresser, who wasn't around to hear her, fussed a little, and generally created a minor scene, but she did it more to release tension than because she was truly upset. Ludicrous as she looked, it was hardly a catastrophe. The burn was tender, and she would have to keep her head covered in public for a few months, but the wigs would hide her disfigurement during the play, and the problem of her own hair showing had certainly been eliminated for the duration of the tour. The only irrevocable damage was the loss of her few moments of peaceful reflection before she went on. They were, as she put it, "shot to hell and gone," but their absence didn't seem to have a negative affect on her performance.

I was too busy either helping her with her changes when she was offstage or shuttling costumes, props, and wigs between the dressing room and the cubicles when she was onstage to catch more than an occasional glimpse of the show, but there was no way I could miss or mistake the audience's reaction. The laughs were long, loud, and came in all the right places, and at the end of the play Mother received a standing ovation that seemed to go on forever. She was forced to take curtain call after curtain call until finally she just stood in front of the curtain, bowing and absorbing the adulation. It was the kind of response that justifies a performer's entire existence, and it brought tears to her eyes.

Eventually the applause began to subside, and as soon as she could be heard above the din, she said, "Thank you . . . thank you. . . . You've been so very kind, I hardly know what to say." It was probably true because she paused and then used one of her old standbys. "I'm not used to getting this much applause with all my clothes on, you know. . . ." It wasn't old to the audience, however, so it got a good laugh.

Mother could have continued with old routines, but instead she decided to break new ground. Fortunately for me, I was in the wings with the mirror, Kleenex, and comb that she used to freshen up between the last scene and the curtain calls, so I got to see it all.

Sweat was dripping off her forehead into her eyes, and she wiped it off with the back of her hand while the audience was still laughing at her old joke. "Boy, it's hotter 'n a firecracker up here," she said when they stopped. "And these wigs don't help, I'll tell you that. It's like working with your head in an oven. A hot oven." The audience laughed, then she continued, but in a different, almost gossipy, tone. "And the trouble they cause. You wouldn't believe it. Just this afternoon, for example, I noticed that my own hair was showing in front, so I had a hair dresser come in to lighten my bangs a little. Well . . . just look what the son-of-a-bitch did to me. . . ." She reached up and removed the wig. Her hair, wet with sweat, was mostly plastered down to her head, but some had been pulled up with the wig and stood straight on end. This was especially true of the few scorched-blond strands remaining in the front. In an instant she had been transformed from a glamorous star into a harridan. There was a collective gasp from the audience, which clearly wasn't sure whether to laugh or to sympathize. Mother quickly told them; she tugged gently at a few hairs and yelled plaintively, "I'm bald, for crissakes!"

It was Mother at her best, broad and earthy but with an honesty that was irresistible. The audience howled. And she didn't give them a break. When the laugh started to die, she pulled at her hair again and said, "John Kenley told me I'd have to make sacrifices if I wanted to go legit, but this is asking a bit much. . . ." And then, "Of course, John's version of legit changes from week to week. He wouldn't dare ask Helen Hayes to go through something like this. . . ."

Eventually the audience was laughed out. Mother finished up with a few words of thanks to John and the cast, said goodnight, and walked offstage. The audience gave her another standing ovation. This time she limited herself to one last bow, but from the reaction it would have been hard to tell which was more successful, the play or the curtain speech. It didn't really matter. When Mother found a gimmick that worked, she held on to it; and she never again appeared in *Auntie Mame* or any other play without giving a curtain speech.

It is an interesting footnote to the curtain speech that Mother never grasped its true appeal. She thought it was the jokes; therefore she constantly experimented with new ones trying to get bigger laughs. She never realized that the audience liked whatever she did as long as she was relaxed and being herself. It wasn't the content; it was she. All she had to do was be natural, and people loved her, but she didn't know that then, and it would be a few years before she learned.

In the meantime, *Auntie Mame* was a smash. It sold out every show, including the standing room, and was the most successful nonmusical Kenley had ever produced. Mother was delighted. It's always gratifying to be a hit, especially with a percentage of the gross, and she left town with close to two thousand dollars more than she had expected.

The two weeks in Warren were remarkable for more than Mother's professional success. While we were there, our relationship was better than it had been in years, or would be for years to come. Actually, we had been getting along quite well since the beginning of the year because I was so grateful for my release from the dormitory — and so determined to prove to her how nice it could be to have me home, lest she change her mind — that I made a point of going out of my way to help her with her projects and around the house. This pleased her and led to her doing other nice things for me, such as teaching me how to drive in Chicago. I, in turn, became even more grateful and helpful, and a very pleasant cycle developed.

One discordant note had sounded repeatedly in the midst of all this harmony: money. The older I got, the more I seemed to need; and regardless of the purpose, just broaching the subject was enough to make her testy. If I managed to convince her to part with a buck, she did so grudgingly, and it inevitably made her irritable and out of sorts. For example, when I asked her for $1.25 per week to cover the cost of laundering the dress shirts I had to wear to school every day, she angrily refused. A clean shirt every day was an outrageous extravagance for a fifteen-year-old boy. After a long, bitter negotiation she agreed to seventy-five cents for three shirts a week, but for the next month she complained whenever I asked for it.

In Warren, however, we didn't argue over money once. This miracle was wrought by Mother's scheme to teach me the value of money by paying me for my work. We had learned our lesson from the book-selling debacle, and this time we avoided all the pitfalls. I was written into Mother's contract, so there could be no last-minute problems with the union, and we had negotiated a deal that was satisfactory to both of us: in addition to my regular weekly allowance of five dollars, I got my own motel room on tour, thirty-five dollars a week for working as her dresser when the show was running, and half-salary for being available to run errands during rehearsal week. This was very good money for a teenager in 1960, especially as Mother paid all my expenses. And best of all, she never begrudged me a cent of it. In fact, on my first payday, she said I was "worth every penny," which was high praise indeed coming from her.

Eliminating the irritant of money was only one of the ways in which my job helped our relationship. When Mother worked, her sole interest was the success of her performance. Because I was helping her realize that goal, I had an important part to play in her life that she plainly appreciated and that I, consequently, filled proudly.

The result was a smoothly functioning partnership that we both enjoyed. On the trip from New York, for example, Mother asked if I would mind cueing her from the script instead of driving. I had been looking forward to the drive, but I knew it was more important that she learn her lines, so I didn't mind in the least, especially after having been asked rather than told. It was the same during rehearsals. Taking

Fu for a walk and getting her tea felt like contributions rather than chores because she never failed to acknowledge my help and let me know that she valued it. There was too little time and too much pressure for such amenities during the performances, but they weren't necessary then. I knew that what I was doing was important, and the work had its own, unique rewards. In order to make the changes in the one or two minutes available, Mother and I had to function like four hands connected to one mind. We rarely spoke; there simply was no time. I could hold a dress open behind her, and she would step into it not only without looking but without thinking while she was changing her wig or fixing her makeup. Cooperating that closely under such intense pressure and doing it perfectly — we never once missed a cue — was as exhilarating as anything I had ever done.

But I risk misrepresenting my character. I was neither a budding workaholic nor imbued with the work ethic. Although I enjoyed these nonmaterial rewards for my work, they were unexpected, came mostly after the fact, and hardly contributed to my motivation. My enthusiastic cooperation was prompted first of all by my salary and then, during rehearsals at least, by the possibility that Mother might help me attain my heart's desire: a driver's license.

In spite of the unique background in which I was raised, I shared with most other red-blooded American boys of my age a passion for cars and driving. Not driving with Mother next to me in the front seat either, but alone and free or with my arm wrapped around a sexy girl. Getting wheels and getting laid were my two obsessive desires.

Before coming to Warren, I had reconciled myself to a long wait for the wheels. I would have to be eighteen before I was old enough for a driver's license in New York City unless I took a special driver's education course, which would permit me to get one at seventeen, but even that seemed an eternity away when I was barely fifteen and a half. Then I arrived in Warren and saw all the apprentices, some of whom were only sixteen, driving. It seemed terribly unfair, until one of them told me how I could get a license of my own while I was there.

Now I knew that as a New York resident I had no business with an Ohio license and that because of my age it wouldn't be valid in New York City, but the dubious legality of it didn't bother me in the least. It would appear legal if I were stopped anywhere but in the city, and I was cocky enough to think I'd be able to convince a New York City cop that I was from out of town and had made an honest mistake. Just as long as I had the official-looking piece of paper.

I foresaw only one obstacle: Mother. Because I was a minor I had to get her written consent, and I knew she would find it all a bit fishy, especially as I was still too young for an actual license even in Ohio. I would have to get a learner's permit and take the road and written tests. If I passed them, the license would be mailed to me when I turned sixteen. In the meantime, I could drive with the learner's permit as long as I was accompanied by a licensed driver. At least, I thought, I would be legal — more or less — when I drove with Mother, and her insurance would cover us in case of an accident.

I stressed the insurance angle when I presented my case over dinner that night. It was the only argument that had any chance of success, but I really didn't expect it to work. Mother, however, surprised me.

"That's an excellent idea, Erik," she said. "But I don't understand why you want to bother with a learner's permit. You already know how to drive."

"I know. But that's all I can get now," I explained for the second time. "I'm not old enough yet for an actual license."

"Oh, that's absurd," she said with an impatient wave of her hand. "I'll go down with you after we open. I'm sure we'll be able to arrange something."

For the rest of the rehearsal week, I was careful to work hard, stay in her good graces, and avoid giving her any excuse to change her mind. Not that she ever threatened to do so. On the contrary, she had me drive to and from the theater every day and practice parallel parking whenever we passed a tight-looking spot so I'd be ready for my road test. I was as delighted as I was surprised by her enthusiastic support, but I was also very skeptical of her plan to have the authorities waive the state's age requirement for me, and I was even afraid that she might queer the whole deal just by asking. I didn't mention my doubts. Mother had no patience with negativism; often it was enough to put her off a project altogether, and I certainly didn't want that. Besides, I was already much closer to my goal than I ever had expected to get, and I figured I had nothing to lose.

Mother had not specified when after the opening she would take me for the license, but she didn't keep me dangling. The morning after opening night, she knocked on the connecting door between our rooms, stuck her head in, and said, "Well, think you're ready?"

"You bet," I said, jumping out of bed and reaching for my jeans.

"Whoa, not so fast. First, breakfast. Then we have to walk the dogs and get dressed. If I were you I'd wear my nice slacks and madras jacket. They make you look so handsome . . . and mature."

That was the first reference she had made to my age, and I had no idea of her plans, but I did as she suggested without question. I had seen her operate often enough to know that she had her ways and that they usually worked.

Warren was not large enough a town for a full-service branch of the Department of Motor Vehicles, but there was a testing station where driver's licenses were processed. It occupied a small, single-story brick building that was set to the side of a large parking lot. We arrived just before noon. It wasn't busy. The parking lot was almost empty, and only two cars were in the line reserved for drivers awaiting road tests. A uniformed examiner holding a clipboard stood next to a car parked in front of the building talking to the driver through his window. When he saw the Rolls pull into the lot, the examiner quickly pulled a form off the clipboard and shoved it at the driver, dismissing him. Then he walked over to the open door of the building and yelled inside, "Hey, Ray! Girls! Come and get a look at what just pulled into the lot."

Mother parked in the first vacant stall and began to touch up her lipstick, oblivious — or so it seemed — to the commotion that was brewing. Meanwhile, the examiner came over to my side of the car, patted the door, and said, "They sure don't build 'em like this anymore. What a beauty. What year is it anyway?" Then he looked inside the car for the first time and added, "Hey, the steering wheel's on the wrong side."

Before I could comment, he was pushed aside by a lean man in his late forties who was wearing slacks, a short-sleeved white shirt with a badge pinned to the pocket, and a tie.

"Fred," the new arrival said to the examiner, "if you'd read the newspaper once in a while you wouldn't keep making such a damn fool out of yourself. Now get out of my way." He leaned in my window and extended his hand across me to Mother. "Saw your picture in the paper this morning, Miss Lee, and it's an honor to meet you. My name's Ray Coombs. I'm in charge here. What can I do for you?"

"How do you do, Ray. You don't mind if I call you Ray, do you?" He beamed his answer as she shook his hand. "Call me Gypsy. I've brought my son down to get his driver's license." She nodded in my direction.

For the first time, he turned to me. "Howdy, son." Before I could respond, he was talking to Mother again. "Well, Gypsy . . ." He paused, trying on the familiarity like a new suit. "You sure came to the right place. Why don't we just go inside and let one of my girls get him started on the paperwork."

Mother opened her door, stuck one leg out, and waited while Ray hurried around the car to help her. She had dressed for the occasion in one of her meet-the-press outfits. This one consisted of an elegant Charles James sheath that was just tight enough to be sexy as well, a Mr. John hat, and a floor-length hemp stole that she flung dramatically around her neck when she got out of the car. A full makeup and one of the natural-looking wigs from the show to hide her singed hair completed the ensemble. She looked great, and not an eye wandered from her as she walked toward the building, and that included those of the people inside who were all crowded in the doorway watching us.

Ray officiously cleared a path for us and ushered Mother directly to the counter which divided the room in half. It was unattended, but two middle-aged women hurried back to their stations from the doorway. These, clearly, were Ray's "girls." He beckoned the older of the two. "Edna, this here is Gypsy Rose Lee. She's starring in that new show they got over at Kenley's. She's brought her son in to get his license, and I want you to take good care of her."

Turning to Mother, he continued, "Edna, here, will handle the paperwork for you, Gypsy. Then I'll take the boy out for his road test. We'll have him fixed up in no time. No time at all."

"Thank you, Ray. You're being very kind. But what about all these people who were here before us. Shouldn't we wait our turn?"

"Aww, these folks don't mind letting a famous star like yourself go ahead of them." Before any could contradict him, he added, "Especially as you won't mind giving them your autograph. Isn't that right? Why, I wouldn't mind having one myself."

"Of course. I'd be delighted. But first, let me get Erik started. Then I'll have plenty of time to sign anything you want." She turned to the woman behind the counter. "Now, Edna, what do you need from us?"

"Well, Mrs. Lee, let's start with your son's name."

"Oh, honey, call me Gypsy. All my friends do. It's Erik Lee Kirkland. That's Erik with a *k* . . ."

"Your address?" Quickly I supplied the street address of the motel. "Date of birth?"

"What?" Mother shrieked. "You can't be serious." She turned to the room and asked in mock indignation, "Can you believe they want to know when he was born? Only the doctor who delivered him knows that, and he's been sworn to secrecy. My God, if that ever got out it could ruin me." She turned back to Edna. "Just leave it blank."

"Oh, I have to put something in, Mrs. Lee," Edna said apologetically.

"Yes, I suppose you must. Let me see if I can remember. I know it was December eleventh. He never lets me forget his birthday. It's the year that gives me trouble." She smiled conspiratorially to Edna. "Just make him as young as possible."

"That would be sixteen."

"Why, that's perfect. That would mean he was born in . . ." She began to count backwards on her fingers.

"Nineteen forty-three," supplied Edna helpfully.

"Good God! Well, if you say so, put it down. Now, what's next?"

It may seem a bit curious that Mother took such a convoluted approach rather than simply lying about the year of my birth, but it was very much in character. She had a peculiar attitude toward the truth: she would bend it, obscure it, exaggerate it, or conceal it without the slightest compunction; but she'd tell a direct lie only if it was absolutely necessary. It was not a moral position but a superstitious one. She said that direct lies always came back to haunt her.

Once past the question of my age, Mother gradually turned her attention to Ray and the others in the office, signing autographs, making jokes, and plugging the show while I completed the rest of the form with Edna and took the eye and written tests. Ohio law stipulates that only the driver and the examiner can be in the car during the road test, but Ray made an exception in our case and let Mother sit in back. Needless to say, I passed. Ray was so busy talking to her that I could have run every stop sign along the route and still passed. Not that I minded. Less than an hour after Mother drove into the parking lot, I drove out with a real Ohio driver's license in my wallet, and that was all that mattered to me.

After Warren any summer stock engagement was bound to be a disappointment, and this was certainly true of Detroit, the second stop on our tour. The notices were good, and every performance sold out, which meant that Mother again earned a few thousand dollars over her guarantee, but the working conditions were terrible. The theater turned out to be a tent, the dressing rooms were trailers reached by a latticed metal catwalk that caught Mother's high heels, one part or another of the set fell apart during every performance, there was room backstage for only one quick-change cubicle, and the management couldn't have been less responsive. In short, we were back to reality.

For Mother, however, all the vexations of the two weeks were completely redeemed by one solitary event. I think she even considered it something of a miracle. She found a wife for Fu Manchu.

It happened by chance. One of the publicity photos that appeared in the local papers showed Fu in Mother's arms; a local breeder saw it and wrote Mother that she had rescued two Chinese Crested females from the pound a few years earlier and would be happy to give one to Mother in exchange for the pick of her first litter by Fu. Mother was ecstatic. She had been looking for a mate for Fu ever since she first got him, and now she had a choice of two.

The breeder brought them to the theater that Saturday after the matinee. Because she had found them at the pound, neither had papers or a known history, but both were definitely Chinese Cresteds. One was clearly younger than the other, trim and lean but with very little crest on her head and no fan on her tail at all. She was snippy, like Fu, and while it was difficult to judge points in such a rare — not to mention ugly — breed, her legs seemed much too long for her body.

The older dog was a walking disaster area. She was bandy-legged, blind in one eye from an old infection, and her tongue hung through a gap on the left side of her mouth where she was missing three teeth. These imperfections, however, were not likely to be inherited by her offspring, and she did seem to have good breeding points: her crest and fan were long and full, and she had a well-proportioned body. She also had a lovely personality. Mother claimed she was trying to compensate for her shortcomings. Whatever the cause, she was sweet tempered and had a pathetic charm that even I found endearing. Mother, of course, found it irresistible. She named her Chu-Chin-Chow after a line from the play.

Miami finished off the summer and almost finished us off as well. The heat and humidity hung over everything like a wet blanket, a hot wet blanket. Business was good, but the audiences were dead. Many members of the cast had left after Detroit because of previous commitments, and the replacements we picked up in Florida were mediocre and worse. And Mother and I had a disagreement on opening night that colored our relationship for the entire engagement.

Everything about opening night was a disaster. The theater was packed, but there was hardly a laugh, the applause was perfunctory, and even Mother's curtain speech laid an egg. Although her hair had grown and the burn healed, she still looked a sight when she removed the wig, but the audience hardly reacted. Then she went into some old standby routines, and they died too. I was watching from my usual spot in the wings with her comb, mirror, and Kleenex; and I could tell she was searching for something that would at least wake up the audience for the drive home; but whatever she tried, failed. Then she glanced into the wings, and I saw her notice me. It may have been instinct or the look in her eye, but I knew I was next, and I dreaded it. I wanted to hide, get away, anything to avoid what I sensed was coming, but I knew it was too late.

"Before I say goodnight, there's someone I want you to meet. He's been helping me backstage, and without him I never could have made it tonight. My very own Patrick. . . ." She waved me on. "Erik, come out here, darling, so all these nice people can get a look at you. . . ."

I did, numb with stage fright, a strained smile frozen on my face. Somehow I managed to kiss Mother on the cheek and walk off with her, arm in arm, but I don't remember it. In fact, I remember only being overwhelmed by a sense of abject terror.

I didn't connect them at the time, but once before Mother had brought me on stage in an attempt to salvage a difficult situation. That had been in 1952 when I was seven. She was playing the act for a month at the New China Theatre in Stockholm, Sweden, and because she had been billed and publicized as a hot and sexy American stripper, she wasn't drawing any women. Mother hated playing to stag audiences. They expected a sex show and inevitably felt cheated by her act. This was especially true in Sweden where they were used to seeing more at their mixed nude beaches than she showed on stage and, worse yet, where her humor was foreign even to the few who could understand English. They didn't even know the act was supposed to be funny. I can still remember the acute discomfort in her voice as she described looking from the stage at a sea of "bewildered, disappointed, leering faces."

After a miserable week of this, she decided on some desperate measures to change her image and, hopefully, her audience. To get some laughs, she hired a interpreter to translate her lines; to draw women, she devised a lottery in which I served as her assistant; and to spread the word, she invited all the local reviewers and columnists back to see the "new" show.

My memories of that night are fragmented. We chose my costume before leaving the hotel. Mother had bought me various national outfits on that trip — German lederhosen, Scotch kilts, a Dutch suit with wooden shoes, and more — but nothing from Sweden, so she decided I should wear my Norwegian sailor suit because "at least they're neighbors." There was a wire waiting for me when we arrived at the theater; it said, "Good luck on opening night. Love, Mother." Before the show, I sat on a folding chair with a fishbowl on my lap next to the ticket-taker. As the customers entered, he put one half of each ticket in the fishbowl and returned the other to the customer, telling him to hold it for a drawing at the end of the show. The customers were all men, and they looked at me quizzically as they passed. I felt very self-conscious. During the performance, I sat in an aisle seat close to the front of the house, still holding the fishbowl, ostensibly to convey the lottery's integrity but also to suggest to the newspapermen in the audience that there was nothing in the show a child — let alone a woman — shouldn't see.

I had seen the act many times, but this was the only time I ever felt uncomfortable. It wasn't the act, it was the men in the audience. I thought they were all staring at me, not openly, but slyly, out of the corners of their eyes. And to make it worse, the act took twice as long as usual because of the translation. In retrospect, it must have been funny, Mother pausing after every line while the interpreter, who stood at the edge of the stage wearing a dark brown business suit, repeated it deadpan in Swedish. However, at the time I was too involved in my own discomfort to notice, and the audience certainly didn't get it or anything else. There wasn't one laugh in the entire act.

I thought it would never end. Then Mother announced the drawing, called me on to the stage, and introduced me. I was almost frozen with fear. The lights were bright, and I was concentrating so hard on not making a mistake that I barely looked around me. Mother told me to draw two stubs out of the fishbowl. I did and handed them to her. She called out the seat numbers. There were a couple of grunts of acknowledgment from the audience. She didn't tell me to do anything, so I just stood on the stage, holding the fishbowl, while she autographed a couple of copies of the Swedish edition of *The G-String Murders* and presented them to the lucky winners. All this was done, of course, with the invaluable but prolonging help of the interpreter. Finally, this too came to an end, Mother put her hand on my shoulder, and we walked off the stage together.

After the show she was so effusive in her praise for my "performance" and in her enthusiasm for the routine that I couldn't bring myself to tell her how much I hated doing it. At seven, I simply didn't have the strength to confront her. Fortunately for me, all the newspapers were highly critical of my presence, and at the manager's insistence she dropped the routine before the next performance.

Although I didn't recall the incident on the opening night in Miami, I'm certain it affected my reaction both on stage and off. Why else the unreasonable feeling of dread at the prospect of a brief curtain call, the terror at facing the audience, or my almost hysterical anger at Mother when we reached the dressing room?

"Don't you ever do that to me again!" I screamed, literally shaking with fury.

"Lower your voice," she snapped back. "How dare you take that tone with me. Apologize this minute."

Mother's control immediately defused my rage but not my anger. I took a deep breath and said, "I'm sorry, but I can't stand being dragged out on stage like that."

"I didn't drag you out on stage. I brought you out for a little bow, that's all." She turned back to me. "Unzip me, would you please."

"Well I don't like it," I said, as I helped her.

"But it went over so well," she argued reasonably, "and it makes a perfect finale for the curtain speech."

"I don't care. I hated it, and I won't do it again."

She changed into her robe, sat facing the mirror with her back toward me, and began removing her makeup before she spoke again.

"I don't understand what you can possibly find so objectionable about taking a little bow, but if you refuse I certainly won't force you. . . . It seems such a shame, though. The audience so loved meeting you. . . ." Her voice trailed off in a tone of resigned disappointment.

I knew she expected me to give in. I wanted to, just to avoid the guilt I felt in disappointing her, but I also knew I couldn't do it. So, feeling guilty, I let the matter slide. To be fair, Mother never mentioned it again, but I felt — or imagined — her silent reproach after every performance. It cast a dismal shadow over the already unpleasant final two weeks of the tour, a tour that would turn out to be the last one Mother and I ever made together.

CHAPTER TWELVE

MOTHER came from a long line of strong, determined, resourceful pioneer women. She never told me a great deal about them, but there was one story she told time and time again, and always with great relish. It concerned her great-great-grandmother, the progenitor of the American branch of the family. With her brother, Louis, she emigrated from Norway and set out for the West Coast in a covered wagon. They made it as far as the Donner Pass in the Sierra Nevada mountains when their party was stranded by a freak, early blizzard.

"It must have been terrible," Mother would say. "Snow and wolves and no food. Most of the party died, but not Grandma." Here she'd remark proudly, "The women always have been the strong ones in our family." Although she never actually said it, Mother rarely missed an opportunity to imply that the men of the family had all been nice but also weak and ineffectual and therefore were unimportant in the overall scheme of things.

"Grandpa used to tell me how the scouts found her. She was dazed and her ears were frozen, but she looked so fat and healthy that they couldn't figure it out. By all rights she should have been damn near starved to death. Then they got her down to the nearest settlement where the local ladies undressed her, and you'll never believe what they found. . . . Steaks! Strapped all around her body.

"They figured it was horsemeat at first, then they noticed the tattoo. It was the Rock of Ages, just like the one Great-uncle Louis had on his hip. . . ."

While the truth in this, as in most of Mother's stories, was probably sacrificed for dramatic effect, she left no doubt that Grandma had eaten human flesh rather than starve, and she made it equally clear that she admired her for it. Not for the cannibalism per se, but for having the strength of will to survive while weaker souls, including her brother, perished. Of course, Mother knew that she had inherited that same indomitable spirit, and she credited it for much of her success in life. It certainly proved its worth after our return from Miami. During the following eighteen months, her life seemed to consist of an unending succession of problems, disappointments, and failures. It was as difficult a period as any she ever faced — her Donner Pass, so to speak — and she was sustained through it solely by her own tenacity and resolve.

This period of misfortune was ushered in by a letter from David Merrick that awaited Mother on our arrival home. In it he reported that *Gypsy* had no advance sale for the coming season, that box-office sales were way off, and that the show was no longer showing a profit. He offered to move the show to a smaller theater in an effort to reduce expenses and keep it running a third season but only if Mother and the other royalty participants would agree to waive 50 percent of their due. Otherwise, he would have to close the show immediately. It is an article of faith among theater people that a show should be kept running as long as possible if only to provide jobs for the cast, musicians, and stagehands. It was, in addition, an article of faith with Mother that 50 percent of something was better than 100 percent of nothing. Everyone, therefore, agreed, and the show was moved to the Imperial Theatre where business actually improved.

Mother and I went to see it in its new home, and she claimed to prefer the intimacy of the smaller theater. She made no such claim about the smaller royalty checks. Not only did they reduce her income to a fraction of what it had been just a year earlier, they were a constant reminder that time was running out. Soon the show would close. She had to find that elusive new career, or at least a way of earning a living.

The future was the most serious problem on Mother's mind that fall, but it was not the most immediate one — I moved into that spot after we had been home less than a week when the inevitable occurred: I took the Rolls from the garage without permission and was stopped by the police. Contrary to my expectations, I was unable to con the policeman into letting me go, and Mother had to collect me and the car from the Harlem Precinct Station at three o'clock in the morning. All things considered, she took it rather well. She ripped up my license, said, "That will be the end of that," and never mentioned the incident again. That, however, was probably because a far more serious incident came to light the very next day.

I had made myself scarce early in the morning and spent the day with a friend from school. When I came home, the house seemed deserted. Then I walked past the door leading through the solarium into the drawing room, and Mother called out to me.

"Erik, is that you?"

"Yes, Mother."

"Come in here. I've been waiting to talk to you." Her voice was low, measured, and ominous.

"What's the matter?" I asked. The lights were off, and she was sitting on the sofa smoking a cigarette in the wan light from the patio. The ashtray was filled with butts, and a cup half full of cold tea was on the Wellington table in front of her. Had her tone of voice not been enough to put me on my guard, the scene would have. We rarely used the drawing room except for entertaining and special occasions. Beautiful as it was, its marble floor, paintings, and antique furniture made it cold and formal, too much so for relaxing. It was, however, perfect for an inquisition.

"Sit down." She pointed to a straight-backed chair across the table from her. "I went to the bank today to get some papers from the vault. There's at least eight hundred dollars missing."

There was no question that I took it. Only she, Erica, and I had access to her safe-deposit box, and my record of stealing money from her went back to when I was five years old and had first been given permission to leave the house alone, provided I didn't cross any streets. That time I took twenty-five dollars out of her purse and blew it on toys at the corner newsstand. I don't remember how my crime was discovered, but I do recall showing her where I had hidden the toys in my clothes hamper and overhearing her tell Boyd how she had insisted the shop keeper take the toys back although they had been opened: "Whatever can he have been thinking of? Selling all those things to a five-year-old who walks in off the street with a fistful of cash. It's shocking! Simply shocking. I told him so, too." I was terribly embarrassed at the thought of Boyd and the shop keeper knowing about my crime, much more so than I was when Mother had Mike the neighborhood policeman stop by the house to have a talk with me. I figured he was used to criminals.

Neither my embarrassment nor the policeman's lecture had any lasting effect. I continued stealing. Usually I took only a five-, ten-, or twenty-dollar bill from her purse, but there were a few major heists. The first of these came when I was eleven. I was supposedly being tutored in French after school, but Mother always gave me a check for the teacher made out to "cash" — no doubt planning to deduct it as makeup or some such business expense from her income tax — so I'd cancel the tutorial, cash the check at the local drugstore, and spend the money on toys or hanging out at the coffee shop with my friends after school. I didn't like doing it. I even tried to stop by asking Mother to make the check out in my teacher's name, but she refused, and I found the temptation too great to resist. This went on for months until she tried to reach me during one of my lessons and discovered the truth. This time she had Bill Kirkland come and talk to me. He was nicer than the policeman but just as ineffectual.

A year later, when I was twelve, I made my biggest haul: sixteen hundred dollars that she had hidden in the étagère in her bedroom. I discovered the money long before I took it; even I found the amount intimidating. Then one weekend a friend from school who was staying over admitted that he occasionally stole money from his father's wallet, and I immediately enlisted him as an accomplice. We plotted all that night, and the next morning I took the money while Mother was making her breakfast tea. Because it was Sunday, we hired a taxi by the hour to facilitate finding stores that were open. The driver was very helpful, and we managed to spend over $700 on cameras, magic tricks, and toys. Then my friend arrived home with all his loot, his parents became suspicious and called Mother, and the jig was up. She did the talking this time. She told me that if it happened again she'd send me to the Wiltwyck School for Disturbed Children.

I knew the threat was hollow, but she also moved all the cash that she had hidden around the house to her safe-deposit box and began keeping only small sums in her purse, effectively limiting my thefts over the next year and a half to an occasional five-dollar bill, none of which she ever missed. It must have been that theft-free period that lulled her into thinking I had outgrown my light-fingered phase. At least, that is the only explanation that accounts for her giving me access to her safe-deposit box. It wasn't a test. That's what I suspected when I saw all the loose hundred-dollar bills at the bottom of it the first time she sent me to fetch her jewelry, and — devious child that I was — I ruled out the possibility by hiding a few of the bills in with her papers and waiting to see if she missed them. When she didn't, I took them; and for the next five months I helped myself to a hundred-dollar bill whenever the spirit moved me, provided it did so during banking hours.

I never understood why I stole from her, other than for the obvious reason of wanting the money, but I knew there was more to it, psychologically speaking, than greed. It was a compulsion. I didn't want to do it, I hated myself when I did do it, I knew I'd eventually be caught, and I was always sorry and embarrassed when I was, but I did it nonetheless. I used to have long internal dialogues over each theft, and they'd always end with my resolving not to take the money, but then I'd take it anyway. It was horrible. I literally had no control.

Then, suddenly, I stopped. There were no more forays to the safe-deposit box, no more lifted five-dollar bills from her purse; I even ignored the thousand dollars that I discovered behind one of the valances while washing her bedroom windows. I'm not sure exactly when the change occurred, nor how or why. I know only that at some point around the time of my release from the dormitory I began to feel it was demeaning to steal from her, and that was the end of it.

Almost. Still ahead lay the denouement of the safe-deposit box caper. I knew Mother would miss the money eventually, and I dreaded the inevitable confrontation. These had always been gut-wrenching affairs for me with tears of guilt and contrite pleas for forgiveness. As the period between the thefts and their discovery lengthened, however, my attitude toward my criminal career underwent a radical change. I began to view myself as the victim and to blame it all on her. Had she been less stingy, I reasoned, I never would have stolen from her. Or, once aware of my proclivity, she should have taken steps to remove temptation from my path. Or, she should have set a proper example. The last was my favorite. As most of the money I had stolen was cash that she had taken under the table to avoid having it taxed, it wasn't exactly honest money; and beyond that, she was pretty light-fingered herself. Nothing major, but the house was filled with "liberated" hotel silverware, ashtrays, and keys, and I was the only boarding student at Riverdale with "Mapes Hotel, Reno" on all my towels and sheets. I didn't object to her stealing, only to her hypocrisy in making me feel guilty about mine. It made me angry. In retrospect I realize that this was simply the most convenient peg on which I could hang all my generalized adolescent resentments, and had we not had our confrontation over my stealing we would have had it over something else. But stealing was the peg I used, and the longer it took her to confront me over my final crime, the more my resentment built; and when the ax finally fell, when she finally announced that she'd been to the safe-deposit box and discovered the eight hundred dollars to be missing, the reaction she got from me was not at all what she had gotten in the past.

At first, I didn't say a word. I sat and waited, willing my anger to build and with it the strength I knew I'd need to stand up to her.

"And you've been stealing my liquor as well," she added. "I've been through the liquor closet. There are two bottles of Jack Daniel's missing, one of vodka, and all my gin."

That, too, was true. My friends and I always helped ourselves to the booze, but I no more considered that stealing than helping myself to milk out of the refrigerator. Still, I didn't know quite what to say, so I remained silent.

Finally, after a long pause, she could take it no longer.

"Well, what do you have to say for yourself? And don't try to deny it. I'm in no mood for lies."

"Why should I deny it?" I said nonchalantly, trying to bait her into losing her temper. I was itching for a fight, but I wanted her to start it. "I took the money last winter, I haven't taken any since then, and I won't take any again."

She was not so easily manipulated. Her hand shook as she lit a cigarette, but when she answered her voice was steady and her attitude reasonable. "Quite frankly, Erik, I'm at a loss. It isn't as though this is an isolated incident, as you well know. We've been down this road time and time again since you were a little boy, and nothing I do seems to help. Bill's talked to you, Mike the cop's talked to you, God knows I've talked to you till I'm blue in the face. . . . I've tried being lenient and understanding in the hope this was just a passing phase, but clearly it isn't, and I don't know what to do next. I just don't know."

"I don't think you have to do anything," I said honestly, trying to be as reasonable as she. "As I said a moment ago, I haven't taken anything since last winter, and I think the problem's over."

"I've heard that once too often to believe it again," she said sharply. "No. This has gone on entirely too long for me to ignore it any longer. Something must be done."

Her arrogance in dismissing what I had said and honestly believed pushed me over the edge. "Has it ever occurred to you that you might be the problem?" I said, my voice rising in tone and volume with every word. "If you weren't so goddamn stingy —"

"Stop right there," she interrupted. "I will not tolerate that kind of language coming from you, nor that tone of voice. Is that clear?"

"I'm sorry," I said quickly, desperately trying to hang on to my momentum. "But if you weren't so stingy with me, I never would have taken the money in the first place."

"I really don't see how you can accuse me of being stingy with you. I send you to the best schools, you have a lovely room, full of beautiful things, a television set all your own. My God! Most boys your age would consider themselves damn lucky to have one-tenth of what you have."

Other times that argument, and its logic, would have stopped me, but not that day. "Sure you send me to the best schools, in hand-me-down clothes. Do you have any idea of how embarrassing that is? The poorest kids at Riverdale dress better than I do."

"I don't believe that for one moment. Why, I've spent enormous sums of money outfitting you for school. Far more than I can afford, let me assure you."

"How can you say that? Look at how we live." Once again my voice rose, and I embraced the room with an angry wave of my arm. "Look at this room. Do you really expect me to believe that we can afford all this, a Rolls-Royce in the garage across the street, and closets full of clothes for you but not a couple of lousy sport jackets for me to wear to school?! Come on."

This time she didn't tell me to lower my voice, but she lowered hers, and I knew she was getting angry. "You may believe whatever you wish. As I've explained to you many times, this house, the Rolls, and my clothes are all part of the way I earn my living. People expect me to dress and live in a certain way. It's part of my image."

"That's just your excuse for spending money on what you want but not on what I want."

"I don't have to excuse myself to you or anyone else. It's my money, I earned it, and I'll spend it anyway I goddamn well please."

"And what about all that cr—— stuff you're always giving me about there being only the two of us and how we have to pull together? Or does that work only one way? You say you earned it. Well, I helped. You've always made damn sure of that."

"And you've helped spend it, young man. A damn sight more than you've earned, too, let me assure you." She spat the words at me. I could feel the bitterness behind each one, and it made me suddenly and unavoidably aware that she resented every dollar I had ever cost her. It wasn't a surprise, but it was an unpleasant shock, like the arrival of a long expected and much dreaded telegram. I had often suspected that Mother cared more for her money than for me, and this proved it to me. My body went rigid and my stomach felt as if it had turned to stone. I couldn't answer for a while; I could barely think. There seemed no reason to continue. I had used all my best shots, and they had failed. Yet I had to keep going, even though I knew the best I could manage would be feeble and weak.

"This may come as a shock to you, but most parents don't expect their children to earn anything. Most parents consider it their children's job to go to school."

"Attending school is a privilege, not a job. And if you were to start treating it as such, your grades might show a much-needed improvement."

"My grades might show an improvement if you'd leave me alone to do some homework once in a while. As soon as I sit at my desk you're yelling down to me, 'Erik, make me a pot of tea,' or 'Erik, do this,' or 'Erik, do that.' I feel like an unpaid servant most of the time."

"You're paid damn well when you work for me, and you know it. But never mind. This is getting us nowhere. Evidently you are unhappy with the way I've been treating you, and I must say I don't much care for the way you've been treating me. This is hardly my idea of a family. . . ."

"Family?!" I shrieked, almost out of control. "We've never had a family. Families are supposed to love each other, and there's no love here. I can't even remember the last time we hugged or kissed good-night."

"Well you can hardly blame me for that. You never were a demonstrative little boy." She paused, but I couldn't answer. I was wrung dry.

"As I was saying," she continued, "you are clearly unhappy living here, and I'm not happy having you around. I haven't the time or the energy to keep constant watch over you, and I certainly can't trust you, so I've decided to send you back to the dormitory when school starts next month. They are used to dealing with boys your age; perhaps they can succeed where I've failed. In the meantime, I'll arrange for you to take your meals separately, and we'll see each other as little as possible."

That came as a nasty shock. She was going to wipe me out of her life completely and, even worse, send me back to the dorm where I wouldn't be able to smoke and I'd have to put up with all the creeps.

"No," I said, with barely a thought. "I won't go back to the dorm."

"You'll do as you're told, and that's all there is to it. Now I don't wish to discuss it any further."

"I won't go back to the dorm, and that's final."

"We'll see about that."

"We certainly will!" I said, stomping out of the room.

On my way upstairs, I decided I would run away rather than return to the dorm, and when I was back in my room I immediately pulled my Vuitton suitcase out from under my bed and began packing. I didn't know where I'd go, but I figured a cheap hotel would do until I got a job and an apartment. Money wouldn't be a problem. When Mother returned to her room, I'd go upstairs, announce my departure, and take the thousand dollars she had hidden behind the valance. It never occurred to me that she could stop me, either physically or legally.

Before I had finished packing, she buzzed me on the intercom and summoned me back downstairs.

"I've been thinking about this dorm business," she began as I entered. "I don't want you to think of it as a punishment."

I've never understood exactly what she meant, but it clearly was an out, and I grabbed it. "How else can I think of it?"

"Seeing how much you dislike being around me, you could consider it a favor."

"You may not be the most pleasant person to live with, but living at home is still a lot nicer than living in the dorm." I had chosen my words knowing they would hurt, and she winced as I spoke, but it gave me no satisfaction. Actually, it made me feel like a heel.

"Well, I'll leave it up to you. I won't force you to live there."

"Fine. Then I'll stay here."

"As you wish. Go back to your room now, please. I want to be alone."

Part of me wanted to hug her, apologize for everything, and tell her that I loved her; but the other part won, so I just went upstairs and unpacked.

The atmosphere around the house was a little tense for the next few days; then Mother was given an opportunity to try out *Curious Evening* on a New York audience beginning October 17, which was only eight weeks away, and the tensions between us were immediately drowned by the greater tensions that accompanied getting ready on time.

Curious Evening had been lurking in the back of Mother's mind, part specter/part savior, ever since our return from Europe. It was the closest she had come to replacing the act. With it she could play a few weeks on the lecture circuit, in regional theaters, or even in small nightclubs whenever she needed to earn some money. It would never command the salary of the act, but it would afford her a similar measure of independence, and she saw it as a nice professional annuity for her old age. Provided, of course, that she could get it to work, and this is what haunted her: Although she had already invested thousands of dollars and months of her time trying one version after another, she had never gotten it quite right. Even the exact nature of the problem eluded her, so while she had shot lots of new footage in Europe and since our return and had devised another fresh approach for the whole film, she wasn't at all sure that the new version would work any better than the old ones. But there were no paying jobs in the offing, and when she was offered free use of the Cherry Lane Theatre in Greenwich Village on five consecutive Mondays, it seemed like a golden opportunity. She put the blackout curtains back on the dining room windows, set up the editing equipment, and went to work.

Mother's fresh approach called for turning the film into a newsreel-style documentary of her life and times by combining her footage with bits and pieces of old newsreels and structuring it all chronologically around newsreel-style title cards. It was an enormous job. First, she had to find appropriate and funny film clips; this took days of wading through thousands of feet of old newsreel footage at various film libraries around town. Then these clips, her recent footage, and her original film had to be combined and reedited into chronological sequence. Humorous title cards had to be written, designed, filmed, and inserted. And, finally, a new soundtrack had to be made and recorded. But that only took care of the film. She also had to write a new script for the narration, and because she wanted a pianist to play silent-movie-style music before and during the performance to further emphasize the nostalgic theme of the show, a composer had to be found and supervised.

Mother excelled at working hard under pressure, but with less than eight weeks from the time she was offered the theater until the first performance, even she had to bring in outside help. It was expensive but worth it; some of the people she found were very talented and made invaluable contributions to the project. Donn Pennebaker, who became famous later in the sixties for his rock music film *Monterey Pop* and other documentaries, worked with her on the editing and greatly improved the pacing of the film. Stan Vanderbeek whom she hired to make the title cards also eliminated many static shots by animating the stills she used from her scrapbooks. Gene Wood helped her with the script, and Sam Pottle composed the score.

At first, no doubt remembering our argument, Mother carefully inquired about the status of my homework before putting me to work, but that didn't last long. It was my job to rerecord the sound track on those sections that had been reedited, so the further we got into the film, the more work there was for me to do. It was fine with me. I much preferred being a part of the action to doing schoolwork. Dates were something else, but Mother understood this and, until the very end, let me off on Saturday nights to go out. Still, it was the only time she ever gave me a curfew. I had to be home by midnight to go back to work.

For all the outside help, *Curious Evening* remained unquestionably Mother's creation. Nothing went into it without her specific approval, and almost everything except for the score — writing music was one of the few things she couldn't do — had her fingerprints on it as well. That she managed to do so much was a triumph of will over substance. I had often seen her drive herself beyond sensible or even believable limits, but never as hard as this. She practically lived in the dining room, leaving it only to visit film libraries or to go to her room for a brief nap when she could no longer focus her eyes. For seven weeks she never took a whole night off to sleep. Often she worked for thirty or so hours straight, collapsed for four or six, and then worked another thirty. The deadline was only partially responsible for this determined effort. There was also a distinct measure of desperation behind it. *Curious Evening* was all she had for the future, it had to work, and by-God-come-hell-or-high-water she was going to make it work!

Given the pressure, it should have been pretty grim around the house, but it wasn't. Occasionally Mother would lose her temper when something went wrong, then everyone would get tense and be on edge for a while, but there was an overriding sense of excitement in the air, like being in a war room at the height of battle, and we were all caught up in it. Mother was responsible for this too. Her enthusiasm was inspiring, and she made us feel not simply a part of something important, but a vital part of it. The entire household was affected. Esther, who normally complained if she wasn't out the door by seven, often manned the kitchen until midnight making food and tea. Erica, unasked, came in on her days off to type editing notes and draft scripts. Only Boyd, who had a real, paying job at the time, was not pressed into regular service, but every night when he came home from work he'd check with Mother to see if she needed any help.

There were even occasional moments of gaiety, such as the one which occurred at three o'clock one morning when we were dubbing the sound over a clip of a particularly silly production number from one of Mother's first Hollywood films. We must have watched and listened to this particular piece of film twenty times in the course of trying to synchronize the sound to the picture, and we were giddy from the repetition on top of too little sleep and too much tea and Coke. Suddenly in the middle of the twenty-first attempt, Mother leaped out of her chair and began to mimic herself on the screen, complete with the song and the dance. What a sight she was in her ratty housedress with an old scarf around her hair, dancing all over the room and singing at the top of her lungs. And poor Boyd. His bedroom was right under the dining room, so of course it woke him up. He arrived upstairs just as Mother was finishing her dance and said that from downstairs it sounded as if someone was being murdered.

"Well," Mother mugged, "I've had my singing criticized before, but never so rudely! And never by a half-naked man in a bathrobe . . ."

You probably had to be there, exhausted, to fully appreciate it, but we all laughed until tears ran down our faces.

In spite of the size of the job, I assumed that we would finish in time for the first performance. Mother never missed a deadline, and in the beginning we moved right along. By the first of October we already had a rough cut through to the end, complete with the new title cards and footage. It was too long, many of the transitions were sloppy, the sound was uneven, and Mother had a one-page list of changes that she wanted to make, but while this amounted to a lot of work, it seemed a not impossible task.

From that point on, however, we stopped progressing. We continued working, God knows, and we actually accomplished a great deal, but for every cut Mother found, she found something else to add, for every problem solved, another cropped up. Whenever we finished with all the changes on her list, we'd screen the film and she'd write up a new one. It was endless, day after day, night after night, looking at virtually the same film over and over again. I thought the boredom would drive me crazy after a while. Only the certain knowledge that it would have to end by opening day kept me going.

I was wrong, of course, all wrong, but I didn't discover it until the early morning hours of Friday the fourteenth. Donn Pennebaker, Gene Wood, Mother, and I were in the dining room. We had just finished one of our periodic screenings of the film. As I returned to my seat after turning on the lights, Mother held her stopwatch out to me.

"Darling, would you please read this for me," she asked, "I've slopped so goddamn much tea on my glasses I can't see through them, and I just haven't the energy left to wipe them off."

At home Mother kept her glasses on a cord around her neck so they were always convenient; inconveniently, they acted something like a napkin and were often covered with crumbs, ashes, and tea. Usually this was good for a laugh, but we had all been working since the previous morning so nothing was funny.

"Two hours, twenty-two minutes," I read off the watch and handed it back to her. We didn't really need to know the exact length to know the film was still too long. The sound, too, left much to be desired; and Mother's list was either two or three pages long, I couldn't tell which. Mother, herself, was in even worse shape. She looked awful: no makeup, her hair a matted rat's nest held atop her head by a soiled bandanna, dirty and wrinkled clothing, but above all tired. So tired. Less than four days to opening, and sometime in there she'd have to sleep. What would she do? I wondered. What could she do?

"Well, boys," she announced, "as far as I'm concerned that's it. It's a little long, to say the least, but even so it's pretty damn good, if I do say so myself, and it'll sure as hell see us through the first show, which is a damn sight more than I'll be able to do unless I rest and get rid of these bags under my eyes. So, unless one of you saw something so glaring that it absolutely must be fixed . . ." She looked to each of us. ". . . Then I suggest we take the weekend off, see how it goes Monday night, and meet back here bright and early Tuesday morning, clear-headed and ready to go to work."

Neither Donn nor Gene said a word, but desperation got the better of me. "But . . ." I sputtered, "how can you show it like this? It isn't finished. We've gone this far, shouldn't we keep going and get it over with?"

"I just finished explaining, Erik, that I must have some rest," Mother answered with a slight edge to her voice at having to repeat herself. "And looking at the bags under your eyes it wouldn't do you a bit of harm either. Besides, the object isn't to get it over with, it's to end up with something we can earn a living with. We can't possibly finish it now, anyway. There are bound to be any number of changes that we'll want to make after we see it with an audience. At least, let's hope so. After all, that's the whole purpose of these five weeks, isn't it."

"I guess so," I mumbled, smothered by equal measures of embarrassment and disappointment. The former for having missed the obvious, the latter at the thought of having to endure the boredom of working on the film for another week and probably longer.

A lot longer as it turned out, and the tedium was even worse than I had expected. It was excruciating. Mother gave five Monday-night performances at the Cherry Lane Theatre. After each, we spent the rest of the week reediting the film. The worst part was the repetition. One week we'd take shots out because they didn't get a laugh, the next week we'd put them back in because Mother felt they had been missed. The only tangible accomplishment of all the editing was to cut forty minutes out of the film; the rest was all fiddling. We'd trim a little here, and a little there, move this scene, change that shot for another one, and through it all we had to keep screening the film over and over again to see how the changes worked. Rather, for Mother to see how the changes worked. I couldn't tell. I hated every frame from first to last. So much, in fact, that I looked forward to going to school, which I got to do every weekday except Mondays when I had to help set up for the night's performance.

Mother had no such respites. Aside from Sunday nights when she forced herself to stop work early and rest for the next day's performance, she continued to work nonstop. I couldn't understand how she managed to keep going, let alone retain any sense of objectivity. For Mother, desperation was a hard taskmaster. Eventually the strain took its toll. Minutes before the third performance, she had an ulcer attack, and we had to hold the curtain while I ran to a drugstore for some Maalox.

Her ulcer kept churning away for the rest of the engagement. She blamed it on the hard work and the long hours with too much tea and too many cigarettes. I'm sure they contributed, but I suspect her stomach would have forgiven all if the audiences had responded differently to the show. More than anything else, Mother saw these five performances as an opportunity to measure *Curious Evening*'s potential. Had the customers stood on their seats and cheered, she would have been delighted. Even if they had walked out in droves she would have had her answer. Instead, the response was muted. The laughs were there but controlled. The applause was more than polite but less than enthusiastic. Only the comments from those who approached her during intermission and after the show were unquestionably positive. Mother was too old a hand to judge by them alone, yet she couldn't disregard them either. The ambiguity was terribly frustrating for her. As she scribbled in her date book after the last show: "Well — I've invested thousands more in the film, spent three months working and reworking it, my ulcer's pumping away, and I'm not sure I *have* a property."

It was hardly an encouraging note on which to end the year.

CHAPTER THIRTEEN

MOTHER spent New Year's Eve on a cruise ship headed for Puerto Rico. She wasn't on vacation. She was going to San Juan to play two weeks in *Auntie Mame,* and she took the boat because she hated flying and avoided it whenever possible. I was not with her — she had decided that I had already missed enough school for the year — but I know from a letter she wrote me that she was unable to find "one lousy, friggin' grape, let alone twelve" on the ship and consequently had to ring in the new year with twelve raisins. It was not an auspicious omen for 1961, but it turned out to be an accurate one.

For starters, the Puerto Rican engagement was a complete fiasco. On opening night, four thousand protesters claiming to represent the local actors' union picketed the theater because the entire cast had been imported from the mainland. It was not an orderly demonstration. They chanted "Yankee go home!" so loudly throughout the performance that the audience could barely hear the actors. Later that night, after everyone had gone home, the theater was firebombed, ruining the sets. The following night, the show went on amid the charred and soggy scenery. Again there were pickets and chanting. There was also a rock thrown through the window of Mother's dressing room that missed her by inches, and she needed a police escort to get through the pickets after the show.

As if that wasn't bad enough a start to her new year, a long-distance problem with me cropped up the next day. We had fought, before she left, over where I would stay during her absence. I desperately wanted to stay at home. One of my misfit friends from school had recently fixed me up with a blind date who turned out to be very nice, very intelligent, and very pretty, with a pale Irish skin, green eyes, a few freckles, and an irresistible figure. The attraction between us was immediate and mutual, and I sensed the possibility of losing my virginity. Success, however, would not be easy. If it came at all, it would require a gentle seduction in a romantic atmosphere safe from interruption, which is exactly what I'd have at home while Mother was away.

Mother knew none of this, but she did know that fifteen was not an age when boys — her boy, anyway — should be left without supervision, and she insisted that I stay at Riverdale. I argued, pleaded, whined, and sulked, but she prevailed, and I moved into the dorm the day before she left for Puerto Rico.

What followed was typical of my behavior over the next few years. I would do anything to get my way. If persuasion didn't work, I'd fight. When that failed, and with Mother it usually did, I'd turn sneaky. I twisted words, wiggled through loopholes in the rules, or disregarded them altogether. Sometimes I was found out; then Mother would lecture me, and I'd revert to my best behavior for a while. Most of the time, I got away scot-free. Either way, I usually ended up with what I wanted, and I considered myself quite a master at getting my way.

In this instance, we hadn't discussed my going home on the weekends. She hadn't felt it necessary to specify the obvious, and I had deliberately not asked because I knew she would forbid it. I succeeded in getting away with the first weekend, when she was aboard ship, although I failed to lose my virginity. On the second Sunday, however, the San Juan newspapers ran banner headlines about "riots" at the theater, and she called me at the dorm to let me know that she was all right, just in case the story had been picked up by the New York papers. The dorm master told her that I had gone home for the weekend. I was too busy to answer the phone — at long last — so after a few tries she called Boyd and left word with him for me to call her. This was before the days of direct-dial; she had to place each of these calls through an operator and then wait from fifteen minutes to an hour to get through or learn that there was no answer. By the time I received her message and got back to her, she had spent the entire day in her hotel room waiting by the phone and was almost incoherent with anger. Then I reacted to her "how dare you disobey me" routine by superciliously pointing out that I hadn't actually disobeyed her because we hadn't discussed the weekends and added that she was getting upset over nothing because I was returning to the dorm as soon as I got off the phone with her. The combination of my effrontery, her frustration of being too far away to do anything about it, her anger at having spent the day waiting by the phone, and her concern over the problems at the theater had exhausted her patience. Wearily she dismissed me with "Oh, I don't care what you do anymore," and hung up the phone. It was an unfortunate choice of words.

That night, the demonstrators blockaded the theater. The police kept a narrow path open, and the actors got through, but most of the customers went home rather than run a gauntlet. Many of the stagehands joined the demonstrators, and some of those who remained on the job were sympathetic to their cause. Thus Mother not only played to a virtually empty house, but props and furniture were missing or misplaced, and at one point a curtain actually fell from the flies during a scene, landing on Mother and a few other members of the cast. No one was hurt, but the warning was unmistakable. After the performance, the producer called the cast together and announced that he was closing the show "in order to prevent violence." Privately he explained to Mother that there wasn't enough money to pay her full salary and that of the cast; she settled for one-third, her hotel bill, and a boat ticket home.

But she was even to be denied the relaxation of the cruise home. When she returned to the hotel, she found an urgent message to call the headmaster of my school. After the usually delay, which must have seemed interminable at three o'clock in the morning, she reached him and learned that I had phoned the dorm master that evening, told him that I wouldn't be returning to the dormitory as my mother "no longer cared" if I stayed there while she was away, and hung up without giving him an opportunity to object. Since then there had been no answer at the house, and they weren't quite sure what to do. Nothing like this had happened before.

Mother covered for me because she thought I might be expelled, but she was so upset by the news that she canceled her boat reservation and caught the first plane home in the morning. It wasn't what I had done that bothered her as much as it was that I had wantonly disobeyed her. Aside from the stealing, she had never had much trouble with me as a child. Overall I had been obedient, polite, and well behaved, especially in her presence. I certainly had never flouted her authority so blatantly. And it was all the more alarming seen alongside my arrest for driving without a license and my impenitence for the theft from the safe-deposit box. She saw a pattern developing, and it frightened her.

I learned all this that Monday after I got home from school and discovered that she'd returned from Puerto Rico. I had no idea that she was back until I saw her luggage piled in the foyer. Caught completely off guard, I walked slowly up the stairs to her room, steeling myself with every step for the pitched battle I was sure would follow. As she did so often, however, Mother surprised me. There was no scolding, no yelling, and no blame. She greeting me warmly, had me sit down, patiently explained her fears, and then asked me for suggestions.

Her quandary was sincere. She had always maintained discipline through the authority inherent in her personality, not just with me but with everyone. Her manner left no room for insubordination, so she rarely encountered it. On those occasions when someone stepped out of line, a sharp word from her was enough to nip the rebellion in the bud. Suddenly she was faced with a full-fledged mutiny from the person closest to her in the world, from the one person who *owed* her obedience, and she didn't know how to deal with it.

I was no help. I pointed out that the whole unpleasant incident wouldn't have happened if she hadn't insisted I move into the dormitory in the first place. She dismissed this notion out of hand. Although she didn't say so, she wasn't really interested in avoiding unpleasant incidents per se. She wanted to reestablish her authority and her ability to bend me to her will. Therein lay the insoluble core of our problem, because I was determined to resist any authority — and hers especially — at all costs. I felt my identity depended on it.

For want of a solution, she decided to let the matter slide in the hope that I was simply going through a phase which would pass of its own accord. It didn't. Less than a month later, my next peccadillo came to light.

Once again, my Ohio driver's license was involved. Her ripping it up had not been the end of it. The next day I had phoned the Ohio Bureau of Motor Vehicles and explained to the clerk who answered the phone that I was on vacation in New York and had lost my license. I asked him to rush me a duplicate, and while I was giving him my vital statistics I took a chance and added two more years to my age. The new license arrived less than a week later. It showed me to be eighteen years old, old enough to drink and drive anywhere in New York State.

A license without wheels is pretty useless, so next I talked a friend into investing all his savings in a clunker that we could use for double dates, commuting to school, and teaching him how to drive. It was to be his car, but I'd have to do all the driving, until he was old enough to get a license anyway. Convincing him was the easy part. Doing it required weeks of running around after school. I had to get a New

York license, using my Ohio license as proof of age. We had to find a car that he liked and could afford. Then it had to be inspected, we had to get insurance, and the car had to be registered. Finally we had the license plates in hand and were all set to collect the car the next day when I had second thoughts. I could have told my friend that the deal was off, but that didn't occur to me. Instead I went to Mother and made a full confession. I'm not sure what came over me. I was probably making a subconscious plea for help. All I remember feeling at the time was fear that I was getting into something way over my head.

This escapade really scared Mother. In her diary she characterized the problem as "grave," and she turned for advice to her friend and lawyer of twenty-five years, Bill Fitelson. He suggested a psychiatrist. Mother saw the doctor and made an appointment for him to evaluate me, but she didn't care much for the idea. She considered my problem one of discipline, not emotional instability. I was too young to be neurotic. In addition, she was more than slightly suspicious of the entire profession.

"I went to see a psychiatrist once, you know," she said when she told me of my appointment, "just to see what it was like. He told me there was no point in my coming back because I didn't need it. I only hope this man is as honest with you."

What she really hoped was that he'd suggest another solution. A more traditional one perhaps, like military school. Certainly a cheaper one. He didn't. After a series of tests, he pronounced me "troubled" and recommended five sessions a week, indefinitely, at thirty-five dollars each. Mother wouldn't hear of it. They compromised at three sessions a week, but she still wasn't happy.

Mother would have found parting with so much money difficult in the best of times, but this was among her worst. *Gypsy* had closed at the end of March, and the road company was, for some inexplicable reason, doing no business at all. Her only income for the year, other than the $1500 from Puerto Rico, had been the $10,000 annual installment from the sale of *Gypsy*'s motion picture rights, and that was long gone.

It would be an understatement to characterize her as anxious over her financial position, but terrified would be a bit strong. When we went over my clothing budget earlier in the year, for example, she became so upset over my request for six pair of underpants that she stormed down to my room and inspected those in my drawers to see if they were as worn as I had claimed. She found two pair that were "perfectly serviceable" and then agreed to buy me only one new pair. When I argued that I couldn't very well make it from one laundry day to the next on only three pair of underpants, she told me that if Harry Truman could find time as President of the United States to rinse out his socks and underwear every night, so could I.

In retrospect, it is funny. At the time, the absurdity of such economies distracted me from the legitimate and real fears that prompted them. Like the little boy who cried wolf, she had cried poverty so often that I no longer believed her. Thus I failed to understand or appreciate the sacrifice she thought she was making in sending me to the psychiatrist. She, in turn, felt I took her for granted and treated her "like a dollar sign and not a person at all." It did not make for a good time between us. It would get still worse.

There was one bright spot in Mother's life in the middle of all this: Chu-Chin-Chow had puppies. Of course, none of Mother's animals simply gave birth, that would have been too easy. Chu's puppies had to be delivered by Cesarean section, and the hysteria involved in getting her to the vet was worthy of a Mack Sennett comedy. Nevertheless, she had five healthy puppies. Three had hair, which was not unusual for the breed; Mother quickly found homes for them. Of the two hairless ones, there was a male who looked just like the father; Mother sent him to the woman in Detroit who had given her Chu. That left a predominately pink bitch that Mother fell in love with the moment she saw her. She named her China Doll and made her a permanent member of our animal family.

That was the highpoint of Mother's year. Misfortune was the rule during this period of her life. Just about everything that could go wrong, did. That she held herself together through it all is testimony to her extraordinary determination and strength of character. Many in her position, confronted with one problem after another in their private and professional lives, turn to booze or drugs, have nervous breakdowns, or just let themselves drift into depression and give up. Mother's grip on herself never weakened. At worst, it slipped a little from time to time, as it did the night Julio came to the house to see *Curious Evening*.

First, a few words about Julio. He was Mother's last, and by far her favorite, ex-husband. Born and raised in Spain, he looked as if he had stepped off a canvas by Goya or El Greco. Tall, dark, and sinewy, he wore his long hair combed straight back and had a gaunt face with strong features, lots of creases, and an intense, brooding expression that contrasted sharply with his flamboyant personality.

His first love was his art. He was a hardworking, dedicated, and prolific painter. Although unquestionably of the modern school, he hated labels and like most painters experimented with different styles and techniques. When he married Mother, he was painting animal studies. Later he went through an abstract period unfortunately reminiscent of Miró, but after that he did the finest collection of his career: seventy canvases of different sizes depicting the destruction of the Spanish armada. All his work was marked by dramatic, unique, and often subtle colors. The unusual oranges and yellows and reds that he used for the burning ships of the armada against the night sky are vivid in my memory today, over twenty years after I saw the paintings. He was undeniably talented, but while he managed to support himself with his art and was represented in the collections of the nation's important modern art museums — no mean accomplishments — he never caught the public's fancy.

He must have been disappointed by his mediocre success, but he never allowed himself to become embittered by it. He had a gusto for life, an embracing warmth, and an ability to transform the ordinary into the magical that made him one of the most wonderful, captivating people I have ever known.

Mother used to tell a story about their honeymoon that was typical of him. They spent it driving to Florida, living out of the house trailer that Mother owned at the time. She had spruced it up for the occasion and, among other improvements, had installed new beige carpeting. On their second morning out, she made her usual thermos full of coffee to drink in the car, only neither of them remembered to take if off the kitchen table. Of course, the bobbing of the trailer knocked it onto the floor, where it broke wide open. When they stopped for lunch, Mother saw the stain on her pretty new carpet and had a fit. Julio looked at it for a few minutes and said, approvingly, "It's a nice design." So it was. The motion of the trailer had not only made it spread lengthwise, it had also made it branch out. Julio outlined the stain with a marking pen, then he bought some dye and drew a triple-faced creature in one part of the stain and made the branches into arms and legs. For added color, he used Mother's lipstick to draw a fish in one corner and an eye in the other. Mother said it was probably the most beautiful carpet in any trailer on the way to Florida.

As a young child, I adored him. He used to cut my hair and then reward me for sitting still by drawing a tattoo on the back of my hand with his colored pencils. I used to keep the hand out of water for days. For my fourth birthday party, he painted huge murals of cowboys and

Indians on kraft paper and covered the dining room walls with them. I had not yet learned to read, so whenever we were apart he would send me "letters" in the form of watercolors depicting what he was doing. Mother framed them; they hang in my office today.

When he lived with us, everything was a major production. I'll never forget morning coffee. He insisted on special beans from a little shop in Chelsea, hand ground in a grinder he had brought from Spain, and then brewed in a special flannel sleeve. He didn't do all this because he was fussy. He wasn't trying for the perfect or the precise, not even necessarily for the best, just for the most enjoyable.

Dinner was an exciting, festive ceremony every night. Julio was the chef. He created elaborate meals with great fanfare and shouting and laughter: paella in a pan so large it covered all four burners on the stove, roast suckling pig complete with the apple, and calamari prepared in its own ink were just a few of his more memorable specialties. Mother was his assistant. She did all the chopping and preparation. He put it together and made it special.

It is hard to picture Mother accepting a secondary role, but Julio was a Latin man with a decidedly Latin view of a woman's place, not only in the kitchen but everywhere, and she went along with it because she loved him. That she loved him is beyond question; the reasons are less certain. I was six when they separated, so my memories of their marriage are fragmentary, and Mother wasn't one to go into personal details. It is, however, possible to make a few educated guesses.

Julio, like Mother, was a doer, and the house was strewn with the results of their various collaborative projects: lampshades made from blackened tin cans with designs punched into them so the light shined through. Julio drew the designs — fantastic birds, fish, animals, and abstract shapes — Mother did the punching. One Christmas, instead of cards, they sent pottery ashtrays that Mother had thrown and Julio painted. And there was the cooking and the excitement, which were all things Mother loved.

Finally, however, it was probably Julio's sex appeal that most captivated her. Women adored him. He could, quite literally, charm them right out of their pants; and then, I gather, he really knew what to do. Mother, of course, never discussed this with me, but when I last saw Julio he was in his late seventies and living with a bright, attractive blonde of about thirty-five who couldn't keep her hands off him. I have also spoken with a woman who knew him before he married Mother. She said he was the best lover she had ever had, and she admitted to having had quite a few.

During their marriage, Mother did all she could to please Julio. She was waiting for him, made up and looking her best, when he returned from his studio at night. She filled the walls of the drawing room with his paintings and replaced all her antique furniture with modern because she felt it would suit them better. His Latin-male sensibilities were offended by the presence of another man in the house, even one as harmless as Boyd, so she had Boyd move out. The one thing she could not do, however, was give up her career. Not that he ever asked it of her. He made enough off his paintings to support himself, but he could never have kept the three of us. Not with Mother's life-style. And that, eventually, is what destroyed the marriage. He was too much a Latin man with too large an ego to go through life as Mr. Gypsy Rose Lee. As he so eloquently put it when asked by a reporter why they had divorced, "I am not cut out to be a prince consort."

Mother was disappointed. She would have liked the marriage to work, and there was always a wistful note in her voice whenever she mentioned their years together. Yet I suspect she was relieved to be free of her role as the deferential housewife. It could not have come easily to her. She certainly was never tempted to reprise it, with Julio or anyone else.

They parted on good terms, and we stayed in touch. Mother and I always went to his gallery openings, I occasionally visited him at his studio, and Mother often called on him when she needed an extra man for a party. She had invited him to the tryout of *Curious Evening*, but he had already left for his winter house in Sarasota, Florida. Hence the special screening. He had just returned to town, and she wanted him to see the film. Few people knew her as intimately as Julio. She felt close to him. More importantly, she trusted him to tell her exactly what he thought of it.

Because the screening would be in the evening, she threw in an invitation to dinner; and because it was for Julio, she planned a special one: Pâté de foie gras, lobster Newburg over rice, a green salad with a walnut oil and vinegar dressing, and a perfectly ripe Pont L'Evêque cheese for dessert, all to be washed down with a vintage Montrachet. She even bought a bottle of his favorite Spanish brandy, Carlos Primera, to go with the after-dinner coffee.

There would be four of us. I was there to run the projector, not that I would have missed an opportunity to spend an evening with Julio, and Mother had invited my girlfriend because it was a Friday night and she knew I always spent Friday and Saturday nights with my girlfriend. Sometimes Mother could be very understanding. It promised to be a very special evening, and we were all looking forward to it.

The day began, however, with the arrival of some devastating news. Upon her return from Puerto Rico, Mother had made a deal to do *Curious Evening* on Broadway for six weeks starting in May. It wasn't a rich deal for her — she had agreed to a small percentage of the net with no guarantee — but she considered it vital to her future. If *Curious Evening* was ever to become the annuity she envisioned, it would have to be reviewed by the New York City critics, and this would happen only if it had a full-fledged New York run. That morning, out of the blue, with less than six weeks before the opening, the producer called her lawyer and announced that he had changed his mind and was dropping the project. He didn't even offer an apology or an explanation, and because the contracts had not yet been signed Mother had no recourse.

It was a terrible blow to her. I had stopped after school to pick up some of Julio's favorite coffee beans in Chelsea, so it was late in the afternoon when I got home, but she was still upset. She was in the kitchen preparing dinner when she told me about it.

"I just don't know what I'm going to do now," she said, her voice quavering. "The opening's been announced in the papers and everything."

"Why did he pull out?" I asked.

"God only knows. I've tried reaching him all day, but he's been avoiding me. He's probably too embarrassed to face me, as well he should be. I suppose he decided it was too risky, although that hardly seems possible. The most he could have lost, even if we didn't sell one solitary ticket, is a lousy ten thousand dollars."

She pointed to the coffee grinder she had bought on our first trip to Spain. It was on a high shelf; we never used it.

"Be a dear and grind the coffee for me."

"Sure," I said, climbing on to the counter to reach it.

"Be careful, darling. The last thing we need is an accident." She paused in her chopping. "I'll probably end up having to use my own money, but the thought of using so much of the precious little we have set aside just makes me sick. If only I knew why he changed his mind. What if he's heard something."

"What could he have heard?"

"Oh, I don't know." She took a deep breath and returned to her chopping. "But I do know that if I don't put it out of my mind, it will ruin the entire evening. There's nothing I can do about it until Monday anyway, so I might just as well wait until then to start worrying myself into an ulcer attack."

I doubt she stopped thinking about it, but she did stop talking about it, and she certainly didn't let it affect her cooking. Everything turned out perfectly, and Julio clearly enjoyed it. If anything, he enjoyed the wine a bit too much for Mother's liking. When he poured the last of the third bottle in his glass, she lightly suggested that he nurse it so he wouldn't fall asleep during the film. He didn't. He knocked it back as though it were a shot of whisky and then made such a fuss about wanting more that she dispatched me downstairs to the liquor closet for another bottle. I doubt he wanted the wine as much as he wanted to tweak her for having had the audacity to imply that he might have had enough to drink.

Julio was in a mischievous mood that night. He also teased Mother about her cooking. He lavished praise on the dinner until she was beaming with pride, and then took all the credit by announcing to my girlfriend and me that he had taught Mother everything she knew about cooking.

"When I met her," he said, "she was eating hash out of cans."

"That's not true, Julio, and you know it," Mother said hotly. "Besides, you've never made a cream sauce in your life."

"Hash out of cans . . . with ketchup on it," he repeated, a twinkle in his eye.

Mother prudently withheld the brandy until after the film, although it might have been more prudent for her to skip it altogether. But then she would have had to forgo her framboise — a raspberry liqueur that was her last remaining alcoholic weakness — and I think she felt that she deserved a treat.

Julio was generally complimentary about the film through his first snifter of brandy, but he began to get warmed up halfway into his second:

"The problem is that there is too much of other people and not enough of you. Who wants to see that idiot dancing with the Indians [referring to a newsreel clip of Grover Cleveland being made an honorary Indian chief]? It's el crappo, all of it. People want to see you. Where's your act? I remember a movie of your act. It should all be in there."

"Oh, Julio. I can't show the entire act, for chrissakes."

"You must show it all. That's what people who come to see you want to see. You! Your legs, your body."

He paused to pour himself another brandy, and my girlfriend saw fit to inject her opinion.

"I think Mr. de Diego has a good point. I've seen the film a few times, and every time I've wanted to see more of your act. I bet there are a lot of people who have never seen it and are curious."

"You see," Julio said, interrupting her. "Exactly what I said." He turned to my girlfriend who was sitting next to him, put his hand on her knee, and said, "You are very smart and very pretty, but you must call me Julio."

"Oh, thank you, Julio," she said, flashing him her brightest smile. She was a very precocious fifteen.

"And you must never wear shoes again," he added, staring down at her loafers. "Your legs are beautiful, those make them look like stumps of trees."

"Really?" she asked demurely.

"Nonsense," Mother interjected sharply, clearly intending to put an end to the topic. "Those shoes are perfect for a young girl."

Julio ignored Mother's hint. He leaned over, put one hand behind my girlfriend's calf, and lifted her leg until her knee was eye level, pushing her against the back of her chair. He removed her shoe with his free hand.

"Look," he said, holding her foot perpendicular to her leg. "School-teacher's shoes make your ankle look like this. A stump! High heels . . ." He moved her foot so her toes pointed toward the floor. ". . . give you leg form, shape. Look at the difference. So feminine. And seductive," he added with a smile.

She giggled nervously. Precocious or not, this was all a bit much for her. It was an ambiguous scene. He was close enough to her leg to kiss it, and it almost looked as if he would, yet he was being perfectly matter-of-fact both in the way he touched her and in his tone of voice.

It wasn't ambiguous to Mother, and neither was her reaction.

"Julio," she said, "leave that poor girl's foot alone, and come over here and rub my back. I've had a stiff neck all day, and you used to give such wonderful backrubs."

It is possible he'd been angling for just such an invitation because he was behind her chair in a flash, rubbing her back.

"Oh, that feels so good," she moaned, opening the top two buttons of her blouse to loosen the neck.

This was the only time I ever saw Mother behave in anything that even slightly resembled an enticing manner, and for her to do so in front of my girlfriend was totally out of character. It can only have been her framboise-loosened ego reacting to the double blow of being rejected by a two-bit producer and then having her ex-husband all but seduce her son's girlfriend right in front of her.

It was clearly time for my girlfriend and me to leave. We were discreetly planning our departure when Mother shrieked. We turned. Julio was leaning over her with his hands down the front of her blouse. She pulled them out and sat up so quickly he had to jerk his chin out of the way of her head.

"I would hardly call that my back," she said firmly. "Anyway, my neck feels much better now, and it's time I went to bed."

Julio tried to persist, but she would have none of it. She hadn't wanted him, that was clear. She may have wanted only to distract him from my girlfriend, or she may have wanted to know that she could still get him. Either way she was satisfied.

He took the rejection in good spirits. My girlfriend and I dropped him off at his studio, and on the way there he spoke only of Mother and only with affection.

The following week, Mother decided to produce the Broadway run of *Curious Evening* herself. Most of the preparations had already been made. All she had to do was sign contracts — and checks — for the theater and advertising agency and wait a month for the show currently in the theater to close. The waiting was the worst part of all. She occupied herself as best she could by making a few final changes in the film and giving a few interviews, but she spent most of the time worrying. She worried about *Curious Evening*, about her future, about her bank account, and about me and my girlfriend. And, since she couldn't do anything about the first three, she tackled the last one.

I had known for quite some time that Mother didn't like the girl. She had never actually said so, but neither had she ever missed an opportunity to mention how nice or how pretty this or that person's daughter was and to suggest that I take them to the movies for a change. I didn't tell her, but there was absolutely no chance of my dating anyone else. Not only was I convinced that I loved my girlfriend, I had become hopelessly dependent on her. It was all very neurotic. As a child I had learned to draw all my emotional sustenance from one person, Mother. Now, as an adolescent, I was doing the same thing only with a new person, my girlfriend. I had made her into the vital source of love and affection in my life. Consequently, I was extremely possessive and jealous of her. For me to date others, if only to keep

Mother happy, would have been to risk her doing the same, and that just wasn't possible for me.

I didn't fully appreciate the depth of Mother's animosity. At first I thought it was nothing more than the proverbial resentment a mother feels for her son's first love. And when, two days after the Julio dinner, she lectured me at length on how "unhealthy" it was for someone my age to devote all my attention to just one person, I felt it was a jealous reaction to Julio's behavior and would soon blow over. It didn't. She became more and more outspoken in her dislike, actually blaming my girlfriend for the decline in my behavior and calling her a "bad influence" over me. Still, I failed to see beneath the surface. In the past Mother had often sought to lay the blame for my misdeeds on my friends. She used different words, but in meaning it remained that old saw: he was such a good boy until he fell in with that group of ruffians. It was so trite, in fact, I didn't believe that she actually meant it. Especially as in the case of my girlfriend, it couldn't have been less true. Like my shrink, she always counseled diplomacy and getting along.

On another level, however, one Mother must have sensed even if she couldn't properly identify it, my girlfriend was truly a root cause of her loss of control over me. As long as Mother had been the source of my emotional sustenance, she had held the ultimate trump in our relationship. If I angered or displeased her, she withheld her love, and I quickly got back in line. When I transferred my emotional dependence to my girlfriend, she lost that power. I didn't care if she withheld her love because I was getting all I needed from a new source. I doubt Mother grasped the psychological intricacies, but she couldn't miss the correlation between her loss of authority and my girlfriend's arrival in my life.

Mother wasn't one to relinquish power, gracefully or otherwise, especially when she felt it was rightfully hers. She was determined to separate me from my girlfriend, and the failure of her initial attempts to persuade us apart only stiffened her resolve. But she wasn't precipitous. She waited for the right moment and the right ammunition, then she pounced.

It was a Monday night. We had finished dinner, Esther had gone home, and we were in the library watching television. A fire had taken the early spring nip off the air, and all seemed well with the world, at least to me. When the news was over, Mother turned to me and said, "Turn off the set, Erik. I want to talk to you." Her tone was ominous, but I had a clear conscience for a change, so it didn't put me on my guard. She continued, "I had to have the plumber in today to fix the toilet in the powder room."

"Oh, yes. I noticed it was almost stopped up over the weekend. I was going to tell you, but I forgot." Stopped up plumbing was commonplace in our house. Most of the pipes had not been replaced since it was built.

"He told Esther it had been clogged by a used condom." I expected a lecture on throwing them in the toilets and started to apologize, but she didn't give me the opening. "Now I want the truth," she continued. "Are you having an affair with this girl?"

"Sure," I answered without thinking. I had always assumed that Mother knew. Just about every Friday and Saturday night I'd bring my girlfriend over to the house, set up my record player in the drawing room, raid the liquor closet, and spend the evening dancing, making out, and making love. Mother always came down at seven-thirty, put the dogs out into the patio, and visited with us for the five minutes it took them to do their business, but after that she never came downstairs. Ever. I took the privacy she afforded us as tacit acceptance of our affair. She was about to correct this misconception.

"I see. Well, at least you aren't trying to lie your way out of this one. I suppose I should consider this an improvement over your recent behavior." She paused to light a cigarette, and I began to defend myself against her comment, but she silenced me with a wave of her hand.

"I've thought all afternoon about how to handle this. My first instinct was to call her parents . . . but I have no idea of what kind of people they are. They might be the type that likes to cause trouble, in which case they could involve the police and make a terrible scandal. And, after all, their daughter is no concern of mine. I then thought of sending you away to school, but it seems a shame to take you out of Riverdale just as you're getting ready to apply to college. Changing schools at this late stage is always viewed with suspicion." She paused with a sigh. "So, I've decided to give you another chance. Again. Provided you'll give me your solemn word of honor never to see her or talk to her again."

"I can't believe you're making such a big deal over this," I said, determined to fight this one to the end.

"You certainly don't expect me to condone such behavior."

"Why not? There's nothing wrong with it."

"How can you say such a thing? It's immoral, it's against the law . . ."

"Since when?" I interrupted superciliously.

"The girl's under age. Her parents can have you put in jail."

"They can not. I'm under age too, so it doesn't matter how old she is."

"I wouldn't be too sure of that. Besides which, it matters to me."

"Why? It's never mattered to you before."

"I never knew about it before."

"What did you think we were doing all this time, holding hands?"

"I certainly didn't think you were having sex with a fourteen-year-old girl."

"Fifteen. And who did you think I was having sex with? Or did you expect me to stay a virgin until I got married?"

It was the only question to make her pause, but she recovered quickly. "I had always assumed that when you got a bit older Bill would . . . see that you were properly introduced. It's customary for fathers to . . ." She paused again, clearly uncomfortable with the topic. "There are houses for that type of thing, you know," she finished impatiently.

Sometimes her Victorianism surprised even me. "That's the most appalling thing I've ever heard," I said with as much outrage as I could muster. "I can't believe you'd rather I learn about sex from a prostitute instead of someone I love."

"Love," she said disdainfully. "You haven't the faintest idea of what that word involves. . . ."

"That's not true," I said, getting upset and showing it.

"And don't think for one minute that she loves you, because she doesn't. It's the farthest thing from her mind. I know. I've been around her type all my life. She's just a scheming little bitch, and she's just waiting for you to make her pregnant so she can get at my money. . . ."

"That's not true!" I shouted. Her accusations were absurd, but I couldn't think of how to refute them. I lost control. Even my voice broke as I continued. "She knows how cheap you are. And she won't get pregnant; that's why I use a rub—— prophylactic."

"If you knew as much as you say you do, you'd know they fail all the time, and if you think I'm going to risk my hard-earned money just so you can roll in the hay with some little tramp . . ."

"She's not a little tramp!" I wailed, tears running down my face.

"This discussion has gone far enough. You're not going to see her again, and that's all there is to it. Now, give me your word, or I'll put you on a train to military school in the morning. It's up to you. I'm too fed up with you to care one way or the other."

"Why are you doing this to me?" I screamed, quite hysterical by this time. "Call my doctor," I begged, clutching at straws. "He'll tell you how wrong you are."

"I don't care what he says. I know the girl, and he doesn't. Now, pick up that phone and tell her it's all over."

"Not on the phone," I pleaded. "At least let me see her one more time so I can explain in person. Please."

"And have her twist you around her finger? Not on your life."

"I won't do it on the phone," I said, gathering all my reserves. "I just can't."

"Fine. Then go downstairs and start packing."

"No, I won't. And I won't go to military school, and there's no way you can make me."

"Oh yes there is. As long as you're a minor you have to do as I say. If you don't, I can take you before a judge, have you declared incorrigible, and sent to a state reformatory. And don't for one moment think I won't! Now, call."

I don't know that I believed her. The words were really unimportant. What mattered was that she remained as strong and determined as she had been at the beginning of the confrontation while I was worn out. She had beaten me down. I just couldn't resist any longer.

So, with Mother standing right next to me, I phoned my girlfriend. It was a short call. Choking with sobs, I told her I wouldn't be able to see her anymore and hung up.

In victory, Mother was magnanimous. She said that she was proud of me for making what she knew was a difficult call and suggested that I'd feel better after a "nice cup of tea." She even offered to make it. I let her. We sat in silence while I drank it. I was numb, but gradually sensation returned, and I became aware of certain feelings. The first, and by far the strongest, was self-loathing. I despised myself for having been weak, for having given in, for having lost. Next I hated Mother. Not passionately, but with an icy revulsion. Looking at her, I shuddered and wanted to get away, as if from something unclean.

Saying I was tired and going to bed, I got up to leave. She presented me her cheek for her customary goodnight kiss. I was aware of wanting to run it through with a ice pick, but I forced myself to kiss her.

"Goodnight, Mother."

"Goodnight, dear." When I reached the door, she stopped me. "Don't forget. You gave your word."

"I won't forget, Mother. Goodnight."

In fact, I had not given my word. That detail had been lost in all the melodrama. Not that it would have made a difference in what followed. I would have broken it without hesitation or remorse. Whatever sense of obligation or honor, not to mention affection, I had toward Mother was destroyed that night for years to come. With that fight, she became the enemy, to be avoided if possible and vanquished when necessary.

It proved very easy to get around her as far as my girlfriend was concerned. I waited in my room until she went to sleep, then I sneaked down to Boyd's apartment and used his phone to call her and explain what had happened. She understood, and we continued our affair on the sly, thanks to Boyd's generosity in letting us use his apartment, without Mother ever suspecting.

In order to keep my affair secret, I began living two distinct lives. Just about everything that Mother would have frowned upon, as well as everything that mattered to me, was in the one that included my girlfriend. Thus Mother was spared the tedious and time-consuming task of shepherding me through my various adolescent traumas. Boyd, with whom I could be myself without fear of censure, handled that job in her stead.

My other life, the "proper one," was devoid of emotion and co-existed with Mother in almost Victorian rectitude, except for a continual quarrel over money. It was all very polite, very distant, and very cold, but if Mother missed the warmth and affection, she didn't show it. Of course, she had other things on her mind.

From my perspective, it was easy to fault Mother for this heavy-handed attempt to bend me to her will. After all, it was worse than unsuccessful, it was counterproductive in that it alienated us so completely. I doubt Mother would have agreed. At the time, she was preoccupied with the opening of *Curious Evening* on Broadway, and a host of other crises were waiting in the wings. Compared to the problems of her career, her life, and her survival, she considered her problems with me mere distractions to be eliminated as expeditiously as possible, and in that sense she was undeniably successful.

PART THREE

CHAPTER FOURTEEN

MOTHER called it "early *Sunset Boulevard*" after the film, and the place did exude a romantic, slightly tarnished air reminiscent of Hollywood in the era of silent films. It was set off by itself, atop one of the Beverly Hills, on an empty, winding street that was bordered with tall cypress trees and ran alongside a high, whitewashed retaining wall. The house itself couldn't be seen from the street, which ended at an old-fashioned three-car garage. Next to it, a wrought-iron gate opened on to a twisting flight of stairs lined with statuary. At the top of the stairs, a paved walkway climbed gently through a rolling lawn, past a huge deodara tree, to an imposing California-Mediterranean house with thick, stucco-covered walls, lots of large windows, and a green tiled roof.

It wasn't a large house. There were only eight rooms, not counting baths and the servants quarters, but because they were spacious and unusual, the house felt very grand and impressive. There wasn't one sharp angle in the entire place. Everything was rounded: doorways, windows, room corners, even the exquisitely tiled shower stalls. The living room was forty feet long, double-height with a beamed ceiling, and had a huge, black marble fireplace. At the far end was a sunken, semicircular conservatory with a stained-glass roof and tall, arched windows that looked out on the deodara tree and the rolling lawn. Outside, under the conservatory windows, a delicate fountain played into a narrow, moatlike goldfish pond. The top floor was one large circular room surrounded with windows. A tiny balcony off the second-floor landing overlooked the living room so a string quartet could entertain unobtrusively.

It was its location that contributed most to the house. Because it was alone on top of a hill, it was very private, and the views were spectacular. Huge windows in the living room, dining room, and master bedroom and narrow floor-to-ceiling windows in the top-floor rotunda looked out on the lush green Doheny estate at the bottom of the hill and, stretching beyond it to the horizon, on all of Los Angeles. It was a beautiful view by day, but by night it was truly fantastic as the stand of weathered eucalyptus trees at the border of the Doheny estate, rustled by the breeze off the Pacific, cast an eerie, forever changing silhouette against the lights of the city.

When Mother first saw the house it had languished unoccupied for over seven years, a small part of a complicated estate, and all this beauty was obscured by the ravages of neglect: peeling paint, cracked and falling plaster, broken windows, rusted plumbing, termites, lantana running wild over the grounds, the deodara a thicket of dead and dying branches, torn awnings hanging drunkenly over the windows, the fish pond dark and stagnant, and over it all the pervasive stink of dirt, dust, and dampness. Not surprisingly, no one wanted to buy it.

Then Mother came along, saw beneath the surface, and fell in love. It was a fluke. While doing *Curious Evening* in Los Angeles she was staying with a friend whose husband dabbled in real estate, and he stopped by the house to check the listing as they were on their way to lunch one day. She hadn't been in the market for a house, and she had always claimed to loathe Los Angeles, but she bought it the next day for $63,500. She justified the purchase, even in her diary, as an investment: "With a few cosmetic touches and a lot of hard work I can double my money in six months, and in the meantime I can support myself on the profit I'll make from leasing the New York house."

Looking back it seems almost mystical, as though Mother and the house were kindred spirits destined to come together at just this perfect moment. The house needed loving care and a lot of hard work; Mother needed a fresh start and an all-involving project to take her mind off her problems. Both were at their fortunes' ebb, past their prime, or so it appeared. In fact, both still had extraordinary potential, and eventually each would draw the best from the other.

That, however, was still years away. At the time, the house was a shambles and so was Mother's life. She had opened *Curious Evening* in New York on May 9 to good reviews, but they hadn't generated any business. None. One memorable evening there were five paying customers in the audience. She closed the show after two and a half weeks and a loss of almost $7000. The reviews did lead to a few dates, and over the summer she had played the show in Saint Louis, Santa

Barbara, Monterey, and Los Angeles, but the reaction was the same everywhere — good reviews and lousy business. She still had a week in Lansing and one-night stands in Grand Ledge and Harbor Springs left to play, but no new offers were coming in, and even Mother couldn't deny the obvious forever: no one was willing to pay to sit through two hours of her home movies, however enchanting the narration. *Curious Evening* wasn't going to support her in her old age. It wasn't even going to earn back its costs. *Curious Evening* was a flop.

I was another of Mother's problems. We were barely speaking. Since the fight over my girlfriend, I had become just short of openly hostile toward her. I didn't want to be around her, and I figured if I made myself unpleasant enough, she wouldn't want to be around me. Thus I became, at least where she was concerned, a greedy, self-centered, morose, uncooperative, unsympathetic young man. Other than to ask her for money or make some other "selfish" demand, I rarely addressed a full sentence to her. I usually answered her in monosyllables, and I did as she asked only with the most obvious reluctance. She called it a "stage" and tried to make allowances, but forbearance was not one of her strong suits, and my plan seemed to work when I refused to go on tour with her and insisted that she send me to summer school for driver's education so I could get my license on my seventeenth birthday in December. She was "appalled" that I could be so "selfish" while she was "struggling for our very survival," and she often reminded me that leaving me alone in New York was costing her "hours of anxiety" and the "astronomical expense" of a union projectionist, but she did it. A summer without me was as pleasant a prospect to her as one without her was to me.

Separation did not improve our relationship. Every phone call degenerated into an argument, usually over money. Few were acrimonious, but all were unpleasant. The call in which she announced that she had bought the new house was typical.

"Oh, darling, I'm so glad you're home," she began, her voice brimming over with excitement. "I have the most wonderful surprise. I didn't want to get your hopes up, so I've waited until I was sure I had it to tell you, but I'm at the lawyers' now, we've just finished signing the papers, and I wanted you to be the first to know. . . ."

"Know what?" I asked, starting to share her excitement. Could she, I wondered, just maybe have bought me a car? Any hopes I had centered around four wheels.

She took a deep breath. "I've just bought the most magnificent house in Beverly Hills. Oh, it's so beautiful! I can't wait for you to see it. The grounds are lovely, there's a spectacular view of the city. Downstairs there's a private two-room suite for you with its own entrance. You're going to love it."

"What do you want with a house in Beverly Hills?" I interrupted, heaping all the disdain I could muster on to the "Beverly Hills." It was more than disappointment. I had never heard her say one nice thing about California. The last time we were there, she had complained constantly about the endless drives to get anywhere, the blandness of the climate, and the vacuousness of the people. She had, in fact, disparaged California so often that I had unconsciously adopted her prejudice.

There was a brief pause. No doubt she was wondering if she was going to have trouble with me over this. When she answered, there was a touch of wariness to her voice. "It's an excellent investment for one thing. For another, it's much cheaper to live out here, and we must find a way to conserve money. The New York house is just more than I can afford right now."

"Well, you can live wherever you want, but I'm never leaving New York." It was less the city than it was my girlfriend, but of course I couldn't say that.

Another pause. When she spoke after this one, no trace remained of her original excitement. It was as if I had turned a switch. She was stiff, cold, and ready for battle. "It's customary for families to live together."

"You were the one who decided to move, not me."

"I don't understand why you're taking such a negative attitude toward this. I thought you'd be delighted. You'll be able to have a car out here, UCLA is less than ten minutes away . . ."

"UCLA!!! I wouldn't go to that intellectual wasteland for anything."

"You have no business criticizing something you know nothing about. UCLA is an excellent college. And it's free, which means a great deal given the state of my finances."

"CCNY is also free, and it's a lot better school. Of course, neither compares with Princeton or Columbia, not to mention Harvard."

"I wouldn't be talking about Harvard with your grades."

"Don't be too sure about that. Of course, I won't have a chance if you take me out of Riverdale just before my senior year. You're the one who's always talking about how important my Riverdale diploma is going to be to my future. It seems pretty silly to throw it away now that I'm so close — "

"I'm not going to discuss anything this important on the telephone," she interrupted. "It will have to wait until I get home. I only called to give you what I think is very exciting news — "

"Well, I think it's awful."

"I'm sorry you're not pleased, but I've bought the house, and it's too late to do anything about it. Now I must go. This nice man was kind enough to let me use his phone, and I can't tie it up any longer."

"Okay then, good-bye."

After a weary sigh, she said, "Good-bye, darling," and hung up.

However disappointed Mother may have been at my reaction, she didn't let it get her down. She had a week's layoff before her next date with *Curious Evening*, and she was determined to spend it enjoying her new home. I know what she did after talking to me from her "garden book" — a diary she kept about the grounds of the house:

I bought garden gloves, snail pellets, a rake, a trowel, and dug right in . . . a few stones behind an Australian tea tree led me down to a secret garden covered over with sumac, sedum, sword ferns, and over them all *lantana*. . . . With my hands, I dug a path through the tangled mess. A rose bush — no blooms but I could see the leaves and thorns — grew against the wall. As I dug my way through it all, the ground suddenly gave way under my feet. The density of the lantana kept me from falling more than a foot or so, but not enough to keep me from plunging into a mud hole above my knees. Rough stones cut my legs as I scrambled up to dry ground. The lantana was delightfully fragrant as I crushed it. The lavender color was pretty. I remembered the hanging basket of it I bought a year before in New York — $25.00 and it died in three weeks. I cried that day when I had to throw it away and here I was literally struggling for my balance in a forest of it. For a while I felt like a millionaire, then I realized I couldn't clear all that overgrowth alone, and I figured what it would cost me in man hours to do the job and I felt poor again. . . . I went to bed on a mattress on the floor and I looked out and down on the city lights glittering through the eucalyptus trees. I tried to imagine how everything was going to look some day. I ached all over. My knees were skinned from falling into the lily pond. [From "mud hole" to "lilly pond" — from what was to what would be in just a few short sentences.] My arms were scratched from the brush. I was sunburned and my nails were broken but I felt a serene happiness I hadn't known in years.

Mother's serenity was short-lived. Her period of misfortune was not yet over. The next installment came in the form of two theatrical producers from New York, Carmen Capalbo and Stanley Chase. They wanted her to play Jenny in the national touring company of *The Threepenny Opera* which they were putting together. It was the best offer Mother had received in years. The Bertolt Brecht-Kurt Weill musical satire about Victorian London's underworld was a classic. It was the longest running show in New York at the time, and it had never been on tour. The role of Jenny, which had immortalized Lotte Lenya, wasn't large or especially dramatic, but it was the female lead, and Mother would get first star billing above the title. She would also get $2500 a week for nine months!!

Mother fretted over the offer for the rest of her layoff. As good a job as it was, and as much as she needed it for her career and her bank account, she didn't want to take it. Because of the remaining bookings for *Curious Evening* and the opening of *Threepenny* which had already been set, she would have to lease the New York house, or at least get it ready to lease and in the hands of a good real-estate agent, make arrangements for me, the cats, and the Afghans for the duration of the tour, and rehearse, all at once and in less than a month. Moreover, she was worried about the score. *Happy Hunting* was too recent and too painful a memory. She doubted her ability to carry a musical with such well-known songs as "Mack the Knife," and she knew that entering into such a long commitment with doubts was the road to disaster. But most of all, she just didn't want to go to work. She didn't want to spend the next nine months doing eight shows a week and living in bleak hotel rooms. She wanted to dig in her new garden, fix up her new house, and start her new life. So before leaving for Lansing, she turned down the offer.

But Carmen and Stanley persisted. Theaters had been booked, rehearsals were starting in a week, they were desperate for a star, and they sensed that Mother was persuadable. They followed her to Lansing, raised their offer first to $2750 a week and then to $3000. They told her not to worry about the rehearsals, they'd arrange the schedule so she'd have time to deal with the New York house. They offered her a voice coach, suites on the road, a personal maid, anything! She took it all, but it was the money that did the trick. Nine months of $3000 a week came to over $100,000, more than Mother was capable of refusing. It was against her better judgment, but she took the job.

Mother arrived home in a state of barely controlled panic, certainly understandable given all she had to do, and we went nonstop until she left for Toronto where the show was opening.

She usually spent weekdays in rehearsal, costume fittings, or working with her voice coach; the rest of the time she devoted to tying up the loose ends of her life. The major loose end, of course, was the house.

226

She had decided to lease it unfurnished and to store all of her furniture and belongings in California until after the tour when they could be moved into the new house. This was hardly consistent with her original plan to resell the L.A. house as soon as she had fixed it up, but in the chaos of the moment that was never mentioned. She may not even have admitted it to herself, but I think deep down she already knew that she would never live in the New York house again. As for waiting until after the tour to make the move, that would have meant giving up nine months' rent, which for Mother was out of the question. I think too she dreaded tearing apart what she had built so lovingly over twenty years, and she liked the idea of getting it over with quickly while her mind was occupied elsewhere.

She planned to have a moving company pack everything, but they are very expensive, and she wasn't about to let them loose in the house until she had weeded out what wasn't worth shipping three thousand miles and storing for nine months. This was the most arduous part of the three weeks. The house was loaded with storerooms and closets, and because Mother hated to throw anything away, they were all more than full, they were stuffed. In the basement were trunks, suitcases, packing crates, and moldy cardboard boxes filled with scenery, props, music, and some stuff so old it had literally disintegrated beyond recognition. There were also the Christmas decorations, thank God minus the cockroaches which had been exterminated, a rusty bicycle, and the remnants of my darkroom. The attic in the front house contained twenty years' worth of mostly broken furniture and lamps, my baby carriage, and ten boxes each of *Gypsy* and *The G-String Murders* which Mother had bought when they went out of print.

Far and away the worst, however, were the closets. Mother had saved almost every costume — complete with shoes, hat, gloves, and accessories — used either by her or by any of the girls in the act and every important designer ensemble she had owned since buying the house in 1943. The sheer volume of clothing this involved was staggering, and beginning her first night home she went through every bit of it. Boyd and I emptied each area in turn, bringing the stuff to the dining room where she separated it into three piles. One consisted of those things she couldn't live without. She was very strict with herself. We had been through closet cleanings before; for the first time this pile wasn't the largest. The second pile, also quite small, consisted of costumes and clothes she felt would be of interest to the Brooklyn Museum, which maintains a large clothing collection. Included in this pile were my kilts, lederhosen, Norwegian sailor outfit, and the other national costumes that she had bought me on our first trip to Europe. I didn't mind. Not surprisingly I felt no sense of attachment to them. What remained was a mountain of old clothes, broken furniture, and junk. Mother called it the "crap pile" until she discovered that she would have to pay someone to cart it to the dump, then it became a "donation" to the first charity that would come and pick it up.

In the two weeks it took to complete the weeding out, Mother somehow managed also to audition movers and real estate agents, find new homes for the Afghans, and settle my living arrangments for the coming year. She even found time to get some publicity for the tour by doing the Jack Paar show, twice! Most of this was pretty easy. The Paar show was always a breeze for her, and with the movers she simply chose the one that gave her the lowest estimate.

The real estate agents, on the other hand, ended up auditioning her. Mother needed a hefty rent just to cover expenses, but the rental market was depressed and many agents refused point blank to handle the house. Even those who expressed interest wanted Mother to make some very expensive improvements. The biggest of these was a new kitchen. The kitchen Mother had installed in the closet off the library when she converted the house's original one into an apartment was ideally suited to our life-style. There were only the two of us, and we usually ate in the library or off a tray in Mother's bedroom. On those rare occasions when Mother actually served dinner in the dining room, we simply coped with the inconvenience of carrying the food down four flights of stairs and through the corridor, something Mother could hardly expect of a tenant paying $1500 a month, as the real estate agents were quick to point out. They also suggested new carpeting throughout the house in the hope it would eliminate or at least lessen the "unfortunate" odor of cat pee, new wallpaper in the stairwell and in Mother's room, fresh paint everywhere else, and refinishing the hardwood floor in the library. Mother tried to get away with agreeing to make the improvements to the order of the tenant *after* the house had been rented, but the agents insisted on the kitchen and carpeting before they'd even show the house, so on top of everything else she had to add finding a contractor, planning the new kitchen, and selecting carpet to her list of tasks.

There was one bright spot. For a change I was not adding to her troubles. Throughout this period I went out of my way to stay in her good graces. I forwent dates in order to help her around the house, I cheerfully did whatever she asked of me, I looked for ways to make myself useful, and I carefully avoided annoying her. There was nothing altruistic in my new leaf. Over dinner on her second night home she asked me if I'd be willing to live in the dormitory while she was on tour. I knew it would relieve her of worrying about me, but I also knew I would loathe it, so I refused, apologetically and not without a measure of guilt. To my utter amazement, she didn't insist or even try to pressure me. Instead she offered me the top-floor apartment in the front house. An apartment of my own at sixteen! It was more than a fantasy; I would never have dared even imagine anything so wonderful. Needless to say I accepted, and from that moment on my enthusiastic cooperation was assured. Far be it from me to give her a reason to change her mind.

Although the first two and a half weeks were the most physically taxing on Mother, it was the last five days, when the movers were doing all the manual labor, that were the hardest on her. It wasn't the noise and confusion; she missed most of that because she was at rehearsals. It was the coming home every night to find another part of her beloved home dismantled. The movers began in the drawing room, packing all the paintings and the chandelier in wooden crates which they made to measure right on the spot. That night, Mother came home to find crates everywhere, her prized marble floor covered in sawdust and excelsior, the walls bare except for rings of soot where the paintings had once hung, and an ugly black hole with two dangling wires in the center of the ceiling. When I came in a few minutes later, she was sitting on one of the crates, looking mournfully about her, tears welling in her eyes.

Day by day, room by room, the house took on an abused look, deserted and forlorn. Every night when she came home, Mother would stop for a while in the latest areas to be decimated and shed a few tears of farewell. She never said it aloud, but she must have wished during these moments that she had never agreed to the tour. Nothing could have made giving up the house easy for her — it represented the only roots she had ever known — but she couldn't even look forward to putting down new roots in her new home. That was too far in the future. Instead, all her precious possessions were going to be moved three thousand miles and stored somewhere, in limbo, while she trouped the length and breadth of the continent, rootless, living out of a trunk in a dismal hotel room.

She dreaded the tour above all, however, because she hated herself in the part. Every day she'd come home from rehearsals feeling less confident. In the beginning she felt out of place with the company, but she thought that would pass after they had worked together for a while. It didn't, but she also began feeling too old for the part of a twenty-six-year-old hooker. Then she was unable to "do anything" with the songs. What it all finally boiled down to was a total lack of inspiration. At best she could get through the part; she couldn't get into it. This sapped her confidence, which in turn hurt her work, and she was trapped in a vicious circle. There was no way out of it either. She could only carry on and hope an audience would provide from without the inspiration that she lacked within.

The brevity of Mother's stay in New York intensified the effort, but it also abridged the misery. The packers began on Monday; on Thursday they finished up with her bedroom. She spent that night, her last in New York, in the spare bedroom of my apartment. There was no rehearsal the next day. The final week of rehearsals was scheduled for Toronto, and they needed the day to transport the sets, props, and costumes. Mother spent it nervously watching the movers load all her worldly possessions on a van and finalizing plans for the new kitchen with the contractor. She had planned to spend Saturday helping me get organized in my apartment, but after the van pulled away she asked if I would mind if she left immediately for Toronto. The thought of spending another night in the house was just too depressing for her.

I didn't mind in the least. Appearances to the contrary, my feelings about her hadn't changed. I found being around her very difficult and couldn't wait to be rid of her.

For a change, loading the Rolls was easy. Most of what she was taking on the tour had gone ahead on the show's costume truck. She had an overnight bag and the three Chinese Cresteds; the cats were staying with me.

Everthing happened so quickly. Before it had registered, I was leaning through the car window to kiss her good-bye and waving at the rear end of the car as it moved off down the street. Then it turned the corner, and she was gone.

I stood alone on 63rd Street, wanting to shout for joy but not quite feeling like doing it. It had been a very difficult three weeks, I was relieved they were over, and I was relieved that she was gone. Yet I also felt as though something was missing, which in a sense it was.

I had just said good-bye to my mother.

CHAPTER FIFTEEN

MOTHER should have followed her instinct regarding *The Threepenny Opera*. It closed in less than two weeks, and there wasn't even enough money to pay her salary. She settled for an antique harp that had been used as a prop in the show, somehow managed to fit it into the back of the Rolls along with her things and the dogs, and left for California after the last performance.

Another flop so soon after *Curious Evening* was very demoralizing, and she hated the loss of income, but on the whole she was relieved to be out of the show. She had not liked herself in the part, and all along she had wanted to be in her new house. She even managed to get there before the moving van, so her things were spared the inevitable nicks from being transferred into and out of storage, and she was spared the expense.

Mother threw herself into her new project, working literally from dawn to dusk clearing and planting her garden and supervising painters, plumbers, electricians, and decorators as they worked on the inside of the house. Meanwhile in New York, I was determined to prove myself worthy of the trust she had shown by giving me my own apartment. I lived within my budget, worked hard at school, and avoided doing anything that might have given her cause for concern, except for continuing my affair with my girlfriend which she knew nothing about. As a result, we began getting along better than we had in ages.

There was, however, one cloud on the horizon — my car. While in New York, well aware that she had me right where she wanted me because of the dangling carrot of my apartment, she had announced that she was dead set against me having a car in New York City because it was "outrageously expensive, totally unnecessary, dangerous, and impossible to park." Consequently she had decided to give me only

$1200 for a car on my seventeenth birthday. If I waited until I went away to college, however, she'd raise the amount to $2400.

I was devastated. I didn't want to wait. For years I had been talking about getting a car on my seventeenth birthday, she had never before rejected the idea, and my heart was set on it. The amounts were almost worse. My insurance alone would cost close to $500. I had been envisioning myself behind the wheel of a Porsche or a Jaguar; now, even waiting until college I'd be lucky to find myself in a used Ford.

While I was still absorbing the disappointment, she went on to announce that she could no longer afford my psychiatrist. I couldn't believe it. This wasn't underwear, this was a doctor! I couldn't have defined what I was getting from my sessions, but I liked them, and I didn't want them to stop, if only because I got to leave school early for them. I couldn't fight her without risking the apartment, so without thinking I tried to shame her into changing her mind by asking if I could use my car money to pay for my doctor. I should have known better. When it came to money, Mother was devoid of shame. She accepted my suggestion with alacrity, and I was stuck.

I hadn't, however, given up on a car. I simply redirected my efforts toward Bill Kirkland. We had a cool yet friendly relationship. Neither of us was demonstrative, so there wasn't a lot of hugging and affection, but he was easy to talk to, and I felt we were close, especially as of late. Since Mother's departure, we had been seeing quite a bit of each other. I had never asked him for anything, he had recently married a very wealthy woman, and I figured I had nothing to lose.

At first, I tried a subtle approach. Before my birthday I explained how I had come to use my car money to continue seeing my psychiatrist, then I waited to see what I'd get. A pair of garters. I thought it was a joke, that the keys were hidden somewhere in the package. But it was no joke, and there were no keys. I should have known right then, but hope blinded me to the obvious. Christmas comes two weeks after my birthday, and I thought he might be dragging out the suspense. On Christmas day I was certain. He gave me an oblong package just large enough for two car keys. Only it contained a pewter box with a carved top, empty. Finally I asked Bill straight out to help me get a car, nothing fancy, just four dependable wheels. He told me that he'd have to think about it.

A few days later he phoned and asked me for my psychiatrist's name and phone number, explaining that he wanted a referral for my half sister who was having problems at school. I gave it to him without a second thought.

At the beginning of my next session, my doctor said, "Bill Kirkland called me."

"I know. I gave him your number. Did you recommend someone else for my half sister, or are you going to see her? Or is that confidential?"

"Is that what he told you? That he wanted to discuss your half sister?"

"Why? Isn't that why he called?"

"He called because he wanted me to tell you that he isn't your father and that you should never look to him for any kind of financial help."

I wasn't surprised. I had had doubts about my paternity ever since Boyd's comment on the night of Mike Todd's death.

"Did he say who my father was?"

"No. But he told me to be sure and tell you that he's always thought of you as his son and this doesn't change that. He'd like your relationship to continue exactly as it always has."

"What an asshole! What a spineless, sanctimonious, hypocritical, stupid asshole!" One of the things I liked best about my psychiatrist was that I didn't have to censor my language around him. Consequently, I often went overboard. "Then why did he tell me, for chrissakes! It might not make a difference to him, but it sure as hell does to me. I hope I never see the son-of-a-bitch again."

I was cold and emotionally detached as an adolescent, and there was much less passion in my reaction than the language suggests. I felt angry with Bill, but I thought it was only because he hadn't had the nerve to tell me face to face. Otherwise I felt unaffected by the revelation. I never asked myself why he hadn't just refused to get me a car instead of denying his paternity. If he didn't want to be my father, that was fine with me. I was delighted not to be the son of such a weak coward. I didn't even want to be his friend, and I cut him out of my life completely.

With Mother I was even more dispassionate. Actually, I was calculating. I realized that this could be a powerful weapon, and I decided to hold it in reserve until I needed it. I knew it wouldn't be long. Time had recently accomplished what Mother could not: I had broken up with my old girlfriend and taken up with a new one. She was a college student. In the dorm where she lived, they locked the doors at a certain hour every night, around midnight as I remember. If she was out, she could either stay out and not be missed or go through an inquisition to get in. She stayed out so often that it seemed only sensible for her to move out and move in with me.

Shortly thereafter, Mother called me from California. She didn't even say hello.

"Erik, what's this I've been told about you having some girl living in the apartment with you?" she asked, her voice shaking with anger.

I knew this was it, and I was determined to make the most of it. "It's not 'some girl.'" I corrected her. "Her name is M————, and I told you all about her in my letters."

"You didn't tell me she was living with you in *my house*. Well, I won't have it, Erik. I want her out of there this minute. Today. Do you understand me! She's not to spend another night there with you. Not one. And you might just as well start getting your things together too, because you're moving into the dormitory just as soon as I can make arrangements with the school. You're obviously not ready to be left on your own."

"I can't believe you're making such a big deal about this. So what if my girlfriend's moved in with me? What's wrong with that?" I was deliberately leading her on. My voice was calm, almost snotty, but my heart was pounding.

"What's wrong with it?" she sputtered. "That should be obvious even to you. It's immoral. That's what's wrong with it."

"You're a fine one to talk about morals."

"How dare you say such a thing to me." She said it softly and slowly without stressing any of the words. Her anger was palpable. "I've lived my life above reproach, and you know it."

It was true, really, and I knew what I was about to do was unfair, but I had gone too far to stop.

"Then how come I'm a bastard?"

"What did you say?" It was a real question, as if she hadn't heard correctly.

The second time was harder. I took a deep breath. "I said, 'Then how come I'm a bastard?'"

Only the slightest pause revealed that I had caught her off guard. She recovered quickly. "Just what is that supposed to mean?"

"Well, Bill Kirkland's not my father, so that makes me a bastard."

"I don't know where you got that idea, but there isn't a shred of truth to it," she said, quietly and matter-of-factly, trying to bluff her way through.

"There's no point in lying. I know it's true. Bill told my psychiatrist."

I waited for her to respond, but she didn't. The silence lasted longer than any I can remember in a conversation with her. Finally, I broke it. "Well?"

She answered immediately and spoke quickly, as though startled from a reverie. "I will not discuss this with you on the phone. It will have to wait until I see you. I have to go now. Good-bye." She hung up before I could say another word.

I had won. There had been no more talk of my girlfriend's moving out or of my moving into the dormitory, and I knew there wouldn't be. Yet I felt depressed rather than elated after I hung up the phone. It was always that way when I fought with Mother. When I lost, I felt weak; when I won, something always took the edge off my victory. In this case, I knew I had scored with a cheap shot. Whatever circumstances and emotions surrounded my birth — and I was certain they involved Mother's love affair with Mike Todd — I knew the word bastard had depreciated them, and in using it I had belittled myself.

I was also afraid that in one very important respect my victory had been self-defeating. I was eager to know all the details about how I came to be born. Mother, however, was generally reticent in personal and emotional matters, and my belligerence would hardly inspire her to confide in me.

I was right, but Mother, as usual, was too fast for me. She gave me the facts so quickly, and they so astonished me, that I didn't miss knowing the emotions behind them until I learned them many years later.

Mother came to see me as soon as she could, which for her meant as soon as she could line up a job that would pay her airfare. It didn't take long. Jack Paar had always liked her as a guest. She phoned his producer, told him she was available, and he booked her for the following week.

It was a very brief visit; she didn't want to be away from home any longer than was "absolutely necessary." She left L.A. on the first flight of the day. The Paar show sent a car to meet her at the airport. She had it wait while she stopped by the apartment to see me, then she went on to the studio, did the show, and made it back to the airport in time to catch the last flight to L.A.

Mother loathed flying, and I appreciated the effort she was making. I was also very excited. And nervous. I wanted the visit to be as pleasant as possible. Rather than risk reopening a wound, my girlfriend and I put all her things out of sight, and on the day of the visit she worked late at the library and called before coming home. I got permission to leave school early that day, hurried home, put out everything I'd need to make Mother a cup of tea, and waited anxiously for the doorbell to ring.

Eventually it did. I buzzed her in, opened the apartment door, and waited at the top of the stairs. I heard her in the hallway below.

"Mother?"

"Yes, dear."

When she turned the corner and I saw her at the foot of the last flight of stairs, I was immediately struck by how tired she looked. It had been a hideous year for her. *Curious Evening, The Threepenny Opera*, giving up the New York house, and now this. She walked slowly up the stairs, using the bannister for support, and I wondered guiltily how many sleepless nights she had suffered through recently because of me.

"Where's your coat?" I asked, making nervous small talk. "It's cold out."

"I left it in the car with my overnight bag."

"I thought you weren't spending the night."

"I'm not, but I can't very well go on television looking like this." So true. She was wearing a cotton dress with a shawl over her shoulders, her hair was tied up with a scarf, and she had no makeup on.

She reached the landing and offered me her cheek to kiss. I did, and I hugged her too. She felt frail and delicate, like a bird.

"Would you like a cup of tea?" I asked as we walked to the living room.

"No, thank you, darling. I don't have much time. I'm due at the station in less than an hour. Getting in from the airport took forever. I can't bear the traffic in this city."

She seemed ill-at-ease; I certainly was. She sat primly on the edge of the couch, got a cigarette from her purse, and lit it. I handed her an ashtray, pulled a chair across from her, and sat down.

She began immediately, speaking quickly and surely, as though she had given the matter a great deal of thought and knew exactly what she wanted to say.

"It's true. I've always intended for you to know; although I would have preferred to tell you myself when you were a little older. And had Bill consulted me I would have given him my reasons, but it's too late for that now.

"In the strictest sense of the word, Bill is not your father." She paused to drag on her cigarette, and I started to comment, but she held up her hand. "Let me finish.

"There is far more to being a parent than the physical act. That's the easiest part. Afterward comes the caring, the attention, the time, the love . . . and the responsibility. And I think you should keep in mind that when it comes down to these *duties*, Bill has performed the role of your father since you were a little boy, even though, as you now realize, he had absolutely no obligation to do so. No reason, even, except that he cared for you.

"I don't know what happened between the two of you that led to this, and I don't want to know. I've deliberately not spoken to him about it. You're old enough to manage your own relationship with him. But I do know that he loves you like a son, and I hope you'll think very carefully before you let the trivial matter of his not being your biological father come between you."

"You're right," I said, "and I agree with you, but as far as I'm concerned I never want to see Bill ever again. The very least he could have done was tell me face to face instead of hiding behind my psychiatrist like a coward — "

"I think you're being unfair," she interrupted. "It is quite possible — I'd say probable, knowing Bill as I do — that he felt your doctor was better equipped to deliver this sort of news. If anyone has good reason to be angry with Bill over the way he's handled this, it's me. The very least he could have done was to warn me before he told you." She dragged on her cigarette and shook her head as she exhaled. "I'm sure it has something to do with this last marriage of his. . . .

"Be that as it may, I think you should give yourself some time to cool off before you make any irrevocable decisions that you might come to regret later.

"Which leads me to my next point: it doesn't matter to me, but if I were you I'd be very careful who I told about this. These things get talked about, and before you know it they're common knowledge. You may not think that matters now, but someday when you're going for a sensitive job or you want to get married, it could come back to haunt you. We know it doesn't make the slightest difference in who you are, but you'd be surprised at how many petty, narrow-minded people there are in the world who will hold something like this against you. I know it doesn't seem possible, but it's true. Believe me.

"Well," she said, standing up and straightening her dress, "that just about covers everything. A good thing, too. I can just make it to the studio in time for a half-hour nap before the show." Clearly she had said all she had come to say and felt much relieved for it.

"Wait a minute," I said. I couldn't believe she was finished. She hadn't touched on *anything* that mattered to me. I was so startled, I wasn't sure how to proceed.

"Yes?" she asked, looking genuinely perplexed.

237

"Who was my father?" I asked, going for the most obvious question.

"I thought you might ask that, and I've decided not to tell you."

"What do you mean? How come?"

"Because it's none of your business."

She said it so simply and with such self-assurance that for a moment I believed her. Whom she had slept with eighteen years earlier was none of my business. Except that in this case it was, as I finally remembered.

"He is *my* father," I reminded her.

She sat back down, lit another cigarette, and considered my argument. I didn't know what else to say, so I waited.

"Very well," she said, at last, "I'll tell you. But only on one condition: you must give me your solemn word of honor that you will make absolutely no attempt to contact him."

"Sure," I said, surprised for the first time all day. I had assumed it was Mike Todd, but he was dead, so it couldn't be him. But then, who? I hadn't the slightest idea.

"No. Not 'sure.' I don't want there to be any misunderstanding about this, Erik. You must promise me, on your word of honor, that under no circumstances will you ever try to contact him."

"So then I'll never meet him?"

"Not necessarily. The day will come when the two of you will be introduced at a cocktail party or will meet somewhere else by chance, and then you'll be able to tell by the look he gives you if he wants to pursue the matter. If he takes the initiative, then you're free to do as you wish. But you must let him make the first move. You're not even to suggest that you know he's your father."

"Then he knows about me?"

"Oh, yes. He's known about you since you were born."

By this time I would have agreed to anything to know. "I promise I'll make no move to contact him, and that if I run into him, I'll wait for him to make the first move. On my word of honor."

There was another long pause. She really didn't want to tell me. But she did. "It's Otto Preminger."

I didn't know what to say. The name meant nothing to me. We weren't a moviegoing family, and Mother had never mentioned him. He certainly wasn't the romantic figure around our house that Mike Todd was. I actually felt rather disappointed.

Before I could think up any more questions, Mother put out her cigarette and stood up again. "If I don't hurry I'll be late for the show." She started toward the door, and I followed her. "Now I hope you'll remember what I said to you about Bill. It would be a terrible shame if you let this come between you." I followed her down the stairs and opened the front door for her. "You won't forget your promise?"

"No, Mother."

She offered her cheek, and I kissed it. "Good-bye, darling."

"Bye, Mother."

Halfway across the sidewalk to the car, she turned back. "Do try to write more often," she called out, "I love hearing from you but these long-distance calls are outrageously expensive and we really can't afford them."

"I will, Mother. Promise."

I didn't see Mother during the next year and a half. She went home after the Paar show and stayed there, gardening and gradually pulling her life together while I stayed in New York where my life fell completely apart.

Because the fuss about my father was so dramatic, it is tempting to think of it as having been traumatic as well and to connect it with my decline. In fact, I had been getting into trouble for years, and what followed the revelation of my paternity was really nothing more than a continuation of what had gone on before, for the same basic reason: my lust for a car.

Having exhausted all other possibilities — except of course doing without — I used all of February's allowance, including my money for food, laundry, and other necessities, to buy a 1953 Ford. It had a bad shimmy in the front wheels, no muffler of consequence, brakes that squealed like a cat in heat, and Christmas tree lights strung around the inside that lit up whenever any of the doors were opened. But it ran. Or it did when I bought it. Afterward it, and I, quickly went downhill.

Because it tended to be especially cranky in the mornings, I tended to be late to school. Frequently it caused me to miss school altogether. I spent one day stranded on the West Side Highway with a broken carburetor. Another I spent in jail because I didn't have enough money to pay the fine for a defective muffler, and I had to wait for Boyd to bail me out. Other days I couldn't afford gas, so I just stayed home, in bed with my girlfriend.

I suffered from a chronic shortage of money, which was simply another aspect of car ownership. My budget never fully recovered from the purchase of the car; repairs, gas, and insurance only wreaked further havoc with it. I was in debt, my bills were overdue, and soon my checks began bouncing. The bank turned to Mother for guidance. So did everyone else. The school was complaining about my tardiness and unexcused absences, the phone company wanted her to pay my bill, Erica felt she should know that I had borrowed a hundred dollars, and the tenant in the apartment below mine was threatening to move because my girlfriend's shoes made such a racket.

All this came at the worst possible time for Mother, who was beside herself with money worries. The New York house had turned out to be a white elephant. She had even put it up for sale as well as for lease, with the same dismal response. In addition, the California house was costing far more to fix up than she had anticipated, and work was nonexistent except for an occasional week with *Auntie Mame* or *Curious Evening*. She hadn't been as close to broke nor as close to panic in years. And now instead of helping, here I was adding to her problems. As far as she was concerned it was "really too much," and she lost her patience with me even before she had a chance to try a measured approach. That, of course, only succeeded in driving us farther apart, so she called my shrink and demanded that he take a "firm hand" with me. He refused and suggested instead that she consider my needs, give me a decent allowance and a reliable car, and stop making such a fuss over my girlfriend. She was so incensed by his unwillingness to consider her position that she fired him on the spot. "I refuse," she wrote me later, "to pay a small fortune for someone to give you advice that I don't approve of."

This left me without any emotional support. Even worse, it left us without a referee, and we needed one. Every discussion degenerated into an argument. Usually the topic was money, but we also fought over where I would go to college, whether or not I would spend my next vacation with her, and other matters of supervision and authority. Generally speaking, she wanted me nearby where I'd be under her control, which was exactly the opposite of what I wanted. It was a continual battle, and the distance between us made it extremely painful. It was easy to fight over three thousand miles but impossible to make up, so each new blow fell on an open wound left over from the last argument. Not surprisingly, we were barely speaking after a while.

My relationship with Riverdale was just a little better. Although I was put on probation for my unexcused absences and came within a hair's breadth of being expelled, I managed somehow to survive the year and to be accepted by Columbia, my first choice college.

Mother was so disgusted with me by the time of my graduation that she refused to come east for it, and I was so angry with her that I refused to go west for my summer vacation. She tried to force me "home" by making me move out of the apartment and cutting off my allowance, but that just strengthened my resolve.

Boyd agreed to let me use his spare bedroom, and to earn some money I took a job as a chauffeur-assistant to Sam Kramer, the original avant-garde jeweler in Greenwich Village. Sam fashioned himself an eccentric by wearing mismatched suits with patchwork silk shirts, keeping a monkey as a pet, and using a lot of glass eyes in his jewelry. In fact, he was just a crazy alcoholic. His brain was pickled through and through. He drank four to five bottles of Irish whisky a day, and in periodic fits of alcoholic rage shot up the store with his .44 Magnum. I didn't care. I loved the job. The only unpleasant part of it was cleaning the monkey cage. I opened up the shop at eleven, swept, waited on the customers, made frequent trips to the liquor store, occasionally chauffeured him about in his Volkswagen, and even learned something about hand-crafting jewelry. It seemed more like a party than work. Sam's friends were always dropping in to visit, my girlfriend was welcome anytime, he kept an open bar, and there was a cigar box full of joints for those who were so inclined. It was my first exposure to marijuana, and I soon discovered that I was so inclined.

Best of all, it allowed me to be truly independent of Mother for the first time in my life. Not having to go to her for money was as though a yoke had been lifted from my shoulders. From our relationship, too. Without the irritant of my constant requests for money, we actually managed to exchange letters free of recriminations and to talk on the phone without fighting or hanging up on each other.

The truce lasted exactly as long as the job. Everything returned to normal the day I registered at college. Mother had never been happy about my going to Columbia, mainly because it was in New York, far from her watchful eye. She had even refused to pay for it initially in an attempt to force me to attend college on the West Coast. She had agreed only after I threatened to attend City College of New York, which was free, on my own. CCNY had no prestige in her eyes, and she was just too much of a snob to let me go there.

Getting Mother to agree to Columbia had taken much long-distance squabbling; getting her check to pay for it was an absolute nightmare. In spite of a notice to the effect from the college which I had mailed to her, she refused to believe that I had to have a check in hand for my tuition and fees when I registered.

"Just tell them to bill me," she insisted.

I did, but of course they refused, and the last day of registration found me exhausted from the long lines and bewildered from the new environment, in a stifling phone booth, begging her to wire me the money or to somehow get me a check before the end of the day. Grudgingly and with a number of ill-humored complaints about the cost of all the long-distance calls — as though the whole thing were my fault — she finally arranged for me to get a check from her lawyer. By then it was after three, but she indignantly refused to pay for me to take a taxi to collect it, so I had to rush half the length of Manhattan and back by subway, fighting the clock all the way. I made it in time, but after my independent summer it was an unpleasant reminder of the price I had to pay for Mother's support.

My first, and only, year at Columbia was basically a replay of my last year at Riverdale. The differences, by and large, were superficial. Like all freshmen, I had to live in a dormitory, but I spent most of my time with my druggie friends in the Village either getting stoned or waiting for a connection. I never made it to my morning classes, and I was only slightly more successful with those that began after noon. My '53 Ford had been replaced by a '55 Jaguar, but it was an even bigger drain on my time and financial resources. Money remained a constant source of anxiety. I was always in debt with my allowance check half spent before it arrived. If it was late — and it often was — my checks bounced all over town, and when I went to Mother in these instances she reacted with long, bitter tirades about my financial ir- responsibility.

I was placed on academic probation at the end of the first semester. That woke me up a bit. So did wrecking my car while stoned on LSD. I turned over a new leaf, the college helped by scheduling all my classes in the afternoon, and I managed a B-minus average on my second semester midterms.

My money problems persisted. The police were after me for some old parking tickets, I had a number of outstanding debts, and there were a few bounced checks that I had to settle. Determined to clean everything up and start fresh, I turned — yet again — to Mother for a loan. She agreed, but only to half of what I needed, and only after a humiliating conversation during which I actually had to beg for the money. The humiliation preyed at me, and when the check arrived I didn't want to cash it, yet I couldn't stay in school unless I did. The police had called at my dorm room with a warrant for my arrest as a scofflaw. I had been out, but they would be back unless I settled the overdue parking tickets.

Mother's check was for just enough to keep me out of jail. It would not alleviate my other money problems. I'd still have debts and bad checks hanging over my head. Even worse, I saw more humiliation stretching before me for as long as I needed Mother's money. I just couldn't face it any longer. School wasn't worth it. Nothing was. So I ripped the check in half and returned it to her with a bitter note telling her that since she obviously loved her money more than me, she should keep it. And my allowance, my tuition, and all the rest. Good-bye.

Then I packed my bags and, at two in the morning, left college — and Mother — behind me for good. Or so I thought, anyway.

CHAPTER SIXTEEN

IN APRIL, 1963, Mother sold the New York house for $175,000. It wasn't close to the $300,000 she had hoped for, but it was the only firm offer she had received in the year the house had been on the market, and she grabbed it. A week later she sent me an offer through Boyd and Erica of a car, a shrink, and total respect for my privacy if I'd come and live with her in California. I didn't even bother to answer. I was perfectly happy right where I was.

From college, I had gone directly to Boyd's, where I dropped off my bags. I used his spare bedroom as a home base, but I spent most of my time in the Village. Because the jewelry business came to a standstill with the end of the tourist season, the only job I could find was that of a short-order cook and dishwasher, but it paid me enough to stay high, and it left me with plenty of free time to hang out in coffeehouses with my druggie friends.

After a month of this, however, I was bored to distraction. Washing dishes is hardly a stimulating occupation, and while my friends spent a great deal of time talking about art, writing, dance, and music, no one was actually doing anything, except drugs of course, and even that grew stale after a while. I didn't know what I wanted to do with my life, but I knew that I wanted to do something, and I was clearly on a dead-end street where I was. Then I had a particularly bad acid trip which emphasized for me the risks I was running, and a few days later I called Mother to negotiate the terms of my homecoming.

She cried when she heard my voice, and she cried even louder when I told her that I was considering her offer, but the tears didn't stop her from going into a lightning-fast spiel about "this perfectly darling little car" that she could get for me at dealer's cost. I'd have to pick it up in New York and drive it out, but she would send the plates to Erica and I should be able to leave in a week, two at the most. In the meantime, she'd get to work on my rooms so they'd be ready for me. And oh, she was so excited, she couldn't wait to see me, and she knew I'd just love it there, etc, etc. It was Mother's bulldozer approach. By acting as though everything was already decided, she left no room for argument. I still had my doubts, and this transparent attempt to manipulate me didn't ease them in the least. I even considered arguing a little just to let her know I was on to her game, but instead I agreed to everything. I was tired of arguing.

Three weeks later, barely two months after my moonlight flight from college, I pulled up and parked near the gate at the end of the cul-de-sac. It was early, around six, but the sun had already burned off most of the morning fog, and the day promised to be quite warm. It was very still. Aside from an occasional birdsong or the buzzing of an insect, nothing stirred. The garage was closed and locked, and the place felt desolate, but "G.R. Lee" was painted in florid script on the mailbox, so I knew I was at the right place.

I got out of my car and very quietly closed the door. I wanted to avoid waking the household, so I could have a few moments to collect my thoughts before I announced myself. I had no idea of what to expect at the top of the stairs, and I still had my doubts about returning to the fold. I knew I would be hard pressed to maintain my independence under the constant battering of Mother's dominant personality. But it was too late to change my mind, and I was too tired to consider it anyway. I had driven from New York in four days and nights on Dexedrine and catnaps. All I wanted was a shower, a bed, and a long quiet rest.

Rest and quiet around Mother? I should have known better. The dogs were the first to sense my arrival. She had left New York with three of them; I was besieged at the top of the steps by twenty, all hairless, all ugly, and all yapping to beat hell. Had Mother been sleeping, that would have been the end of it, but she was up on the porch of the house, engrossed in watering three huge hanging baskets with a hose. She yelled automatically at the dogs to shut up, then she turned to see what was causing the commotion.

"Oh, my God," she shrieked when she saw me, "Erik! I didn't expect you for hours."

She started toward me, then she realized that she had the hose in her hand and started to put it down, then she changed her mind and headed for the valve to turn it off, then she changed her mind again. In the meantime, her yell, coupled with this little dance of indecision and the arrival of a stranger, had inspired new levels of hysteria in the dogs. They dashed back and forth between us, jumping up and scratching our legs, yapping and peeing from the excitement of it all.

"Will you shut up!" she yelled at them, this time slapping her thigh for emphasis. The dogs only jumped higher, dashed faster, and yapped louder.

"Oh, what am I going to do with this goddamn hose?" she asked herself. "To hell with it," she answered in the next breath. To me, she added, "Darling, don't move. I'll be right there."

She ran with the hose to the valve, which was next to the side of the house. On the way, she stumbled over a dog. It yelped indignantly. "Well, what do you expect, for chrissakes?" she asked it. "If you'd get out of my way, you wouldn't get hurt."

She turned off the water and then hurried to me, gently but impatiently pushing the dogs out of the way with her feet and talking to them all the while.

"Flower, get out of my way. . . . Damnit all, Chu, will you let me get to my son. . . . And shut up! All of you!"

It was a madhouse, and I felt right at home. When she finally reached me, she hugged me so hard it almost hurt.

"Thank God! You're really here. And all in one piece. Thank God!" Although Mother could blaspheme like a sailor, she believed strongly in God and often thanked Him for special favors. This was one of those times. Even I was moved by the love and relief in her welcome, not to mention the joy. When we stepped back to look at each other, we both had tears in our eyes.

"You're up bright and early," I remarked, making nervous small talk.

"I've been up for hours. We're in the middle of a hot spell, and I try to be out here by four so I can finish the watering before the heat of the day."

"You're kidding."

"Not at all," she said seriously. "It's vital. When the sun gets too high, the drops of water act like little magnifying glasses and burn the plants all to hell. On top of that, the heat causes half the water to evaporate before it gets a chance to soak in and do some good, and with what they charge out here for water I try to make sure every drop counts."

Mother hadn't changed, although she did seem a bit more extreme. From three dogs to a herd. Getting up early used to mean six, not four. And her appearance! She had never cared how she looked around the house, but this was a new low. Her hair, perfunctorily tied up with the usual old scarf, was bleached totally blond, except for the half-inch at the roots where it had grown out, and it looked as if it hadn't been brushed or washed in a week. Most of her false nails had broken off entirely, those that remained had grown away from the cuticle leaving narrow gaps that were filled with soil from her gardening. She was wearing the top of a two-piece sunsuit, panties, a full-length apron covering her *back*, and a short carpenter's apron around her waist in front, its pockets overflowing with gardening implements, cigarettes, and dead twigs and leaves which she had absentmindedly pinched off plants and trees as she passed them. She wore rubber overshoes, and her glasses, as always, were hanging around her neck and opaque with dirt.

I couldn't help but smile. She noticed. "Would you believe this outfit? I've worn through the ass of every swimsuit I own from all the bending over I do working on the garden, so now I'm reduced to wearing panties with this old apron over my back to keep the cops out." Then she gave me the once over and added, "You don't look so hot yourself."

"I can imagine. You should see how I feel. I haven't had a real night's sleep in four days. I can't wait to take a shower and go to bed."

"The last thing you want to do is go to bed now," she lectured officiously. "You'll sleep all day and then you won't be able to get to sleep tonight, and tomorrow you'll be just as tired as you are right now. You'll be much better off if you force yourself to stay awake at least until late this afternoon. Then when you go to bed, you'll sleep through the night, and you'll wake up in the morning rested and right on schedule."

"Who has a schedule? Besides, I'll never make it to this afternoon. I'm ready to drop right now."

"Oh, that'll pass. Believe me, I know what I'm talking about. God knows I've driven through the night often enough. Come on into the kitchen, and I'll make you a cup of tea. That'll revive you. And maybe these goddamn dogs will quiet down while we're inside."

Without waiting for me to answer, she turned and marched up the path to the house, shoving dogs out of the way with her feet and nipping the stray dead leaf off a plant as she went. I followed, more than slightly annoyed. Here I was, home less than ten minutes, and already she was bossing me around. Over something as stupid as a nap, no less.

Looking around the kitchen didn't help my mood. It was fully equipped with every appliance imaginable, all new and all obviously expensive. I remembered the countless long-distance arguments over money when she would accuse me of not understanding how close we were to the poorhouse, and once again I felt all the old resentments bubble to the surface.

She busied herself making tea and missed my pique entirely.

"Oh, my God!" she exclaimed out of nowhere. "I almost forgot. I have a surprise for you."

"I'm too tired for a surprise," I said sourly. "What is it?"

"I'm not going to tell you. That would ruin it. Close your eyes."

"Oh, Mother," I complained impatiently. She mugged a pout, but I knew she meant it, so with an ill-humored "All right," I closed my eyes.

I heard her scurry about; then she put something on the table in front of me. "Your favorite," she announced dramatically. "I got it for you yesterday at the Farmer's Market."

I opened my eyes. In front of me sat a huge slice of lemon meringue pie.

I loathed lemon meringue pie, I had always loathed it, and I had told Mother that I loathed it countless times, but it had never penetrated because it was *her* favorite. For my entire life she had refused to accept that I could dislike something that she loved. She had always dismissed every opinion of mine that differed from hers, be it about lemon meringue pie or anything else, as some sort of temporary aberration that would pass as soon as I came to my senses, and it had always infuriated me. This time was no exception. I wanted to scream.

Then I looked at her. She was standing over me, waiting eagerly for my reaction, beaming love. In less time than it took to think the thought, I realized that she couldn't help herself. She genuinely loved me, and in her own way — such as getting me the pie — she tried to show it, but a short-circuit in her psyche prevented her from empathizing, from making that step outside of her feelings into mine. She was the STAR, the one whose opinions, values, and feelings counted, and she had been one for so long that she was incapable of being anything else. In short, she was a prisoner of her own ego.

As quickly as it had come, my anger disappeared and with it all my old resentments. It wasn't that I forgave her. Forgiveness really didn't enter into it. Rather I came to accept her and to accept that she sure as hell wasn't going to change. I would just have to take her love as she gave it. And since the last thing I really wanted to do was disappoint her or hurt her feelings, I picked up the fork and took a healthy bite of pie.

"Isn't that just about the best goddamn pie you've ever tasted in your entire life?" she asked enthusiastically.

"Sure is," I answered automatically. Then I found myself laughing and taking another bite. It actually wasn't that bad.

Neither, as it turned out, was staying awake for the rest of the day. Mother made it easy by keeping me occupied. She began as soon as I finished my pie by giving me a tour of the house and grounds. Because of my deep emotional attachment to the New York house, I was prepared to hate the new one, but I couldn't. It was simply too beautiful.

For the most part she had transplanted the furniture and paintings from New York room by room, yet everything seemed to work better in its new surroundings. The juxtaposition of the Regency and Victorian antiques with the Mediterranean-Mexican adobe architecture in the living room was surprisingly successful. The clutter of beautiful things against a semitropical background reminded me of photographs I had seen of colonial residences in India during the British raj. Generally speaking, it was the light that made the difference. The New York house had looked in on itself in order to exclude the dirt and noise of the city. As a result it had been pretty gloomy. This house welcomed the outside with its gardens and spectacular views, so it was gloriously bright and cheerful, and all of Mother's things sparkled as though a shroud had been lifted from them.

My rooms were not what I had expected. Mother had led me to believe that I'd have a separate apartment of sorts; in fact I had two rooms right off the foyer in the back of the ground floor. They were the only rooms without a view in the house, and the promised "private entrance" was nothing more than a pair of french doors leading to the rear garden. When locked, they couldn't even be opened from the outside. To be fair, there were compensations. Mother had given me the French Provincial furniture from the library of the New York house which I loved, the rooms were painted a wonderful deep red, the study had a working fireplace, and the overall effect was warm and masculine. I was actually quite pleased with them.

Her tour of the house was perfunctory compared with the one she gave me of the garden. Inside, she showed me each room and then we moved on. Outside, she dwelled on each plant, referring to it by its Latin name, telling me when she had planted it, how she thought it "liked" where it was, where she had had it before in the case of those she had moved, who had given it to her in the case of those plants she had received from friends either whole or as cuttings, and so on. Considering that she had planted the bejesus out of her half-acre, all this took some time, and since I knew nothing of plants and gardening, most of it went right over my head. Once again, however, I could not deny the beauty of what she had accomplished.

The front of the hill from the house down to the roof of the garage, which formed a sun deck, was mostly covered by a lush dichondra lawn, yet wherever the eye rested flowers were in bloom. Roses predominated, of every color and size imaginable. Next to the small swimming pool, a large bed containing over fifty rosebushes of thirty varieties separated the hill from the sun deck. More were planted between the far edge of the lawn and the top of the retaining wall, and small rosebushes bordered both sides of the paved walkway through the lawn up to the house. Under the huge deodara tree in front of the house, she had planted all sorts of shade-blooming plants with small, delicate flowers. Calla lilies, night-blooming jasmine, and two magnificent camellias — one was over eleven feet tall — filled the flower bed that ran between the side of the house and the path as it approached the front porch, and the porch itself was edged with pots and hanging baskets full of various kinds of beautiful plants.

Where the paved walk ended in two steps up to the porch, a small flagstone path branched off to the right. Bordered throughout with different types of flowering plants, it continued all the way around the house. First, through the kitchen garden which was planted with tomatoes, herbs, and more flowering plants to the kitchen door; then around the back of the house to my small garden which was shaded by an Australian tea tree and planted with the same types of shade-loving plants she had used under the deodara. The path continued through a bower of mature rhododendrons back to the front lawn, but a short branch off it led behind the tea tree to three steps that descended to what Mother called her "secret garden." It was a tiny, secluded niche dug into the hill and planted with irises and a few ferns around a small fountain that contained water lilies and a family of frogs. I had to take Mother's word for the frogs because there were none to be seen when she gave me the tour.

"They are all quite shy," she explained. "Even my shadow disturbs them. But there are three for sure. I saw them early yesterday morning. There were two huge ones and one small. The biggest one croaked.

It was a tiny croak — like a faggot frog — not a bass croak at all, but perhaps his tone will improve as he practices."

The other, larger fountain that curved around the outside of the conservatory at the end of the living room was also dear to Mother's heart because of the resident wildlife, only in this case it was goldfish rather than frogs. While cleaning out the years' accumulation of mud and debris from the pond, she had discovered a number of culls that had survived in it since the house had last been occupied. Since then she had added more and, using Pavlov's method, tamed them by ringing an old schoolmarm's bell before every feeding. Now they assembled in the center of the pond whenever she rang it, even though she had cut down on their food because they were all too fat. She had named them, too. "Sammy Davis, Jr." was a black cull with only one eye, "Jackie Gleason" was the fattest fish in the pond, "Dean Martin" appeared to be drinking all the time, "Queen Victoria" had bulging eyes and a long trainlike tail, and Mother swore "Lazarus" had come back from the dead after having been out of the water for ten minutes.

Lazarus would have been an appropriate name for Mother, too. When last in New York she had seemed old and exhausted, worn out both physically and emotionally. Now she was tanned, looked healthy, and radiated a peaceful contentment that I had never before seen in her. For once she wasn't frantic, just energetic and full of *joie de vivre*. She delighted in her new life, even the mundane facets of it, as I learned that afternoon when she dragged me along while she ran some errands.

That she even went shopping was something new. In New York she had rarely left the house. Occasionally she would venture out to a favorite antique shop, only to return reciting a litany of complaints about the noise, dirt, and chaos of the city. For the most part she stayed home, ordered everything by phone, and either had it delivered or sent me to pick it up. All that had changed in Los Angeles. She loved getting out and about. She had even bought herself a special car just for "going down the hill" into Hollywood and Beverly Hills. A Fiat "Jolly," it was a tiny baby blue car with open sides, wicker seats, and a fringed canvas top. She claimed to have bought it to spare the Rolls the inevitable parking-lot nicks and dents, which was no doubt true, but she also loved the look of it and the rush of air as she tooled around town in it.

When she left the house, Mother made only the most perfunctory improvements in her appearance: a cotton dress (the same one she had worn throughout Europe five years earlier), a little lipstick, and a clean scarf neatly covering her hair. Still, she looked a hell of a lot better than the Beverly Hills matrons we saw who had clearly spent their entire mornings getting made up and coiffed just to hit the grocery store. Mother looked real and, above all, happy. She seemed to be having the time of her life.

Our first stop that afternoon was the Farmer's Market for a quick, stand-up lunch of tacos, then we went to the Akron, one of her favorite stores in Hollywood. The Akron is a chain of giant cut-rate emporiums filled to overflowing with whatever the buyers can get at a discount, from Spanish olives to pillows, dishwashing liquid to roofing tiles. It was, needless to say, just Mother's meat. This day she was after canning jars — the Rangpour lime tree was "coming due" — and outdoor-furniture pads, both of which she had seen advertised in the Sunday paper. And as long as we were there, she also picked up a little barbecue and a long-handled shovel that she had needed for weeks but denied herself because they cost "nine ninety-eight at Beverly Hills Seed Company! Ten dollars for a shovel, can you believe it?" This one was seven, Mother was delighted, and of course I believed all of it. From Akron we went to the aquarium store to pick up a pump for the goldfish pond, and while we were there she also bought a new "bubble head goldfish" that she couldn't resist. She called this one "Margaret Truman," but I don't remember why. Then it was on to Home Silk to buy some fabric for chair covers that she wanted to make.

Last, but far from least, we did the grocery shopping. This was a favorite part of Mother's routine. She liked it so much that she went to three markets: an expensive one in Beverly Hills for delicacies that she could get nowhere else, a supermarket for standard items like canned and paper goods, and finally a little neighborhood market in Hollywood for her produce and meats.

Mother was quite a regular at the little market. She knew all the salespeople by name, and those who waited on her went out of their way to oblige. The produce man had set aside half-a-dozen baskets of raspberries for her; she ate two while she did the rest of her shopping, carefully keeping the wrappers to show to the checkout clerk so he would charge her for them. The butcher had a shopping bag full of bones saved for the dogs and had already put together an order of beef hearts, liver, and kidneys that Mother used to make a stew for the dogs instead of giving them dog food. The fact that the butcher had gone out of his way to save her the bones didn't stop her from complaining about the price of the stew meat, but to be fair her complaint didn't induce him to lower it either. Clearly they had gotten to know each other pretty well.

Finally it was time to go home and late enough, once she had made me a light supper, for Mother to let me go to bed. As usual, of course, she turned out to be right. I slept right through the night and woke up bright and early the next morning feeling great.

Life with Mother in California wasn't quite as she had suggested it would be. I certainly didn't have enough privacy to "entertain" girls in my rooms, and she never again mentioned the promised shrink, but neither turned out to be important. We quickly settled into a comfortable, pleasant routine.

Her career was still in the doldrums, but there were signs of improvement: the occasional Joey Bishop show, a vodka ad, and even a few days on a film. Nothing major, but enough to keep her spirits up, especially as she wasn't worried about money. The sale of the New York house had not only lowered her expenses, she had taken the mortgage, and it provided her with a sizable and dependable income. With the pressure off, she relaxed and enjoyed herself. Pleasant days she spent working in the garden, not-so-pleasant ones she puttered around the house, put up preserves, and the like. In the evenings, she sat in front of the television and worked on her quilt until nine o'clock when she went to bed.

On the phone from New York, I had mentioned getting a job to pay off my debts, so she had put out some feelers in the jewelry business and elsewhere. The jewelers she arranged for me to meet were not at all encouraging. I quickly discovered that it is one thing to eke out an existence in Greenwich Village handcrafting jewelry but something else entirely even to sell it in Beverly Hills. They all suggested I go to school to study art and design, but as school didn't interest me in the least, I dropped the jewelry idea entirely.

Mother's next scheme for me was typical of her. She had it all planned out for me to open my own business cleaning neighborhood swimming pools. It would be your basic skim-the-bugs-off-the-top-and-vacuum-the-bottom service with one twist: she had come across a new type of pool disinfectant based on iodine instead of chlorine, and its advantages would be the hook I could use to get people to switch from their current service to mine. At least, that is the way she saw it. Actually, it wasn't a bad idea, but I was hardly ready to start my own business, so I let that idea slide, too.

Then her hairdresser suggested I work for a friend of his who owned a telephone answering service. This was ideal. I worked the graveyard shift, which left my days free to sit in the sun and visit with Mother and my evenings to enjoy a limited, and innocent, social life.

In short, it was a quiet, restful summer devoid of crises or arguments, just like the old days of my childhood. Of course, there was a price. Around Mother there could be only one opinion — hers — so I had to defer to her in all things, just as I had as a child. It wasn't difficult; I wasn't really in the mood that summer to assert myself. But I knew it couldn't last. It is one thing to step back into childhood for a visit, another to remain there forever. Eventually I would have to leave, to make my own way; and as the summer drew to a close I began to think about my next step. A job was out. The possibilities open to an eighteen-year-old out of high school didn't interest me. School was also out. I doubted anyplace would accept me with my record, and more than that I didn't want to sit in a classroom. I wanted to be out in the world. Out and far enough from Mother to be my own person.

So I joined the army.

Mother drove me down to the induction center on the last day of September. We had parted before, always with a measure of bitterness on one side or both. This time there was no bitterness, and we parted as friends.

I didn't want to be stigmatized by being seen stepping out of the Rolls, so I made her stop around the corner. We hugged, and she started to cry. Not sob, just a few tears. I promised to write, got out of the car, leaned through the window to give her one last kiss, and walked away. Once I turned and waved. She was dabbing her eyes with an old balled-up Kleenex and waved back.

Then I turned the corner.

CHAPTER SEVENTEEN

LIKE the average civilian soldier, I hated the army, but it was a liberating experience of sorts, being on my own and away from Mother's influence. Not that I was as far from it as I had expected. She found numerous tax-deductible excuses to visit me in Germany where I was stationed. Once, much to my chagrin, she even arranged to do *Curious Evening* for the troops on the base. And, of course, we exchanged frequent letters. Hers were always typewritten, having been dictated to her secretary, so the arrival of an envelope addressed in her nearly illegible scrawl clearly presaged something out of the ordinary. Nonetheless, I hardly expected news that would entirely change the course of my life.

Otto, she announced, would be getting in touch with me. Somehow, he had heard that I knew he was my father, and he had asked permission to contact me. She had given it, but only after exacting his promise — which she expected me to honor as well — to keep the true nature of our relationship a closely guarded secret. Clearly rumors were beginning to spread, and she was afraid they would lead to a full-fledged scandal.

Her reproach was unmistakable but unfair, even though I was responsible for word having gotten out and, eventually, back to Otto. She had left it up to me to tell whomever I wished about my parentage, although she had warned me of the possible consequences to my future, and I had told a number of people because I thought it exciting and romantic. These were new rules; however, I understood the reason behind them. She had recently begun a daytime television talk show aimed at the woman's market, and she was afraid a scandal might adversely affect it. I planned to abide by her rules, too. After all, I was now far more interested in meeting Otto than in telling people that I was his illegitimate son.

Two days later, a note arrived from Otto. He would be in Paris later that month to open his latest film, and he invited me to meet him there. Of course, I accepted.

I spent most of the next weeks trying anxiously to assemble a wardrobe that would be suitable for Paris. I wasn't about to wear my uniform, but most of my civilian clothes were very casual, jeans and the like. On the dressy side, I owned one ratty sport jacket, a pair of slacks, two shirts, and a raincoat that was positively disreputable. My civilian shoes, fortunately, were serviceable although quite worn. The problem was compounded by a severe shortage of funds. Army salaries have never been lavish, and I have never been much of a saver. Between my compassionate commanding officer who arranged an advance on my salary and some astute begging from my friends, I managed to scrape together enough for a new suit at the PX and a round-trip, second-class train ticket to Paris with enough left over for some pocket money and a box of candy for Otto's wife.

When I wasn't worrying about my clothes, I was of course worrying about meeting Otto. I remember wanting him to like me and to approve of me, but most of all I remember wanting him not to feel obligated to like me.

It was sometime after nine o'clock at night when I arrived at Otto's hotel, the Plaza Athénée. It is one of the finest and most beautiful hotels in Paris, and although I had experienced first-class hotels with Mother, I felt decidedly out of place when I entered the lobby in my new PX suit. At least I had had the foresight to carry my raincoat.

I presented myself at the desk, gave my name, and said that Mr. Preminger had reserved a room for me. There was an immediate flurry of excitement. The concierge abruptly ordered a bellboy to take my bag, told me he would have it brought to my room, and came around the desk to escort me to Otto's suite. As he was leading me to the elevator, I mentioned that I wanted to go to my room first, but he explained that Mr. Preminger had been calling the desk every ten minutes to ask if I had arrived and had left strict instructions that I be shown to his room "immediately." By then we were at the door to Otto's suite. The concierge knocked and then opened it for me in response to a booming, faintly Teutonic *"Entrez"* from within.

For a brief moment, time seemed frozen, and the tableau remains vivid in my memory today and probably forever. First the suite, what

I could see of it anyway. A foyer and a sitting room beyond it. Both were magnificently furnished with antiques and resembled, on a more intimate scale, the apartments I had seen in various French châteaux. There were huge arrangements of flowers everywhere, and off to one side of the room was a room-service cart laden with caviar, vodka, and white wine. Otto was standing in the middle of the room, wearing a dark blue suit. He appeared to have been pacing and caught midstride. I had recently seen a small photograph of him in *Time* magazine, so I was prepared for a heavy-set, bald man. No photograph, however, could capture the strength of his presence. He emanated power. His wife, who was seated on a sofa looking in my direction, came as an even greater surprise. I had seen no photograph of her, but I had assumed that Otto's wife would be matronly and middle aged. Hope was in her early thirties, tall, slim, stunningly beautiful, and wore an elegantly simple black dress.

"Why didn't you let me know what plane you were taking?" Otto demanded gruffly. In retrospect, they seem like strange first words for a son you've never met, but they didn't seem so at the time. I knew he had been waiting impatiently for me, and his reaction seemed perfectly normal. I was, after all, used to impatience. "I would have come to meet you at the airport," he continued, only slightly less gruffly.

"I didn't think of it," I answered, tossing my raincoat on a chair in the foyer with a nonchalance I wasn't feeling. I didn't want to admit that I had taken the train because it was cheaper, and I felt I had started off on the wrong foot.

"Well, you're here now, and that's all that matters." We shook hands, then he put his arm over my shoulder. "Come meet my wife."

He introduced us, and I gave her the candy I had bought in the PX. It seemed like such a quaint offering for such an elegant, sophisticated woman, but she thanked me with a gracious warmth that would always characterize her acceptance of me.

I was too nervous to notice that Otto was equally ill-at-ease. We made a little polite small talk. He asked me about my flight, offered me some caviar, which I declined, and then suggested we go for a walk. I felt very much under the gun and leaped at the opportunity to be outside, doing something.

As we were leaving, he pointed to my raincoat and asked if I wanted to wear it. It was chilly out, but I decided I would rather be cold than embarrassed and declined.

"If my son doesn't wear a coat," he announced proudly, "then neither do I." It was a declaration of love and acceptance, and I felt the warmth of it even through my self-conscious reserve.

We spent the next two hours walking the streets of Paris. It was a clear, crisp night, and the illuminated buildings and monuments stood dramatically against the black sky. It would be impossible to imagine a more romantic setting for a first, intimate conversation between a father and son.

I was still tongue-tied. Fortunately Otto did all the talking.

"I would have contacted you long ago, you know. It was your mother who insisted we not meet." He then continued with the story of my birth from his point of view. He was clearly a little uncomfortable, and when it came to discussing Mother he went out of his way to be gallant, but he seemed determined that I know the truth.

"My affair with your mother was very short. We met at a party given by Lady Mendl and after that we would meet in her dressing room in the evening. She had a bungalow, and I think she was living there. I remember she used to make dinner for us on a little hot plate. Then one day I phoned her, and the studio told me she had left and gone back to New York. It was so abrupt, I thought perhaps I had done something. . . .

"When I was next in New York, I tried to call her again. This time her secretary answered and told me she was in the hospital. When I reached her there, she said, 'Congratulations. This morning we had a son.'

"I immediately went to the hospital to see her, and offered to support you. I had always wanted children, but my wife at the time didn't want any. Your mother wouldn't take anything from me.

" 'I don't need your money. I have money of my own. Erik is going to be *my* son. He's not even to know that you're his father.'

"She said I could visit you from time to time, but only as a friend. We agreed to say that I was your godfather if anyone should ask.

"When you were little, I used to come see you at her house on Sixty-third Street whenever I was in New York, but then she remarried. An artist, Latin American or Spanish, I think, and he objected to me, so she told me not to come anymore.

"I saw her in Europe a few years after that. She was no longer married to the painter, but she felt it would be better if I didn't see you. I asked that she at least put something in her will, so that you would know about me if something happened to her. I don't know if she did or not. But that doesn't matter anymore, does it. Now that we know each other." He put his arm over my shoulder.

Briefly I put my arm around him and said, "No, it doesn't." I didn't really know what to say or do, and I was still tense and nervous, but Otto's unequivocal acceptance was very gradually getting to me.

Then he asked me what I wanted to do with my life. Whether it was the question that put me on the spot because I didn't know the answer or just misfortune, I stumbled and tore the sole of my right shoe loose all the way from the toe back to the heel. Of course, I didn't want Otto to know, so for the rest of our walk much of my attention was devoted to walking in such a way as to keep the sole from either bending back or slapping the pavement.

It was very funny. Even at the time I couldn't miss the humor. Moreover, it was a strange sort of blessing because it took my mind off my self-conscious tension and directed it toward something mechanical. So as I walked rather oddly down the Champs Elysées while attempting to explain my quandary about the future, I actually began to relax with Otto. I told him that I hated school, that the army had trained me to program computers but that I thought it would be a little tame after my childhood in show business, and that my mother assumed I would be working with her on her television show, which was out of the question. I didn't know what I wanted to do, but fortunately I had nine months before my discharge to decide.

That's when he offered me a job with him when I got out of the army. It would be, he explained, an opportunity for me to learn the movie business and for us to get to know each other.

I waited a few weeks before giving him my answer, and I discussed it with Mother, but I knew I'd take the job the moment he offered it. More than anything in my life, I wanted to find out what it was like to have a real father.

CHAPTER EIGHTEEN

Six MONTHS later, I was discharged from the army. I had recently married an American girl whom I had met in Germany while she was there on vacation, and we settled in New York where Otto maintained his offices. There I began a new life as his assistant — and secret son.

The years that followed were as exciting as any in my life. Working with Otto wasn't always easy, but we forged a relationship which is one of the mainstays of my life. More than a father, he became a loving and loyal friend.

My marriage was less successful. It lasted only four years. However, it did produce a splendid young man who became Mother's delight. She was never without her album of his baby pictures, and she would drag it out of her purse on the slightest provocation.

Mother and I remained close. Not as close as in the old days, but close in the manner of parents and grown children who are leading separate lives yet still like each other. Business often took me to Los Angeles, and then we spent a great deal of time together. Occasionally I'd even stay at the house. When I was in New York or on location with a film, we'd talk on the phone at least once a week. I always made the call — Mother's reluctance to part with a buck never waned — except once when she called me at the office.

"Erik, they've found a spot on my lung," she announced, not beating around the bush or even saying hello. "They want to operate immediately, but I've told them I have to wait until you can get here. How soon can you come?" She sounded insistent but not panicky.

"Let me check with Otto."

I did, and he had me in a limo headed for the airport within the hour.

I called the house when I arrived and learned that she was already in the hospital. I rented a car and went to see her. She had just finished executing a new will when I walked into her room, and she handed me a copy.

"They've promised me that this surgery is quite safe, but I didn't want to take a chance. I made my last will when you were a little boy, and it was hopelessly out of date. . . ."

"How serious is this?" I asked, kissing her.

"They won't know until they open me up and take a look around, but the surgeon told me not to worry. From the X-rays, he thinks he'll be able to get it all."

"Then it's cancer?"

"Oh, yes. They've known that from the beginning."

I didn't know what to say. When she used the word "spot" on the phone, I had assumed it was TB or something else serious but curable. Not cancer.

"Can I do anything?"

"Just your being here is enough for now. Well, I'd better ring for the nurse and tell her that you've arrived, so she can give me my pre-op sedative. I've kept everyone waiting until you got here."

The nurse gave her the shot. As it was taking hold, she told me to go home rather than wait at the hospital. It would be hours after the operation before I could see her, she explained, because she'd be going into a special postoperative intensive care unit just for lung surgery patients. "They have to be careful we don't catch cold . . ." she said as she nodded off.

I waited until they wheeled her out of the room, and then I went to the house. From my visits I was accustomed to all the changes and additions she had made over the years, yet as I walked through it that afternoon I saw them all as if for the first time.

She had screened off the conservatory at the end of the living room, and it was now home for over a hundred finches and other small birds. Their song filled the house from dawn until dusk, which is why Mother referred to them as her "alarm clock." Not that she ever needed one.

The dining room table was, as usual, strewn with the remnants of her latest project. Now it was souvenirs she had collected on her last USO tour to Southeast Asia. She had made three tours, always by herself instead of with a group, to visit small hospitals and forward firebases where the large shows, like Bob Hope's, never stopped. In the hospitals, she'd visit the wards and climb into bed with the boys to pose for Polaroid snapshots which she'd autograph. "Sort of like a sexy grandmother," was the way she explained it.

I remembered the last time I had seen her. She was in New York to accept an award as USO Woman of the Year. She looked terrible and explained that she had been suffering with horrible headaches for months, yet in spite of the pain her main concern was that the army might not let her go on her next tour. Shortly afterward, she sent me a letter from Tokyo that I still have. In it she wrote, "The doctors (five of them) after not finding a 'reason' for my constant headache since August finally decided to let me go on my hospital tour, and I'm so glad they did. I keep up just fine on Darvon with the help of the courage and bravery of the men I visit my own silly aches and pains seem to dissolve."

The little breakfast nook off the kitchen had been transformed into a tropical fish hatchery. There was one large, custom-made tank and around it another five that she used for breeding or holding sick fish. The tropical fish phase had preceded the bird phase, however, and I could tell from the algae that had built up on the glass of the tanks that Mother's interest in this area was waning.

The workroom behind the kitchen was now her editing room, and her film collection had grown measurably, mostly during the three years of her daily television show. The TV show had been Mother's greatest professional success in terms of audience reached and probably in terms of appreciation. Her "ladies" as she called her viewers, loved her. She was perfect for television, this time around, because she had finally learned the secret of her curtain speech: she was herself. And that is basically what her show was, a half-hour curtain speech. She shared her life with her "ladies." She read them letters from me (even such highly personal ones as that in which I told her I was getting married), discussed her face lifts, shared her interests and hobbies, introduced her show-business friends from the famous like Judy Garland to the not-so-famous like *Ziegfeld Follies* beauty Iris Adrien, and all with her unique, infectious enthusiasm. She did cooking shows; making jewelry out of bread-dough shows; bird, fish, flower, and dog shows; shows with writers like Tom Wolfe; and shows with artists like Andy Warhol. Any topic that interested her was grist for the show, and whenever she couldn't get the topic to the studio, she'd take her home movie to the topic. In this way she did shows on garage sales, quilting bees, and even my wedding in Germany.

Outside, the garden behind my old rooms had been completely fenced to create two outdoor aviaries, one for pigeons and the other for large, exotic birds including a cockatoo, a toucan, and a few parrots among seventy or so others. At one time she even had two peacocks, but they made so much noise honking at each other that an irate neighbor sneaked in one night and kidnappped them. As I looked at all these strange, wonderful creatures through the french doors, it occurred to me that they might not have been fed, so I got one of the special "bird pies" that Mother baked every week and took it out into the aviary. When Mother did this, they ate out of her hand, but they weren't used to me so I just broke up the pie and left it on the ground for them.

Upstairs, on her bed, was her second finished quilt. The beginning of a third lay folded on her sewing basket next to the chair that she used for watching television. And on the far side of her bed, the entire table top was devoted to photographs of her grandson.

Everywhere, of course, there were dogs. She was determined to breed enough generations to get them accepted by the American Kennel Club. She had not yet succeeded, but looking around I figured she had to be close enough to smell success . . . among other things.

All this life. Everything she touched was so full of it that I recoiled at the thought of her dying. It just didn't seem possible.

I returned to the hospital and waited by the door of the pulmonary intensive care unit for word, but the nurses who came and went hadn't seen or heard of her. Finally, after three increasingly frantic hours, I called her doctor's office and learned that she was already back in her room. She was awake when I got there.

"I've been waiting for you by intensive care," I explained. "What happened? Why aren't you there?"

"Because they took one look and sewed me back up. It has spread too much for them to operate." She was close to tears but holding them back. This was a time for fighting, not crying. "They've told me not to worry . . . yet." She continued. "There's a good chance they'll be able to knock it out with radiation. We'll know more about that later.

"Now," she changed the subject, "how long can you stay with me?"

"Otto told me to stay as long as you need me."

"Isn't that nice of him. Well then, I'd like to have you here at least until I get this radiation thing organized. And first thing tomorrow, I want you to call Arm and Hammer. I did a commercial for them last month, and they haven't paid me for it yet. I took a bath in baking soda and said it was good for my skin. Well, they sure as hell won't be able to use it when word of this gets out, and they're just as liable to try and hold on to my salary. It's ten thousand dollars, too, and God only knows when I'll be able to work again. So I want you to call them tomorrow and ask about my check. There's a letter on the desk with the man's name on it."

I laughed to myself. It felt so good to see her acting so true to form.

When I left Mother later that evening, I visited her doctor to find out exactly where she stood. He told me it would kill her for sure, but he refused to tell me how long it might take. I explained that I lived in New York but could arrange to move if it would be a year or less, but he told me she might hang on for years. Why he said that I'll never know. Nine months would have been a miracle, and in fact she died in five. And because of him, I missed most of those months with her and got only snatches instead.

I must have gone back and forth between New York and Los Angeles at least a dozen times over the next five months. On each visit, she had visibly deteriorated. In the beginning, she was able to get around the house and walk into her radiation treatments, then she was bed-ridden in her room and needed a wheelchair. When she became too weak to make it down the stairs from her room, we tried using a stretcher, but the stairs were too narrow so she moved into my old rooms on the first floor. Then came the oxygen tanks, the electric bed, the round-the-clock nurses, and all the other signs of serious illness.

During all of this, she never gave up. She never once admitted that she might lose the fight and die. I sometimes wished that she would, so that we could say good-bye, but all she ever said was "I'm going to beat this thing, Erik. I'm going to beat it." Everyone helped her maintain the fiction by leaning on the back of the scale when she weighed herself so that she'd think she was gaining weight instead of losing it.

Toward the end, she began to get nerve blocks to help with the pain. Once the doctor came to the house to adminster it. He had to give her injections in her back, and he asked me to hold her. Very demurely, being careful to keep her breasts covered, she dropped her nightgown off her shoulders and leaned against me. She had always been frail, but now there was nothing to her except dry skin and bones. She was being eaten away from the inside out. Worst of all was the smell of the illness. She knew it, too, and tried to hide it with perfume. That, of course, only made it worse. After the doctor finished, we put her back to bed. Then I went outside, sat on the front stairs, and tried to keep from fainting. When the doctor passed on his way out, he apologized for having asked me to help. I only hoped that Mother hadn't sensed my revulsion.

Later that night, she called for me. We had said goodnight earlier, and I had gone up to the rotunda where I was sleeping. When the nurse called up to me, I put on my robe and went downstairs.

"I can't sleep, darling." She patted the bed next to her. "Please come lie here next to me for a while."

I lay down next to her in the darkened room. The only light came from the nurse's reading lamp in the study next door. Mother dozed or thought; I never knew which in those days.

"How are things between you and Otto?" she asked suddenly. It was the first time she had ever inquired about Otto or our relationship.

"Wonderful," I answered. "He's been great through all this, you know? He gives me all the time I need to visit you, and he always finds an excuse so the studio pays the way."

"I'm so glad." She squeezed my hand. "I sensed he was a good man, in spite of his reputation. That's one of the reasons I picked him. That and his mind. I could have had a child by Mike anytime, but Mike had a mean streak that I didn't want my child to inherit. . . ."

She paused or dozed. I held my breath and hoped she would say more, but I didn't dare ask.

"It was after Mike left me," she finally continued. "I felt so alone that I decided to have something no one would ever be able to take away from me. I'm so glad it's working out."

She dozed briefly, holding my hand, until the pain woke her. The nerve blocks took care of only some of it.

"Nurse," she called. "Nurse, is it time for my shot yet?"

"Just a little while longer," I lied. She actually had close to an hour to wait. Throughout her illness I had a running battle with her doctor about her pain medication. He claimed that if he gave her all she wanted, she'd roll into a ball and sleep her life away. Instead, she spent her last days watching the clock and waiting for her next shot.

"But it hurts so," she cried. "Oh, God! It hurts so . . ." She kept repeating, "It hurts so," like a mantra until she dozed off. Moments later, she woke again and asked for her shot.

"Soon," I lied.

"But it hurts so much, and I'm so tired. I don't know how much longer I can fight this pain. It's so awful."

I thought she was finally admitting that she was dying and said, "It'll be over soon."

"What do you mean?" she demanded, instantly alert and clearly frightened. I had meant, of course, that her struggle would soon be over, but I could tell that she didn't want to hear that, so instead I lied and said that it was almost time for her next shot.

That was the closest I came to saying good-bye to her. She died while I was en route for my next visit, so I don't even have any parting words. When I think of her last days, however, I usually remember one of her first visits to the radiation clinic. The night before we had celebrated her fifty-sixth birthday. She was always taken the moment she arrived, and we were walking past all the patients who were waiting in line for their turn.

"You know, Erik," she said quietly, "when I look at all these people I can't bring myself to berate God for giving me this horrible disease. I've had three wonderful lives, and these poor sons-a-bitches haven't even lived once."

AFTERWORD

A FEW months after Mother died, Otto and I were stopped by an acquaintance of his as we were leaving his office in New York. Before Otto had a chance to introduce me, the acquaintance said, "And this must be your son."

This happened very often, no doubt because of the strong resemblance between us. As always, Otto quickly corrected him.

"No. He's my assistant. Erik Lee Kirkland."

As we were walking down the street after having parted from the man, I remarked on how silly it seemed to keep maintaining a fiction that so few believed.

"Well, it's entirely up to you," Otto said quickly. "Nothing would make me more proud than to adopt you."

Three months later, on March 10, 1971, he did, and I became Erik Lee Preminger.

ACKNOWLEDGMENTS

I wish to thank the many, dear family friends who shared with me their memories of Mother and in particular Boyd Bennett, Hope Davis, Erica Dorf, Bill Fitelson, Ed Gustin, Lelah Halton, and Georgia Sothern.

I also wish to thank Alan Brovar, Arthur Hoffman, Floria Lasky, and Genevieve Young. Each in his or her own way helped me through the many difficult years I spent writing this book. Without them it would have been a longer, a harder, perhaps even an impossible task.

There are five whose unique contributions deserve a special mention (at the very least):

My friend David Columbia who initially convinced me that the story was interesting enough to tell.

My father, Otto, who insisted I tell it first in a book.

My friend and agent, Steve Sheppard, who got me going again every time I faltered and threatened to give up.

My wife, Brigid, who never doubted that I would finish and never asked when. Her faith sustained me.

And, above all, Mother who believed that a child belongs with his mother, which is how I got all the stories in the first place.

Thank you all.

INDEX

274